How to Agent Your Agent

Nancy Rainford

HOW TO AGENT YOUR AGENT
Copyright © 2002 Nancy Rainford

LONE EAGLE PUBLISHING COMPANY, LLC™
1024 N. Orange Dr.
Hollywood, CA 90038
Phone 323.308.3400 or 800.815.0503
A division of IFILM® Corporation, www.hcdonline.com

Printed in the United States of America
10 9 8 7 6 5 4 3 2 1

Cover design by Sean Alatorre
Book design by Carla Green

Library of Congress Cataloging-in-Publication Data
Rainford, Nancy
       How to agent your agent / Nancy Rainford.
              p. cm.
       ISBN 1-58065-042-2
       1. Acting--Vocational guidance. 2. Theatrical agencies. 3. Motion picture authorship--Vocational guidance. 4. Literary agents. I. Title.

       PN2055.R35 2002
       792'.028'023--dc21   2001050215

Books may be purchased in bulk at special discounts for promotional or educational purposes. Special editions can be created to specifications. Inquiries for sales and distribution, textbook adoption, foreign language translation, editorial, and rights and permissions inquiries should be addressed to: Jeff Black, Lone Eagle Publishing, 1024 N. Orange Drive, Hollywood, CA 90038 or send e-mail to info@ifilm.com.

Distributed to the trade by National Book Network, 800-462-6420.
IFILM® and Lone Eagle Publishing Company™ are registered trademarks.

For Zoë

Contents

CONTENTS

Acknowledgments

There are so many people to thank—so I'll blame the billing on my editor and just get started: First and foremost, my husband, Tim—a gifted actor, writer, husband, father and friend—who urged, inveigled, teased, threatened, pushed, prodded and ultimately challenged me to write this book. I love you. Thank you: Mom, my toughest editor and biggest fan; Dad, my favorite entrepreneur; Sabrina, for your passion, determination, eloquence, and fierce loyalty; Michael, for your endurance; Dickie, because I know you will read my book. And Zoë, my love, who allowed Mommy time to work. It is for Zoë, Alex and Nick that I strive to set an example of "Yes, you can."

I have the absolute *BEST EDITOR* (no bold, no italics, no small caps—I know, I know!) in the entire world. I always wondered why editors were thanked so zealously and now I know—Lauren Rossini: smart, funny and a damn good writer. Jeff Black and the entire Lone Eagle staff, especially Carla Green for her layout. Oh, Hopwood, you are so patient, and such a great client, partner, friend...a GIANT talent. Thank you: Rhonda Dotson for your great work, your unfailing friendship (and your dining room table); Bruce Haring for guidance; Grant Show for fodder; the ever-positive Linda Sivertsen, along with Mark and Tosh; Tom Fox, the Boatmans, Iris and Emanuel, Barbara and Richard, the McGuigans, the Zayers, Dagmar, all the Rainfords; the Yates family—Doug, Missy, Jacqui and Sammy; the Kaminir-Kellys, the Krings, Maria Smith, the

Hardys, David and Liza, the Dearborn clan, Jean Levine, Annie Thomas Schwartz, Jane Schwartz, Chris Albrecht, Alex Soffer, Tracey Pakosta, Heidi Feldman, Howie Gold, Barry, Dina, Jay and Mike, Richard and Sherry, Tommy and Tracey, Vince and Teryn, Brian and Elizabeth, Lee Daniels, Kerry Jones, Roxanne; and no, Jennifer, I didn't forget you. All the talent agents, managers, casting directors, producers, directors, and attorneys I've worked with and for, especially Allison Jones, Gretchen Rennell, Marcia Shulman, Robert Morton, Pervis and Edgar, Ashton Springer, Kass and Woo and John Sloss and Associates. Thanks to *all* my clients throughout the years—especially Christine, Kim, Jada, Conrad, Michael, Lucy, Geoff, Joe, Juney and Sven—and particularly the first thirty clients of the Rainford Agency, who took a chance on me when all I really had was passion and chutzpah. Peace.

Introduction

Oh good, you opened the book. That means you either want an agent, you have an agent, or you *are* an agent. If you want an agent—any sort of agent—read this book before you venture forward. "Talent agent" is an all-encompassing term for every type of agent in the entertainment business. The term is most often associated with actor's agents for television and film, also known as theatrical agents. If you're a writer you look for a lit, or literary, agent. Stage actors seek legit agents (as in legitimate theatre), and of course there are also commercial and voice-over agents.

It doesn't matter what you call them, agents are agents. And because agents are *always* agenting, you—as the "talent"—need to be skilled in the art of agenting. You need to know what you want and why you want it (because the right agent for your boyfriend is not necessarily the best agent for you), and then you need to know how to go about getting what you need.

If you have an agent, you need to get the most out of him or her. This book will teach you how to follow an agent's point of view, how to speak the language and how to get (and keep!) your agent's attention. Anticipate how agents think, and you will better understand how they work. Understand how they work and you can get them working harder on your behalf. Don't just hand your career over to someone—get involved and stay involved. Remember: agents can't "make" you, so don't let them "take" you.

How to Agent Your Agent

If you *are* an agent, stop right here. You probably don't want to see your tricks, schemes and manipulations in print. Or read a book that tells your secrets and bares the soul of your chosen profession. Don't get me wrong, there are some terrific agents who are hard-working, honest, diligent, creative, informed, respected, loyal and successful. But too many other agents still need reminding that they are the employees in the relationship with talent, and all agents would do well to remember to treat their clients with respect for their craft and compassion for the difficulties of the business that performers deal with daily—inside and outside of the agency. So agents, put the book down. Everyone else—pay attention.

I have spent a lot of time with and around agents. I've been one, and even had one, so I know firsthand that *agenting your agent* is essential. Expecting someone to be more attentive to your goals than you are is foolish. It's your responsibility to be proactive with your career. Agents may often be the brunt of bad jokes, but let's face it: a good agent is an invaluable component of your package. Agents have access to every area of the entertainment business, they are instrumental in showcasing your talent where it might not otherwise be seen, they negotiate your deals and they speak on your behalf.

Even if you think your agent is great, you just might be able to make them better. For varying reasons, no two the same, Jada Pinkett, Anthony Geary, Juney Smith, Christine Elise, Michael DeLano, George Jenesky and Michael Nouri all made me a better agent. Moreover, being an agent made me a better casting director, a better manager, and now—many years later—a better producer.

With a degree in Television and Theatrical Producing, from a college in upstate New York without a clue about the industry, I moved to Los Angeles with the intention of working in entertainment. Not unlike a young actor heading west to seek fame and fortune, I was determined to make it. My first break was a temp job at The Wilhelmina Agency, where I was quickly hired full-time to work in the Theatrical Department. "Willy West" as we called it then, was a renowned top modeling agency, with a burgeoning acting roster. Most of the credit for the Theatrical Department belonged to agent (now manager) Joan Greene. Her departure, just prior to my arrival, was the source of many heated conversations, brought about when the remaining agents shifted into "damage control" mode. The unspoken rule is this: when an agent leaves an agency, co-worker loyalty, friendship and integrity fly out the window in favor of protecting the agency from a mass client exodus.

Faced with disaster, agents immediately go to great lengths to ensure that the talent stays put. And they are hyper-vigilante. They will bad-mouth, sweet talk, exercise emotional blackmail and even re-write history in a desperate attempt to usurp any influence the departing agents may have held over clients.

At the time, "Willy" clients included Kevin Costner, Crispin Glover and Heather Locklear, who, as I recall, was a focus of the discord. The agency wanted nothing more than to rid themselves of Joan while keeping Heather (and her commissions) on-board. It speaks to both Heather's and Joan's sense of loyalty and trust that they are still together as client and manager so many years later.

Wilhelmina has gone through many transformations since then, but in the early '80s, it was a fun place to work. Beautiful people, lots of parties and even more money. In the summer months, the agency hosted a Happy Hour every Friday from 3 o'clock until closing, complete with shelves of alcohol and trays of food. Clients and staff would mix work with pleasure right there in our West Coast offices. (Incidentally, I would be fired from Wilhelmina some eight months later during a Happy Hour fiasco—more on that later.) It was at my post behind the front office reception desk that I committed my first industry no-no: I refused a very intoxicated man entrance to the agency, despite his proclamations of "owning the place." As it turned out, technically, he did. Oops.

My second on-the-job reprimand came on the heels of inviting a client to the Happy Hour festivities. Clients were invited, but *not* all clients and *certainly* not that client. Because, as I was told, "all clients are not created equal." The big moneymakers were treated with kid gloves; they were not stopped at the front desk, but were announced as they buzzed in. Scripts and materials were delivered to their homes, not left in the agency lobby for pick-up. Their resumes were written, edited and photocopied by us, for them. We paid their *Players Directory* fees, and they had a standing invitation to Happy Hour.

My third infraction, the *coup de grâce* that triggered my last frozen lime daiquiri at 3:15 on a Friday afternoon, was precipitated by my inability to "get it." I worked for three agents in the Theatrical Department as their sole assistant. We had about ninety clients, and I thought every one of them was important. So, when a call came in at noon trying to locate an out-of-town actress (for a job I knew she needed) I paged Paul, her responsible agent, who was out at lunch. He didn't return the page. The other agents were out, and by 2:30 the casting director was panicked, so I paged him again. In fact, I paged him repeatedly until he returned to the office around 4:30—freshly showered, gym bag in hand and *furious*. Evidently his pager was to be considered a prop; because, Paul told me in no uncertain terms, "even if [his] mother is poised on the edge of a cliff prepared to jump," I was not to page him ever again.

The hype generated by the minds of agents made short work of my innocence. Especially when they fired me on that fateful Friday afternoon. For twenty minutes—before *finally* getting to the point—they agented me. They raved about me personally, praised my work and my professionalism; they even liked my shoes. I listened in disbelief while they declared love, loyalty and friendship, and expressed their dismay (as if it wasn't their decision), that they " had to" let me go. "Oh, and please stay for Happy Hour."

Such was my introduction to agenting. I've learned a lot since those crazy '80s days, and while artists are definitely more business savvy today then they were back then—there are still a load of myths to dispel and plenty of catching up to do. Every artist—in whatever stage of *stardom* or *starvedom*, from the unsuspecting novice to the been-around-the-block star—should learn to agent their agent…and you should start right now.

Enjoy,
—N.R.

A Note to Non-Actors

Throughout this book you will find many references to actors. If, as a non-actor, you think any portion of this book does not apply to you, I ask that you allow yourself to think again. Yes, crafts like screenwriting or costume design may be more tangible, but we both know that nothing is as simple as "here is my script/here are my sketches, like my ideas or not."

An agent does not have to believe your script is brilliant in order to sell it—but an agent *must* believe he can sell it. Actors, writers, directors, models, musicians, quarterbacks or crew-members: anyone who has, wants, or needs an agent or manager can use the information in this book. Just like an actor, you will need to fuel and sustain your agent's enthusiasm for your product.

Actors audition, writers take pitch meetings, and quarterbacks throw touchdowns. For actors, pictures, resumes and tapes are the tangible necessities of the business. For writers, it's your spec script, writing sample, treatment and ideas; for musicians, it's your demo tape; for models, it's your portfolio. All require agents to lay the groundwork, to provide opportunities, to excite the buyers and negotiate the deals. Remember that whether literary, theatrical, commercial or legit: *talent* agent is the common denominator. So, please, take the few extra minutes to read the chapters you may think do not apply to you. Where I write actor, insert your craft; if I say audition, think pitch-meeting, go-see or lunch meeting. Ultimately, the more you know about the basic nature and inner-workings of agencies and agents, in whatever capacity, the better equipped you'll be to agent *your* agent.

1

The Water Is Filled With Sharks
- Agents -

Alec Baldwin had been with the same agent for nine years, steadily building an admirable career that led to the lead role of CIA agent Jack Ryan in *The Hunt For Red October*. The film's success promised a sequel—actually three sequels, as reported in the November '91 issue of *Premiere* magazine: "...negotiations with Alec Baldwin to make *Patriot Games*, the first of the three planned sequels...dragged on for nearly one year. No sooner had they agreed on a price of $4 million per film and started the nitty-gritty of contract negotiations than things started getting extremely nitty. Among Baldwin's demands was a reported $700,000 in perks, extra pay for overages, and a contractual guarantee barring *Premiere* magazine from the set or from even having any contact with the Paramount Publicity Department." Just when it seemed the studio would give in, the picture Harrison Ford was scheduled to do fell apart. In an instant, Baldwin was out and Ford was in. Not at all surprisingly, Baldwin fired his agent.

A young unknown actor is about to screen-test for a television pilot. The deal and all of its particulars fall well below industry standards, even for a newcomer. The actor's responsible agent, *moi*, recommends that the client pass. But the agent negotiating the deal stands to get a hefty end-of-year bonus if the pilot goes to series, and so encourages the client to accept. During a staff meeting, the negotiating agent announces to the owner of the agency that an unknown actor with no prospects for future offers has been advised to pass on a deal by his responsible agent. Without further discussion I was given two options: Call the client during the staff meeting and persuade him to take the deal, or, drop the client from the agency.

A young writer gets a load of attention when her short film is recognized at a respected indie film festival. Agents are clamoring to take meetings and anxious to sign her. She signs, and shortly thereafter delivers a terrific feature film spec script for the agent to shop around town. He loves it and sends it out to a handful of studios, confident the script will sell over the weekend. It doesn't. Two weeks later, the agent's enthusiasm for the script diminishes to polite fondness, which quickly fizzles to complete non-interest. Two months later the writer can't even get the agent on the phone.

A middle-aged actress leaves her agent. The series that made her a household name has long since been cancelled. The TV movies are only trickling in. She wants film auditions, and she's looking for an agent who can get them for her. She walks through the door of a prospective agency and they know exactly what she wants to hear. They listen politely as she extols her loyalty to her last agent, despite the agent's failure to open any doors for her in feature films. She gives a number of excuses for the previous agency's failure. Around the room everyone is busy reacting. Some of the agents shake their heads at her misfortune, while others hurriedly jot down ideas. When the agents speak, it is with a mixture of excitement and pity. How *excited* they are to have this *opportunity* to work with *such a fine actress*, and what a pity that just weeks ago there was the *perfect film role* now lost to some other actress. They are *eager to get started* and *available for her at any time*. She signs, and immediately the TV agent begins browbeating the film agents to get an audition for our fading TV star. Not for reasons the actress heard in the meeting; they don't think for a second that she has a shot at a feature career. The meetings are to appease the actress as a client. The agents call in favors, pull strings, and do whatever is necessary to get the meetings—because this actress still has a few movies-of-the-week and maybe even a series left in her, and that means cash on the hoof to the agency. They need ammunition to induce her to get back on the TV money train. Once she's had a few meetings with "film people," the agents can convince her that *television* is what she needs for renewed exposure, and exposure will give her power; then the *real* film opportunities will open up. "Look at Helen Hunt and George Clooney," they say, "Trust us."

Trust your agent? Can you? Should you? Are they the scoundrels they're reputed to be? Liars and cheats? Or all-powerful, smart, savvy...and indispensable? Will they work harder if you ask them to be a godparent to your child? Will they let you down when the going gets tough? Are they sharks? Barracudas? Vipers? Or, are they professionals with only your best interest at heart? Who *are* they? What, why, and how do they think?

Some people are born agents, others work very hard to become agents. I agent when I buy a car, rent an apartment or go to a yard sale. I can still walk into almost any room in Hollywood and pick out the agents. Agents can read upside down, and can hear around corners. They will introduce themselves without provocation and engross themselves in multiple conversations at one time. They are problem-solvers, negotiators and master-jugglers. Only an agent can get away with falling asleep in the front row of a 99-seat theatre while trying to woo the actor performing onstage. And only an agent would have the chutzpah to praise a writer for a script that hasn't been read. A seasoned agent knows what you're going to say before you say it, and can sense exactly what you want to hear when you walk in the office. They can sell you your own idea. A good agent, by definition, is one who has mastered the Three S's: **Sign. Sell. Service.**

Sign

An agency's power is determined by the clients they represent, therefore, there is a constant need to sign new talent. Finding new or undiscovered talent (the next Mel Gibson, Julia Roberts, Shane Black or Alan Ball) is challenging, exciting and rewarding—everyone gets a chance to earn money, and an opportunity to climb the ladder of power. For a small or mid-size agency, one "breakout" client is enough to put the agency, and the responsible agent, on the map.

Years ago, I worked for an agency with a "10 percent" policy. This meant they would only allow 10 percent of their client list to consist of "developing" actors. Everyone else had to have a body of work. Today many of the large star-driven agencies have agents or departments geared toward developing young careers, while others let smaller agencies develop the talent before they swoop in and take over.

The success of a client enhances the reputation of the agency, which in turn attracts more moneymakers. Agents are rewarded with bonuses, more signing power and increased visibility within the industry. An agent with a substantial client list can demand more money and be more selective about where they choose to agent, or the agent can toss off the agent hat and step into a management or production role with ease. Along with the benefits of "breaking out" new talent, come the increased risks of losing that talent to larger or more powerful agencies. Most larger agencies have offices in other cities (even countries) or at the very least the "reach" to splash around in larger talent pools. Using their access and leverage as enticements, they can easily acquire talent from smaller agencies.

To maximize opportunities, agents are constantly active.

Screenings, festivals, showcases, plays, ski trips, parties, lunches, tapings, television, and yes, believe it or not, reading, are all part of an agent's routine. In the field, at the studios, on the golf course or the cell-phone, anywhere in or out of an office, wherever there is information to be found, an agent can justify being present. Aside from signing new talent, agents are expected to sign working actors and recognizable talent, and in many cases, stars. Acquisition meetings, as they are commonly termed, consist of staff meetings implicitly designed for signing talent. After deliberating over who and why, the agents then devise ways to pursue and eventually "acquire" the talent. Maybe one agent knows your manager. Maybe another sees you at the gym. Maybe no one knows you at all but needs to have names on their list when they go into the meeting. An agent may know your agent, know you're happy with your agent, and know your agent works hard for you—none of that will stop a determined agent from trying to "poach" you away from your current agency. An agent's signing power is of the utmost importance to any agency. Stealing clients from a competing agency is neither accidental nor a stoke of luck. It is always orchestrated and deliberate. Agents will woo talent for *years* until they sign.

SHARKS WITH HEARTS
If an agent is hesitant to "go after" a potential client
because of an existing friendship with that person's agent,
a different agent might be assigned the task.
But the task will be done.

For small agencies, one or two clients can make the difference between staying open for business and closing the doors.

SHARKS WITH HEARTS
Abe Lastfogel, legendary William Morris agent, established
a policy of not stealing clients from non-threatening
smaller agencies. That was a long time ago; I can tell you
first-hand that this policy is no longer in effect.

Larger agencies can also suffer losses when "raided" by an equally large agency.

In 1992, The Agency for Performing Arts (APA) suffered a series of setbacks. The most devastating was marked by the sudden death of a respected,

5

well-liked agent and founding partner. Industry rumors circulated about the agency's inability to sustain the loss. While many mourned, others scoured their resources for access to the agency's client list, and launched an aggressive assault to steal clients. The powerful Creative Artists Agency (CAA), which could have easily acquired any number of artists, respectfully and publicly took a hands-off stance.

Segue to 1999, again CAA takes a hands-off approach, but this time toward its own former president & founding partner, Mike Ovitz, along with his newly formed management and production company, Artists Mangement Group (AMG). CAA publicly announced its decision *not* to do business or share clients with the management company, forcing many of their clients to choose between the two. While it was the hot topic of industry gossip at the time, the players, the circumstance, and the needs change so frequently in Hollywood that company enemies today can easily be forming partnerships tomorrow.

Let's assume you are not being pursued or wooed by agents. How do you get one?

RULE 1: There Are No Rules.

Gimmicks don't work. Strangers have boldly arrived at my door with more than their pictures and resumes. Dozens of roses, bottles of champagne, baked goods, pencils, pens and kazoos. Hopeful artists sent crystals and poetry, promises and money, even shoes filled with candy (to get a foot in the door). I have received more letters, phone calls, faxes, FedExs and telegrams (including a singing hooker-gram on Halloween) than I care to remember. Some were cocky, some were clever, some rhymed and many were the brunt of jokes, but *none* of them worked. Still, I looked at every picture and resume that came through my door. Some sooner than others and many were glanced over briefly, but they all got opened. An agent who signs you because you sent a gift basket is not the agent you want.

A younger agent at a reputable agency asked everyone in the talent department to meet with an actor that the agent wanted to sign. Before the meeting, the agent let it be known that the prospective client had the financial resources to create his own work. "He gets cast," we were told, "because he puts up money for the production." After the meeting, the agents agreed not to represent the actor and the young agent is assigned the task of letting the actor know. Instead, every agent receives an individual gift basket with a Thank You note and bottle of very expensive champagne. Suddenly, the agency is representing the actor.

Though most smaller agencies will open and look at all submissions, larger agencies usually require a referral—it really depends on the agent. If your submission is addressed to an assistant, especially one who wants to be an agent, your letter will be opened; eager assistants generally leave no stone unturned. Though submitting to the assistant won't guarantee you an audience with the boss, it does guarantee that the submission will get into the hands of the person you're most likely to speak with on the phone. On the other hand, an assistant who works for an agent who can't be bothered...might not be bothered either.

If you're going to send an unsolicited picture and resume or query letter, keep it simple and smart. Always mention your referral, and if you don't have a specific referral, try something like this:

Dear [insert agent's name],
Your name keeps popping up as someone I should contact....

The agent has to feel as if you are their discovery. Don't tell someone you're the best thing to ever happen to their agency—even if you think it's true. Right off the bat, you've insulted them and made an annoyance of your-

A NOTE TO WRITERS
Keep in mind that looking at a picture and resume is a lot less time-consuming than reading a script, or even a treatment. Most agents will not accept unsolicited scripts. (Though most agencies will accept submissions from attorneys.) Unsolicited work is too labor intensive and potentially too litigious. Agents don't want to be sued for stealing your idea and they don't want to waste their time reading bad scripts. If you have to send something unsolicited, send an interesting query letter. Maybe you had a good review, a clever article or won a local contest—use something that demonstrates your talent as a writer to pique an agent's interest in meeting with you. Even writing for the school paper can work in your favor. For instance, Harvard University's The Harvard Lampoon *jumpstarted the careers of many a* Saturday Night Live *writer. (Be sure your work is registered with the Writer's Guild of America before submitting. If your query letter results in an agency wanting to read your script, very often they'll have you sign a standard disclaimer.)*

self. Don't tell them you want a relationship "like Jack and Sandy."[1] They've heard it before and they don't believe it. Don't tell them you're a young James Dean (unless your picture is the spitting image of Dean at fifteen, you're over eighteen but play younger, and the role of young James is being cast and the producers have seen everyone in town except you). You won't get the meeting. Don't tell them how to sell you. You have to be their idea.

Agents Always Need to Sign Talent

Use your resources. Agents do. When agents are looking to move to another agency, they have everyone they know, in any position, in almost any area of the industry, call on their behalf. You should do the same. Ask everyone to call—everyone. Lawyers, editors, actors, writers, directors, producers, studio heads, casting directors, even other agents—anyone who can and will speak well of you. Don't wait; those calls should be made before and after you've met the agent.

SHARK ATTACK
A client of mine was referred to a top lit agent at a top literary/theatrical agency. Before the agent would set a meeting, he wanted material. After allegedly viewing the

---

[1] Jack Nicholson and Sandy Bressler, whose client/agent relationship is older than this author.

*film my client had written, directed and starred in,
the agent passed. He told me he couldn't really get behind
the material, so there was no need to meet my client.
The tape was returned to me by the end of the day. Four
days later, the agent called back. Shortly after dismissing
me and my client, he'd heard about this great movie and its
hot young writer/star/director through the grapevine and
from several of his clients. He asked me to re-send the tape
so he could watch it again because, as he now put it,
"I think I like it more than I thought." We had already
signed with a different agent... but it didn't hurt
to make sure the new agent knew that we were
getting repeated calls from the competition.*

Legally, agents can't accept kickbacks for sending actors to a coach, photographer, lawyer, etc., but it's still a common practice to make referrals. If you're new in town, use it. New York and Chicago, both regarded as cities with great talent, carry weight. Seattle and Portland are also popular. Canadian actors are usually well received. With the box-office success of many foreign films, Hollywood has become more receptive to artists with accents. If you're a recent college graduate, use that to your advantage. Young is *always* in. In Los Angeles, the cachet of UCLA and USC go without saying. Yale, Harvard, Northwestern, Brown, Wesleyan, and, of course, NYU are popular as well.

Most agents will accept calls from the Dean of Theatre, or from a Creative Writing professor at a respected university—have them call on your behalf. If college wasn't your route, don't sweat it. You don't need a degree to be an artist. Don't look at what you haven't done as a handicap, instead, use what you *have* and what you *have done* in your favor. Explore your own uniqueness and bring that to the forefront of your sell. Eventually you will get meetings. Take them.

BEWARE THE SHARKS

In Hollywood, meetings are "taken" not held. Take them with legitimate agencies only. For actors, an agency should be signatory to the Screen Actors Guild (SAG); licensed, bonded and regulated by the State. Literary Agencies are signatory to the Writers Guild of America (WGA) (for a nominal fee, non-members can register their scripts and treatments with the WGA). (A complete list of signatory agencies can be found in the appendix at the back of this book.)

SHARKSKIN SUIT

Remember, agents don't interview, they "meet with" for representation. Dress in whatever makes you feel and look your best. Be comfortable.

Initial meetings are usually with one agent. If you're unsure of his or her status, ask. How long have you been with the company? Where were you before? How long have you been an agent? Ask the questions you need answered, but try to do it within a conversation. This isn't a job interview, it's a meeting. An initial meeting to see if either one of you has something that might benefit the other. Try not to panic. I've met actors who literally shook through meetings. The agent translation: He/she is green, and not ready for auditions. If an agency doesn't think you can handle an audition, they are never going to believe you can get a job. If you can't get a job, you can't make money. If you can't make money...next! Confidence is a necessity, but how and why you impress an agent is not always with your work or your looks, and whether that matters or not is up to you. Be pragmatic. During an initial meeting, after you've impressed Agent A, he or she may ask Agent B to join in. Stay calm. This is your time to assess the agency. Don't let their apparent excitement sway your judgement. It could be that the agents have heard that a competitive agent or agency is interested in signing you and their egos have to "win." You don't know their motives—and they don't know everything.

SHARK BAIT
I know an agent who is always drawn to variations of the same man—her husband. Any guy similar in stature, coloring and basic demeanor, she invites back to meet the other agents, or urgently calls other agents to her office to meet her "find." On the flip side are actors who have been passed on by agents for committing the unconscionable crime of looking like someone's ex-husband or ex-wife.

I've told actors whom I genuinely wanted to help, but was unable to sign because no one else in the agency was interested, to meet with an agent who specifically loved to steal clients from me. Turnabout being fair play, I've also sent actors I wouldn't rep for all the money in the world to that same agent. The motives of agents are not always what they might seem.

It could be that Agent B's willingness to meet you is selfish. Perhaps later that day Agent B has a meeting with an actor he wants to sign. So Agent B might pop his head in, say hi, or even spend some time with you... depending on how much help he'll need later from Agent A (an example of agents agenting agents). At the end of your meeting you may hear a very familiar, "let me talk to the others...." Don't expect any agent to stand behind the conviction of this interest; don't give them that much power. Their interest in you must be massaged by the interest of others. If you don't hear from them and you're still interested, have someone of (at least some degree) importance call on your behalf. For example, if you have a friend who works for a casting director or production office, ask that friend to call. How quickly an agent calls back is often determined by their assessment of the competition. If the agent believes you have options and the options are good, you'll hear from him or her pronto. If the agent sets a time for you to meet the other agents, he or she may really want to sign you; but the agent might also be on the fence and want someone else to make the decision. Maybe the agent owes a favor. Maybe the agents need to inflate their "acquisition" lists. Or maybe it's the only way to get you out of the office or off the phone.

Agents Will Never Tell You They Don't Want to Sign *You.*

They will tell you they have too many clients, or too many people in your age range, or your "type" and it "wouldn't be fair" to you. They will say they can't get all the agents to agree, and though they really want to work with you, it isn't their decision alone. During pilot season, the agency "isn't signing any new clients," after pilot season "business is slow." Agents will say *anything* but *no.* There are instances when an agent will really want to sign an actor, and the other agents refuse. It's frustrating, and if it happens often enough, the agent will eventually move to another agency.

> *Anthony Geary was starring in a production of Jesus Christ Superstar, working with a young actor named Geoff Meek. We represented Anthony, but Geoff didn't have an agent, so I sent him out on a few auditions—the next thing we knew he was testing for a series. At the time, I was still just an assistant, so when I pitched and pushed and suggested we sign Geoff, the other agents scoffed. Days after we passed on Geoff, he landed a long-term contract on a New York soap, and continued to work from that day forward. He credits me with starting his career, and I blame those agents as the reason I never formally repped Geoff.*

Don't believe everything you hear. Walk into an agency with a three-picture deal, an on-air series, or a script that's been optioned, prepared to commission the agent who signs you, and you will not be turned down. Regardless of how many actors or writers they represent—where there is work, there is money and prestige, and wherever you find both, you also find agents.

Today's agents want tape. You may not have tape, or it may be outdated, or maybe it's just not good. If it's not good, don't show it. Five minutes of poor quality, mediocre-performance tape can feel like an eternity. If you only have one great two-minute scene on a ten-minute reel, show the two great minutes. Use what works and leave the rest behind.

Getting an agent to go to a play can be difficult (especially if it's an obscure theatre in the middle of nowhere), and taped plays usually wind up looking like a muddy mess. Unless it's a one-man show (generally speaking), plays are meant for the stage. Many actors will offer to do a scene, either in the agent's office or during an acting class where the agent can audit. If the acting coach is reputable, auditing is more enticing—it's a great opportunity to scout other talent, and that's exactly what they're doing; agents are the original multi-taskers. Regardless of the motivation behind auditing, the effort is indicative of what you might expect from the agent in the future. If the agent makes the effort to watch your scene, that agent might also make the effort to see you in a play, and make a call on your behalf. I have

> **MUSICIANS, DIRECTORS, ET AL:**
> *Listening to unprofessional tracks or viewing a bad demo reel is not an agent's idea of a good time. With technology today, presenting a polished video, cassette or even CD is worth the extra effort. Don't send a demo tape with every song you've ever written or every image you've ever shot; give the agent a sample of your best and make sure your query letter indicates that you have more material.*

signed clients based on scenes, though I've never been a big fan of seeing them in my office. No matter where you do it, doing a scene is a risk. If you're willing to take the chance, first, be prepared—don't do a scene that you aren't familiar with just because you think it's a good scene. If you're bad in it, you've wasted everyone's time. Second, be good. At the very least, be as good as your scene partner.

SHARK BAIT

One of the most memorable scenes I've witnessed was performed by a young actress and her boyfriend. At the time, neither had any substantial credits. He was so subtle and brilliantly funny that her performance seemed even worse than it might have, had she chosen a less talented

*scene partner. Unfortunately, it was her audition.
After the scene I scrambled to the* Players Directory *to find
out who represented the boyfriend I now desperately
wanted to sign. Today you wouldn't need a directory to
recognize Matthew Perry, whose performance I never
forgot, but I wouldn't recognize the actress even if
she married my brother. Conversely, I may have left
an equally unremarkable impression.*

Don't shoot yourself in the foot. If an agent is happy to sign you, but doesn't want to see your scene, let it be. Because even if you're good in it, it doesn't mean you can act. It means you did a good scene, one that you may have been doing for the past year. If you were bad, maybe you just did a bad scene, or maybe you didn't have enough time to prepare. Even if it isn't your fault, it doesn't matter—agents just remember *bad,* and you don't usually get a second chance.

Choosing the same scene an agent has recently sat through can also be dangerous. How many times can you hope an agent will laugh at *Lovers & Other Strangers*? Ask before you leap: "Is there anything you guys don't want to see...?"

The scene that best shows your acting chops may not be the best scene to bring to the table. Unless you can blow them away, most agents are looking for more than your ability. Agents want to see that you can get hired. They want to see your charm, your hook, your humor...*your potential to get work.*

A NOTE TO WRITERS

It is so easy nowadays to shoot something you've written, either on DVD or videotape, that if you can, you should. Tape is a great tool, but keep in mind how many other factors can potentially cloud the focus of your writing—like casting , performance, direction or editing. If all aspects are brilliant and garner attention, so will your script. If any element leaves something to be desired, your piece may suffer. Also, the in-it-for-the-long-term literary agent will want to see more than a tape of something you wrote; they need to read your words. Keep it professional.

Nothing is more annoying than a sloppy presentation. The information is out there; learn how to professionally structure your script or treatment. Use your spellchecker, but don't rely on it; know the difference between its and it's— most importantly, let other people read your script before you send it out. **Edit. Edit. Edit.**

14

Maybe the scene just doesn't work in an office or conference room with six people sitting around a table staring at their watches. Maybe your audience just got screamed at by the agency head and they're not in the mood to meet with you. Remember Agent B who popped his head in during your first meeting? Well, that afternoon, your Agent A nixed Agent B's actor, and now *you* are the payback.

What I'm trying to say is, first, there are no rules and second, it's not all about you. Even when it seems it should be. It's your deal, your job, your trailer, your contract, your butt on the line; still it's not all about you. This is why *you* need to look out for *you*.

Let's say you've piqued the agent's interest. Regardless of whether the agent wants to sign you, he or she now wants to tell you why their agency is the better choice. This is the "the way we work" speech—and it is basically the same at every agency for every actor or writer.

If it's a mid-size agency competing with a large company, the speech goes like this:

"The difference between us and Huge Agency is that we work as a team. In larger agencies your 'key agent' covers specific areas. For instance, if your key agent covers Disney TV and Paramount Films, and you're right for a project at Universal, your agent must sell you to the agent covering that project at Universal. Of course, that agent has their own 'key clients,' so you'll never be their priority, not until after they've exhausted their own list. Agents at larger agencies are motivated by and strive for the year-end bonus—money generated by booking their 'key clients.' That's not our policy. *We* divide the town instead of dividing the agency. Larger agencies work with huge client lists. So you're actually competing within your own agency if you sign with Huge Agency! Here at Mid-size Agency, we work to develop the artist's career. At large agencies, if you don't land a pilot or film, they drop you. Not here. We're in it for the long haul."

A large agency would turn that around to sound like this:
"*We* represent the writers, the directors, and the producers. We've got the clout to get you in on every project. We've got everything. Smaller agencies just don't have the manpower to cover the town. Do you know how many projects are out there right now? We do, because we control the product. We get the information before anyone else in town. We can 'package' you into films and TV. We represent someone on almost every television project or movie produced."

The very largest agencies may only respond to direct questions, and not bother to sell themselves. After all, you're supposed to want to be with them. (The soft sell shifts into hard-drive when a big agency is wooing a star. But if you're not an established star [yet!], they're in the driver's seat—if you allow them to be.)

A small agency has a different approach:
They claim "You won't get lost here at Small Agency, the information is available and everyone's got access to it. We'll use that information for you, not just our stars. We're a hands-on agency, almost like managers. You can get us on the phone. We don't have ten actors just like you, so you'll be a big fish in a small pond. There's enough competition outside the agency; the last thing you want to do is compete within the agency representing you."

There is a place and a need for agencies of every size. Still, every actor, every writer, every director will eventually yearn for the big agency experience. The lure of playing in the big game, with the big kids—where big money, top choices and unlimited opportunities abound—is a powerful one. Delivered scripts, holiday parties, power lunches. For some that gets old, for others it's the top. It's more than just a matter of personal taste; the truth is that you want to get work and keep working. So, as your situation and circumstances change, so must your choice of representation. Your agents, your personal manager, your business manager, lawyers, publicists, photographers—everyone will change.

SHARK BITES

When I first became an agent, I met with Chris Albrecht, who is now President of HBO. At the time he'd recently left a successful agenting position at ICM, and at this meeting he offered me three bits of advice:
(1) "No" is the most powerful word an agent can use.
(2) "No deal" is better than a bad deal.
(3) All your clients will leave you.
I left his office vowing to heed his words about the deal stuff, but knowing he was wrong about the client thing.
He wasn't.

RULE 2: You Will Leave All Your Agents.

This may sound like a fatalistic approach toward creating a relationship—unless you understand that agents work with the knowledge, the fear, and the certainty that, no matter what they do, or how hard they work, you *will* leave[2]. Think of it as dating someone you know you won't ever marry, or renting a house you'd never dream of buying. You may be in love and very comfortable, but everything is shaded by the fact that it's not a permanent thing. Eventually, no matter what they do, you *will* leave your agent. Agents who don't work under this assumption are the exception, and are doomed to repeated disappointment. Concentrate on the time that you and this particular agent will be working together, and work to get the most out of it. Pay attention to your business, because no matter where you take it, no matter

---

[2] The rule is proved by the exception—and today there are but a few exceptions left.

> *Many actors sign with a commercial agency that also has a Theatrical Department, thinking that if they book jobs commercially the agency might sign them theatrically. On more than one occasion I was forced to sign an actor theatrically because the Literary Department "needed us" to sign the client. From time to time some agent in the Lit Department would bombard the Theatrical Department with requests for acting auditions for the writer. Anything was acceptable, just get the writer an audition. In today's market, agencies are hard-pressed to successfully enforce the "sign with us across the board, or not at all" rule; there is too much competition and talent is too savvy. Just because one area of a company is successful doesn't always mean the other is as well. Choose them separately, and with care.*

who your agent happens to be at the moment, it is always *your* business.

There is an agent out there for everyone in every phase of every career. I know I've beaten out other agents and signed actors based on criteria other than my agenting ability. But I'd like to believe it was my agenting ability that kept them with me. Actors have signed with me because I am a woman, thinking female agents were more nurturing. Clients have left me because I'm a woman, thinking they needed a man in a man's business. I've signed actors because my dog used to go to work with me, and a Golden Retriever with a wagging tail somehow lent to my credibility. I've probably *not* signed other clients because there was a dog in my office. Think of the criteria you use to choose your agent, and remember that agents are just as susceptible to whim.

This is still a business, and like any business, there is supply and demand, and there are always options. "Any" agent is not better than no agent at all. Don't sign with someone just so you can say you have an agent. You didn't come to Hollywood to get an agent. You came to get a career.

Focus Your Energy on the Work

Work begets work. If you work, agents will come. Everyone hates agent-hunting. But choosing an agent is as difficult as you decide to make it. Know what you want from an agent and for your career.

Freelancing with various agencies is commonplace in New York, although more and more agents are presenting even the bi-coastal actor with agency contracts. In freelancing, it's standard practice that the agent who initiates the audition and negotiates the deal, subsequently collects the commissions. It's first come, first served.

In Los Angeles, agents sometimes "side-pocket" clients, which may sound good, but the term side-pocket infers only that you have friends at an agency who submit your pictures and resumes and sometimes field inquiries. Or, they might not do anything on your behalf except allow you to use their agency letterhead on your résumé. While there are no signed contracts, Los Angeles agents tend to assume that no one else is simultaneously side-pocketing the same client, which can get sticky.

> *I've seen actors lose out on auditions because they were submitted by too many agents. If no one calls to pitch the actor the photos are tossed aside because the casting director is reluctant to get involved in a dispute.*

Though side-pocketing is acceptable, the practice is limited in Los Angeles. Most side-pocketing in Los Angeles occurs when the agent (or more often than not, the agent's assistant) has no authority to sign, isn't convinced he should sign, or can't get the actor to sign contracts. (Many agents also side-pocket personal friends, and friends or relatives of clients, producers, and directors, etc.) Actors routinely boast of being side-pocketed at one of the "big" agencies. If that's you, unless it's your choice and you're getting plenty of auditions and work, don't rest on those laurels; no one with any power is fooled by the façade.

If you *are* side-pocketed, it's best to present yourself as being repped by a specific person at an agency. In other words, rather than saying, "I'm being side-pocketed at William Morris," try, "I'm repped by Aggie Agent at William Morris." If you aren't specific about the office covering you and a casting director or development exec calls to set up a meeting, he or she will speak to the agent who is covering the project or ask client information for your responsible agent. Either way, if you're not on the agency client list, no one at the agency will have heard of you, and very often the search to bring you in ends there.

If you don't want to sign an agency contract because you're afraid you might get screwed, don't be. It's so easy to free yourself from unwanted agency contracts (even after you've signed) that you don't really have to worry about making a huge commitment. Your goal should be to find an agent enthusiastic and powerful enough to commit to your career all the way—at least for the time being. You *can* get an agent. Getting one is nothing compared to getting the best out of one.

Sell

All agents are expected to provide opportunities for their clients to work. On occasion, agents can create jobs that might not otherwise exist.

"Packaging" is a common term used to describe the circumstance whereby agencies or management companies place one or more clients on a project. Putting together an attractive "package" is a common sales tool designed to remove some of the "uncertainty" from a project, and to shift the responsibility if it fails. For instance: Joe Young Writer has a great script but no resume and no clout. Under normal circumstances, a network or studio might be reluctant to buy his script and commit large sums of money. Enter the agent representing a star actor and a prolific writer/producer/show-runner, both of whom are looking for a fresh idea and willing to commit to Joe Young Writer's script. With these two new elements attached, the risk is diminished and the project becomes viable in the eyes of the network or studio money men.

Regardless of how or to whom an agent sells, sell they must, or they will lose the client. It's easy to sell an actor into the next project if he's just starred in a blockbuster film or written a box-office hit. It requires a bit more skill to sell that actor into the same project if he's just been fired from a soap opera.

Remember the middle-aged TV star who changed agents because she wanted to work in feature films? Creating a film career for that actress is a lot more work then putting her in a series or television movie. The dollars she can generate in television far outweigh the monies she might reasonably earn doing small roles in large pictures, or larger roles in any independent film. Not to mention that it's a lot easier to sell her to prime-time than it is to sell her to Scorcese. Signing her was guaranteed money—*television* money.

RULE 3: Agents Don't Like To Make Work... They Like To Make Money.

A writer I know is repped by a reputable agency. While a client there, he has created a network TV pilot and had two feature scripts optioned by respectable production companies. None of these accomplishments have been due to the efforts of the agency. Prior to signing with the agency, he'd written, produced and directed an award-winning independent feature film. Now the client needs work, but his responsible agent can't get the other agents behind him. The agent suggests that if either of the client's scripts go into production, or if the client sells something else, then the other agents might perk up. In essence, the agent is suggesting the client get work on his own as a way to induce the other agents to work on his behalf!

SHARK TRICKS
There are instances where an actor or writer needs to make money, regardless of how short-term that income may be, and without concern for any long-term consequences. The responsibility of the agent is, first, to offer a professional opinion, and next, to achieve the immediate goal of the talent, while minimizing any negative long-term effects.

Money is a powerful motivator, even for agents who genuinely have the client's best interest at heart. The obligation to sell is equally powerful. Once an agency contract is signed, regardless of an agent's personal opinion of the client's talent or ability, the agent is obligated to procure employment. In many cases agents will find themselves representing actors or material in whom or which they have no interest. If the owner of the agency says his daughter's best friend is now a client; it doesn't matter that she's never taken an acting class in her life, or that she's got the personality of a spoon—agents are expected to sell.

How do you sell someone when you have no faith in their work? You pick up the phone and you make the calls. You push, you cajole, you plead, you laugh at bad jokes, you ask for favors, and you get your clients in the door. For many agents, selling an actor is like selling anything else: you find the hook, and then you feed the line. If you're selling a car and its one distinguishing feature is spoke wheels, you sell the spoke wheels. For other agents, it's not about the hook at all, it's just about the way they sell. The talk, the patter—the schmooze, if you will. The same schmooze they use on you when you call. You bought it, why wouldn't someone else? Savvy agents are adept at turning a phrase. Even if they have no knowledge of the actor's craft, and no heartfelt desire to get him or her work, the money motivator can make them sing like canaries. It's the *action*.

SHARK SCHOOL
One agent runs his agency by the credo of "throw them against the wall and see who sticks" He never tries to fit the role to the actor; he sells everyone for everything.

Selling actors you believe in would seem the easiest route, but they pose the same obstacles and require the same skills as repping anyone else. The only difference is the agent's personal interest. Hopefully, that passion will encourage the agent to go the extra mile, but ultimately selling is selling. The easy sell requires no work. The passionate sell has staying power. Selling a Monica Lewinsky was easier during the Clinton administration than it is today. Five years prior to that her name meant nothing in the media world; she was just another college kid. On the other hand, selling last year's Oscar® winner is a breeze—but can just any agent negotiate the particulars of that deal and satisfy those creative tastes? Pay attention to the other people your agent represents and where your agent sells. If you meet with an agent who represents eighty actors and half of them are in your age range and working steadily, simple logic says that this agent can get work for people in your age group. But be more specific: if the work is primarily on soaps, is that the agent's only strength? And how will that help *your* future career?

SHARK SCARE

One agent met a young actor who clearly showed promise, but was still turned down for representation. "I'm like Don King," the agent declared, "I don't represent talent on their way up, I get 'em when they're up...and ride 'em down."

To whom and where your agent sells should be a major consideration in your choice of agents. Many theatrical agents limit their selling to casting directors, while others completely ignore them. Some lit agents sell to development execs and can't get a decision-maker on the phone. Others concentrate on independent studios rather than major studios, or cable rather than network. Good agents don't completely rely on or dismiss anyone. In this business, the rulers change fast, but the truths holds steady. The practiced agent knows how and when to use all available resources. And don't think for a second he's not using them on you. Selling, by agent definition, encompasses far more than merely soliciting work.

For the agent, finding or devising the hook that makes the talent stand out—in an industry with talent to burn—is crucial. But how far should (or can) you stretch the truth?

A segment of CBS' *Sixty Minutes* described the "meteoric fall of a teenage prodigy whose career ended abruptly when the entertainment industry learned that her true age was thirty-two."

Entertainment Weekly online wrote: "In addition to fooling *Felicity* producers, Weston also duped her agent, manager, lawyer...even *Entertainment Weekly*, which put her on that year's "It List" and quoted her as saying, 'In many ways I am Felicity, so I hope to portray this generation in a realistic light.'"

Yes, Riley Weston, AKA Kimberlee Elizabeth Kramer, fooled a lot of people—but her manager wasn't one of them. In fact, her manager is her ex-husband. And though she takes credit for devising the ruse, he sold her scripts and the wunderkind angle to studios, talent agents and the press—and he sold them well.

It worked beautifully until it didn't work at all, and as quickly as Ms. Weston grew to fame, the walls of fame came crashing down around her. Could she have done it without her manager/husband? Were there others who knew or suspected but kept quiet and didn't ask—was that the best, or only way to sell the client?

The fact is, if her purported age was the only reason her work was considered worthy, none of it speaks well for the writer, sellers or the buyers. If her work stood out on its own merit, should it matter how old she was when she wrote it? Ms. Weston can, and should, work again—all she needs is a little re-inventing. And there are many agents and managers willing to take the chance.

Service

An agent can sign, and an agent can sell, but they'll lose a client if they don't service. Proper servicing requires personal and professional attention, while responding to the individual needs and circumstances, traits and moods of the actor.

Personal attention shouldn't mean finding a discreet drug dealer for the addicted actor, though it may mean putting him in rehab.

An actress I once represented landed an on-air series, despite the fact she reeked of alcohol each time she auditioned for the part. Before testing at the network, she signed contracts with a 'drug clause'—that she never read. By the third episode, the producers enforced the clause and she was mandated to check-in to rehab within a week or lose the job. Her manager and I approached the subject with her cautiously over lunch at her home. She ranted, raved, cursed and performed for us. Swearing that she hadn't had a drink *in years* and that she'd *never* done drugs (uh huh), she then stormed off to the restroom. The manager took a tentative sip of her lemonade. "Vodka," he announced, quickly taking another healthy swig before she returned.

Another more famous actress has a little problem with kleptomania. Something everyone is aware of—from her agent, publicists, friends and family to salesclerks and store managers; it's common knowledge. It's not that she can't afford to pay—but she has a strong compulsion to steal. Periodically, the actress is banned from stores, until her agent arranges (without her knowledge) to have the bills are sent to her husband, whereupon they are paid promptly and without question.

When David Caruso left *NYPD Blue* to pursue a film career, he was lambasted by both the public and the industry. In *TV Guide*, Caruso made a compelling statement about his decision to leave the show. Ultimately he "wanted a chance at bat." The opportunity to crossover from TV into film was at hand—he wanted to take the chance. The decision to leave the show was reportedly Caruso's, but how culpable were his agents in the decision-making? If they were, say, "less than enthused," would speaking up have cost them the client? Regardless of their opinions—right or wrong— once the decision was made, you can bet they picked up the phone when he called, and defended, approved and supported him publicly. Three years later he was back and working again in TV. But evidently some folks haven't forgotten.

While I was writing this, an actor I know had an audition for a guest star spot on *NYPD Blue*. He arrived at the casting/production office, signed-in...and noticed David Caruso's name on the sign-in sheet. Producer humor.

Servicing requires availability. To an actor, whose well-being and liveli-hood is dependent on others, an agent should always be on hand. Have you ever called an agent and been told she's not available because she's on the phone with another client? No, and you never will. It's always a casting call, a staff meeting or a producer, director or conference call—but it's *never* anoth-er client. Don't believe it. Your average mid-size talent agency represents at least one hundred actors, and if they admit to that number, you can tack on at least another forty to fifty more. And that's not even beginning to count the clients who think they have an agent, despite the fact that their files have actually been stowed away in a back room for months.

Every single client in every single agency wants individual, personal and professional attention. Even if your name hasn't crossed your agent's lips in a week, she'll tell you she just had a conversation all about you. Agents need to make every client feel like a priority—while at the same time, seizing every opportunity to make money. Though you may not want to hear that Amy Actress just landed a series, her landing that series has now opened another door for your agent. If used properly, that door may lead to a new opportuni-ty for you. The reality is that unless they're in the midst of negotiating, rarely is an agent's conversation about just one person. That's not cost effective. In an effort to make you feel special, an agent might tell you that she has been on the phone all day talking about you. If that's what you need to hear to make you feel "serviced," that's what you'll get.

Of course, the more actors work, the more servicing they require, and the more difficult it becomes for an agent to take credit when other people are also involved. For instance, if an actor signs with a manager, a publicist and a lawyer, that's four people trying to keep their client, each trying to appear more necessary than the other guy.

RULE 4: Success Has Many Parents; Failure Is Always an Orphan.

No two agency clients have the same needs, but they do have common denominators. They must at all times feel confident that their agent knows more then they do about the business. Good agents do. They stay informed, and stay in the loop. If you call your agent about a project your friend's been in on and leave a message with the assistant, your agent is a fool to call you back without information. You wouldn't be calling if you thought he was on top of things, so if your agent calls back without a clue, he's only validating your fear.

Know this: agents bluff.

They bluff because the minute they cease to appear to know more than you do, or than your friend's agent does, they risk losing you as their client. How can you tell when they're bluffing? Ask specifics. Have you ever been satisfied by hearing, "You were submitted"? Of course not. You want to hear that your agent knows the producer and has an inside track at the network. When an agent is negotiating your contract, you want to hear that they have a friend in business affairs. You want to have confidence in your agent. Some agents do know more, and a lot of agents bluff. Whether the bluffers are servicing their clients or saving their butts...depends on the client.

SHARK BITE
I once represented an actress on a popular series. Sometime during the first season, word got back to me (through a number of reliable sources, including her own publicist), that she was earning an unfavorable reputation with her less-than-decorous behavior on the set and in public. So, before things got worse, I gently took her aside. I was servicing my client, but I knew very well the

result would be one of two things. Either she'd thank me
for my honesty (not very likely) or fire me
in denial (very, very likely).
She fired me.

There are no rules to servicing a client. What one agent might find abhorrent, another would consider common practice. It is amazing what an agent will do if the client is important enough. Equally alarming are the demands actors will make to prove to themselves that they wield power. The motivations for an agent to *sign*, *sell* and *service* are *power*, *money* and *necessity*. An agent doesn't leave her child's graduation to take an actor's call because she loves the client. She does it out of necessity, because the client leads the way to power and financial success.

2

Cats and Dogs
– Agents vs. Managers –
(Who are they kidding? They're one and the same!)

Early on, I was given good reason to dislike and distrust managers. Edgar Small, who originally gave me my agent stripes, was wary of managers, and on many occasions used what I termed his "bull's-eye theory" to demonstrate. Imagine a target, with the actor in the center of the bull's-eye. Surround the center with a number of rings, placing the agent inside the ring closest to the actor. Fill the other rings with the rest of the team: lawyer, publicist, accountant, friends, family, therapist, stylist, trainer, nutritionist, masseuse, whatever. Now enter the personal manager, whose goal is to make his way to the target. For the manager to succeed, everyone else has to move out a ring or two, including the agent—who is often replaced entirely. From this inner ring, managers gain a position of influence over everything—including securing a more subservient agent, one who will assume a position outside of and with deference to the manager. When percentages are assigned, say 10 to 20 percent for the manager, 10 percent for an agent, 5 percent for lawyers, 5 percent for business managers…that's a lot of people on the payroll. Staying inside the inner circle is really the only way to ensure job security.

RULE 5: When A Client Signs With A Manager, Sooner, Rather Than Later, That Client Leaves The Agency.

It's simple math. No one decides to pay double commission because they have extra money floating around. Either your career is not moving and you *want* the muscle, the middleman and the guidance; or your career is flying and you *need* the middleman, the muscle and the guidance. Both spell trouble for your agent, because one way or another it means you are dissatisfied with the agent's performance.

Once the seed of doubt is planted, a newly acquired or long-standing manager is the agent's Grim Reaper.

The need to be closest to the bull's-eye is the bottom line of the agent/manager relationship. And it can work to the client's benefit. If your agent and your manager are vying for your loyalty, both should be working diligently to prove worthy. That's a good thing and works in your favor. If they aren't competing then valuable time is wasted while each blames the other's inadequacies or schemes to take credit and earn brownie points. That cannot help your career. When an agent and a manager work cohesively for the good of the client (thereby also benefiting themselves), great things can happen.

For agents, it's a nice change of pace to be able to hand off some of the "bad cop" rap to a manager, and have someone else run interference when a client is dissatisfied. For a manager, having an agent solicit and negotiate can free the manager to orchestrate and develop. It *should* be a symbiotic relationship—if the business wasn't wracked with paranoia and guilt, which it is. If you have an agent and a manager and you are paying two commissions; you want two efforts on your behalf. Whether those efforts are united or divided, they need to equal two when combined, otherwise you are wasting your money.

The perception in the business is: unless you are a major talent or an independent creator (meaning you generate your own work) having just a manager and no agent is unfavorable. That doesn't mean you should run out and grab the first agent you meet, because equally ill-perceived is the actor with management and negligible agents. And managers want the prestige of working with a substantial agent who can open doors, assume some of the workload and access information.

> I made a test option deal for a young actress whose quotes[1] weren't worthy of mention. Happy to have an invitation to the ball and gun shy about the art of the deal, the client wanted to accept a sub-par deal and wouldn't give me the power to say no, which I needed to move the deal forward. I couldn't sell her out, even though she wanted me to, because I knew that if I did, once she got on that set and chatted with other actors, she'd realize her deal stunk and blame me. So, I used her manager in the Bad Cop role. I told Business Affairs that I hadn't yet spoken with the client, but that her manager wasn't budging and there was no way he was going to accept this deal. I had to go back to the manager with something acceptable or we were both going to lose this deal and I was going to lose my client. It worked and we forged ahead. Needless to say, the client was shocked by the significant improvement in the deal and promised next time not to get in the way (easier said than done). (For more on the 'Power of No,' See Chapter 6.)

Stan Kamen was a big time agent at William Morris who, at one time or another, represented every major star— Barbra, Warren, Goldie, Jimmy Caan, Kirk Douglas, David Niven—before he passed away in the mid-eighties. It never hurt Stan Kamens, the manager, that the two names were often confused.

If you sign with a manager who feels your current agent is lacking in any of the above, you'd better start drafting that teary-eyed, goodbye-to-my-longtime-agent letter, because securing a new agent is that manager's first order of business.

---

[1] An actor's quote refers to money the actor has received in the past for work in a comparable medium. (See Chapter Five for more details.)

You Have an Agent and Want a Manager

If, over the course of time, you mention to your agent that you may need or want a manager, he will know whether it's time to suggest one or if he can still talk you out of it. If he can, he will. An agent who is paying attention will know by the way you suggest it if this "manager thing" is already a *fait accompli*. If you ask more than once, then someone's been talking. Most likely you've met with a manager who is trying to sign you. Obviously, if you ask about a particular manager, your agent will assume you've already met or at least had a conversation with the manager. The reaction will vary depending on the manager and your importance to the agent.

A young client of mine once did a guest star stint on an episodic show that was shot out of the country. The mother of the lead actress was a manager who represented some recognizable actors, and to her credit she saw my client's potential. My client returned from the gig having been and (continuing to be) hounded by the manager and the manager's daughter. She did not want to sign with the manager, but she also didn't want to deal with having to tell her, so she asked me to intervene. As a courtesy, I met with the manager...and for the next two years she tried to wrestle the client from my roster, never once trying to establish a relationship with me. The more the client worked, the more determined was the manager. Eventually the manager saw her opportunity when I left the agency business. Concerned that I might consider management, the manager cleverly told the client that she was "desperately" trying to use her connections to set *me* (me!) up at another agency. She convinced the actress to sign contracts with the manager to protect herself during this lapse time, then urged her to meet with other agents at "my" suggestion. The manager then called me to say she had done her best to convince the actress to wait for me, but the client was desperate to sign with a different agent. She lied, but the actress had signed papers and so, for the time being, financially had to live with the consequences.

Agents who want to hold on to a client will recognize when it's time to stop fighting and start accepting the idea of a manager. Once it has been determined as the only way to retain the client, the agent will suggest managers, and set meetings. Meetings with managers who have worked with the agent before, and who will hopefully have an allegiance because the agent put the actor with the manager. What your agent wants you to find is a manager he or she can trust!

If your agent suggests that it might be time for you to get a manager, it is for one of the following reasons: Your agent is having difficulty getting the other agents to work on your behalf—and having agents at odds within the agency is tricky but having a manager nag is acceptable; or, your agent knows you are unhappy and is worried you'll leave the agency. When your career really starts to blossom, agents know that it's just a matter of time before you get antsy. Bringing in a manager is often an effective way to keep you with the agency, while satisfying your need to expand. If none of these seems plausible, consider the idea that your agent may be looking into management. Again, agents who are paying attention can sense when they are about to lose a client—long before you think they know. If it is a foregone conclusion that you are out the door...well then, damage control becomes a whole 'nother ball of wax.

The first question a manager will ask is, "Who is your agent?" If you've spoken more than once with a manager and that manager knows your agent but doesn't call your agent to express interest, it's the agent's first sign that the manager's plan is to move you to another agency. A call after-the-fact, stating "I'll be managing the actor from now on" is usually the next clue. If a manager calls an agent out of the blue to get together, that manager has designs to represent someone specific and the agent can probably tell you immediately which actor the manager wants.

One manager initiated lunch meetings with me three times over the course of ten years. Each time she called, I knew which client she was after because I knew the clients she represented and knew her taste in actors. Not once in those ten years did she ever call and ask me to meet with any of her clients, so I steered my clients away. It was never a question of her skill, but rather a question of her principles. We never shared a client, but we've known one another a very long time.

If a reputable manager calls about a client, regardless of any past relationship, the agent should (and usually will) take the meeting or have the lunch. If the agent doesn't, it can be used against him later—also, in this business, it never hurts to make more friends. An agent who knows a manager is pursuing his client should call the manager first. If nothing else, it's an opportunity to make another contact. If the manager does not return the call, the agent will quickly pass that tidbit on to the actor, thereby planting a seed of doubt. Establishing communication forces the manager to work with the agent before pulling the client.

SHARK CALLS

Underlying all this communication is ego and game playing. Take for example, the Telephone Hierarchy Game—who calls who, how often, and with what results. This is a blood sport in Hollywood, and taken very, very seriously. Picture this: During a delicate negotiation a conference call is required. Scheduled to be on the call are the talent's agent, manager, and lawyer, along with the studio exec and head of Business Affairs. The call is orchestrated by the office of the studio executive who invariably calls the manager first, then the agent, followed by the lawyer and the person in Business Affairs. Not until all parties are connected and holding does the studio executive get on the line. The inference being that those of least importance stay on hold the longest. Naturally, no one wants to be first on the phone...no wonder it takes forever to get anything accomplished!

If an agent is trying to establish a relationship with a manager because he or she is actually wooing another client the manager reps, the result might be that the agent will work harder and be particularly attentive to increase the chance of winning the other client. If, on the other hand, it's the manager with the strong desire to work with a particular agent, then the manager will be "on top of things" so as to establish his or her credibility with the agency. Managers generally don't let you sign with an agency they're unfamiliar with unless they don't have many agent contacts, the agency is one that is big and powerful, or, they don't want to waste the contacts they have on someone they feel is not quite ready.

Sometimes a manager and an agent actually *want* to work together, and are searching for the right client. Or, the agency's reputation is such that the manager believes it would behoove both the manager and the client to sign with a particular agent or agency. Many managers insist that agents not

I once managed an actor who was being courted for a production deal by two companies. One is a traditional studio/production company, the other a production/management company. During the bidding war that ensued, the studio people insisted that I would lose my client if I chose the management firm. "They will steal him, and you won't be protected." The studio people were absolutely right.

speak directly with the client, but instead relay everything through the manager (remember the bull's-eye!). Some agents accept and even welcome this arrangement, as it relieves them of the obligation to explain, pamper, coerce or police the client. The agent can then concentrate on the business aspect of the client's career and leave the personal to the managers. As an agent, I always hated this type of arrangement (unless the client was really obnoxious). As a manager, it worked to my benefit because I was never out of the loop. The downside to an arrangement like this is in instances where information is passed to the manager either by the agent, studio or network, which the manager is then asked to address—*without* re-telling the pertinent details—to the client.

Judgment Calls

These are a manager's job, and the relationship you choose to establish with your manager will determine his or her response. Some people want to know the truth, others simply do not. Regardless, I encourage you to maintain communication with your agent. It's just smart business. Unless you have a personal relationship with an agent, you will not get the perks of personal attention. Ultimately, the decision is always in the hands of the talent. If you can't stand the timbre of your agent's voice or tolerate the bile that spews forth from it—but he kicks butt with your career—then leave the talking and communicating to your manager.

Until recent years, agents barely tolerated the inclusion of managers and remained eternally hopeful that at some point the actor would tire of paying added commissions and leave the manager. Times have changed, and while managers now play an obvious, and often important, role in the field, generally agents still don't like them. Ironically, more and more agents are opting for the more accessible, less regulated, and more lucrative manager's role. Some have even gone so far as leaving agencies they have built and heading into management. This doesn't mean they behave any differently, act any more kindly, or tell fewer untruths. It just means they now do all these things with less regulation, and often with larger comissions.

- In March 2001, Writers & Artists Agency founder Joan Scott resigned from the agency she built over the course of a thirty-year career and opened a management/production firm.
- In July 2001, Susan Smith, of Susan Smith & Associates (longtime agent of Brian Dennehy and Kathy Bates), closed shop and opened a management company.
- J. Michael Bloom, after twenty-five years, sold his agency (and with it his name) in 1998. One year later he left the company and started another agency, Meridian Artists. In July 2001, that agency closed, and another re-opened within weeks.

Some agents have switched back and forth between manager and agent. If an agent has built solid relationships, earned a respectable reputation in the industry and reps quality talent, it doesn't matter which hat the agent wears when making the calls.

There are about 250 talent agencies and about 650 management companies. This is not so surprising when you consider the restrictions applied to agents. Unlike managers, agents—*all agents*—are licensed (by the California Department of Industrial Relations), bonded, regulated, and signatory to the guilds. Agents can't produce, they can't work as casting directors or actors, they can't work from home[2] and they can't commission more than 10 percent of a performer's gross earnings. Agencies can't own or be owned by producers or distributors.

And the regulations don't end there. Specific banking criteria must be adhered to and strict bookkeeping records kept. In addition, by law, client files must be stored and accessible for up to three years after the actor is no longer a client. Agents must work from a designated, identifiable office, which is subject to inspection by state employees. There is a letterhead stipulation, and agency owners and officers are bonded, fingerprinted and registered with the Federal and State Government under the category of Employment Agency.

Managers, on the other hand, are completely unregulated regarding any of the aforementioned.

1. Managers can produce[3].
2. Managers can be casting directors, actors, acting coaches, hairdressers, spouses, parents—you name it. Anyone can call themselves a manager.
3. Managers can work out of their bedroom, their kitchen, their car or a post office box.

---

[2] A home office must have a clearly marked separate entrance.

[3] The Writer's Guild is working to eliminate this as a vanity credit if the manager is not actually performing producer duties, which are very specific.

4. Managers can commission at any rate you agree to pay.[4]
5. Managers have no rules.
6. The only thing managers *cannot* do is act as agents. Which means (by definition) it is unlawful for managers to solicit work or to negotiate deals.

If a manager picks up a phone and calls a producer or casting director and pitches an actor for a job, that manager is violating the law. If a manager sends an unsolicited picture and resume, that manager is violating the law. And if an actor's manager negotiates a deal on the actor's behalf, that manager is violating the law.

And yet, managers do it all the time. It may be against the law...but it's evidently not a crime.

Managers enjoy the freedom of involvement in multiple levels of one's career, with no official policing. California Law prohibits a licensed agent from doing any work in show business other than agenting. As I write this, the Association of Talent Agencies (ATA), backed by some very powerful agencies, is working feverishly to eliminate many of these Guild restrictions, and it appears they may succeed. The agents want the reigns loosened, and argue that that the Guild's financial interest rules are outdated and impede an agency's means of attracting capital. The Screen Actors Guild leaders believe that loosening those financial restrictions will create an undeniable conflict of interest. Rumors of agencies abandoning the franchise agreement (which expired in October 2000), were met by SAG warning members not to sign general service contracts with agencies that chose to disregard the agreement.

In an effort to make some gesture toward agents during the threat of strike in June 2001 (which ended with a fizzle), SAG representatives initially included stronger language and enforcement of the policy that requires producers to deal only with agents in their negotiations with talent. Those demands did not become anything concrete, and so the battle continues.

---

[4] Most reputable talent managers abide by industry standards and do not commission higher than 20 percent. The music, modeling and sports industries have different standards.

Agencies have banded together to protect themselves and broaden their reach. Managers, for the most part, are leery of losing their freedoms. Most agree a restructuring is imminent but the face of the "new agency" has yet to be seen.

It is a catfight, albeit (so far) a very polite one.

> *Incidentally, it is no secret that the near-threat of a writer's strike in 2001 played a major role in thwarting a SAG strike the same year. Both guild contracts expired within months of one another, the first being the WGA, a notoriously united guild. Had the WGA stood firm for a strike, SAG would almost certainly have followed suit. The Writer's Guild settlement paved the way for the SAG settlement.*

Most buyers will not close deals with managers unless the talent doesn't have an agent. Some managers actually make deals and use a lawyer to close, thereby technically staying within the letter, if not the spirit, of the law. This practice diminishes the need for an agent and protects the manager from you, the client.

Why would a manager need to be protected from a client? For one thing, unlike the agency contract, which is standard and regulated by the Guilds, managers generally draft their own contracts. First-time agency contracts are limited to one year, with a clause that allows the actor to get out of the contract. Many managers require a three-year binding contract, without any such "out" clauses. But guess what? You don't have to agree. Like all contracts, you, the client have the right and ability to negotiate for more favorable terms. For example, if you meet with a manager who really wants to rep you, but insists on taking commissions on commercial jobs, even though they don't have any influence over your commercial work—just say No. Find another manager. Hesitant to commit to three years? Cross it out and sign for one. If you can't come to terms, find another manager. If you do agree to the terms and you fire your manager before the end of your contract, you could be paying commissions long after the manager is out of your life. There are two exceptions: Your manager agrees, or, you can prove the manager either solicited work on your behalf, or negotiated deals.

Since it's not a crime for managers to break the law, the only recourse a dissatisfied performer has is to sue. If the performer wins, the manager may have to forfeit all commissions.

But, proving that your manager has violated any laws is a difficult task at best.

Finding a buyer willing to testify to receiving unsolicited pictures, résumés, scripts or phone calls won't be enough. Even if you have a copy of a written submission your manager sent, check out the wording; if the manager is smart, it says, "Per your request, enclosed please find X, Y, or Z." The manager is off the hook. Those three words, *per your request*, infer that the manager did not solicit, but was in fact requested to send. If a manager calls a buyer and talks about a wonderful actor or writer he represents, even though we know it's a pitch, and the buyer knows it's a pitch, *legally*, when the buyer says I'll meet the actor, the *buyer* has solicited the client, via the

> *In June of 1999, comedian Gary Shandling and long-time manager Brad Grey settled the 100 million dollar lawsuit Shandling had filed against his manager of eighteen years. Shandling had accused Grey of "triple dipping" into the revenues from Shandling's* The Larry Sanders Show. *"According to Shandling, Grey unfairly gained fees and commissions, not only as his manager, but also as the show's producer. And as Grey's 'cornerstone client' for many years, Shandling contends the manager leveraged him to gain lucrative production contracts, such as one to produce NBC's* Just Shoot Me."[5]

manager. Of course, until the relationship sours, you *want* your manager soliciting to get you work, every-single-living-breathing-minute-of-the-day. You want him making calls, writing letters, sending material and doing everything he can to justify being paid his commissions.

[5]Handling and Grey Settle, Daniel Frankel 7/2/99 eonline.com

The day after I stopped being an agent, I was solicited by actors seeking management. Years later, the soliciting continues (and it *is* flattering), because friends, family, and even ex-clients all assume that hiring a manager who was once an agent is a two-for-one deal. You get an agent (with all that implies) who, as a manager, has more time to devote to your career, fewer clients for you to compete with, and you can call them any time of the day or night.

Actors and writers sign with managers because they're easier to obtain. They're easier to obtain because there are so damn many of them and that's because there are people willing to sign with managers for no better reason than to say, "I have representation." The same reason actors will sign and stay with an agency that does nothing for them. Because representation implies legitimacy. If legitimacy is what you're seeking, be selective. In the world of managers there are tons to choose from, so choose carefully.

If you don't have an agent, whether you're hoping a manager can get you one or take the place of one, you still have to agent the manager. They are the same animal.

The Agent/Manager Relationship Shouldn't Be (But Is), Rivalrous.

Make sure you're the one benefiting from it. If you have an agent and a manager, decide for yourself what you hope to get out of each—who picks up where the other leaves off—and then get the best of both. Otherwise you're just wasting your money.

If you think of your agent or your manager as your confidant, remember that he or she will always be concerned with whether or not you can, or will, generate income. That means, if you call your agent swearing you've given up and you'll never write another word or set foot in a casting office again, don't be too convincing—unless you really mean it. Face it: if you thought your representative was incapable of furthering your career or supporting your endeavors, wouldn't you be looking to make a move? Yes, you would.

3

Dancing Bears
- Agents and Auditions -

Writers and other non-actors: Don't think for a second that you don't audition! Flooding the town indiscriminately with your script will not get you a job. "I loved his spec/demo reel/triple lutz/whatever..." will not pay your bills. You need to get in front of the people who have the power to say: "You're hired." You need pitch meetings. Pitching story ideas or scripts is the essence of the writer's audition. If you depend on your agent to get you work—then you need your agent to get you "auditions" in the form of pitch meetings. A great idea is not enough. The buyer needs to feel confident that your brilliance and creative thoughts can be executed and transformed into dialogue and action on paper. You, along with your agent, have to convince the suits that you are the writer to make that transformation. Your agent should be selling that before you walk in the room. And when you walk in the room, just like an actor, that's your turn to shine—make the most of it. Get what you want from your meeting. Read this chapter, put yourself in those actor shoes, and agent your agent.

"I've sent him out a million times."   *"My agent never sends me out."*
Who's lying?

The truth? Your agent *is* sending you out on every possible audition. Your agent *isn't* sending you out on every possible role you think you're right for—

and no agent ever will. Because you aren't right for every role you think you are, no actor is. If your agent truly *never* sends you out...get a new agent. The lack of auditions is an actor's biggest complaint. If you're not getting offers of work, or creating work on your own, then you need auditions to get jobs.

Using the numbers theory, an agent should get as many appointments as possible for an actor; after all, agents don't make money if you're not working. So why can't your agent get you more auditions? For one thing, the easiest actor for an agent to sell is the actor who needs no selling—the hot-actor-flavor-of-the-month. If that's you, skip this chapter and go directly to Chapter Six; in six months, if you're not working on a film, haven't signed on for a series or the auditions seem to have dwindled down to nothing, *then* come back and read this chapter.

But if you're *not* the hot-actor-flavor-of-the-month, pay attention.

Scenario: A friend—same age, same type, and with credits similar to yours—has an audition for a nice role in a film. At the audition are fifteen other guys just like you. You call your agent, and nine times out of ten, what do you hear? "You were submitted." If you've been in the business for about twenty minutes, this might be a great relief to you. "Oh goodie, I'm up for the role!" If you've been around any longer than that, then you know that *"You've been submitted"* is infuriating. As if that's supposed to alleviate all your worries about getting your shot. With computers, faxes and instant access to information, if it were that simple, you could submit yourself (and, depending on your agent, that submission might carry just about the same weight).

"You were submitted" means:

My assistant pulled your picture and résumé, stuck it in a manila envelope and attached it to the twenty-five other client photos beneath a submission sheet—noting the role I thought you'd be right for—and sent them to the casting director. I hope. Once there, the casting assistant or intern will eventually open the pack and stack those pictures right alongside the other agency submissions, in whatever haphazard order of importance the casting director has decided to use that day. Now, we're just waiting for the casting director to flip through the photos, pluck yours out of the pile, see that you're right for the role, and call you in to audition. See how easy?! Sell your clothes and go to heaven, the job is practically yours!!

Wrong. What's really happened is that your agent has bought a little time. Don't waste a call to your agent asking if you were submitted. That should be a given, because if you're right for a role and you weren't submitted, your agent's not going to cop to it. Unless the role has been cast, cut or changed, there is no sound reason for your agent to admit that he or she omitted your picture and résumé from the pile.

Submitting is the easy part. Come on; you don't want to know if you were submitted, you want to know when

> **A NOTE TO WRITERS**
> *If you're a writer, and you have a spec script that fits perfectly with the genre of a new television series, call your agent. Don't expect your agent to remember the content of your spec. Remind them. Excite them with the possibility of making money. Encourage them to submit your script and get you in to meet with producers.*

you're getting the audition. If you're an actor, try starting the conversation like this, *"I know you submitted me for* (name the role and project); *have you had a chance to talk to* (casting, producer, director, anybody) *about getting me in?"* From time to time, add a little flourish (agents do it all the time)—if your friends are telling you about projects you're right for, tell your agent you've gotten a couple of calls and you think "We" should check it out. If your agent is easily impressed with the opinions of others, then gather the opinions of others and present them. "A guy I know who works at Endeavor, he thinks I'm right for this role; what do you think?" Or, "a friend I know at Fox read my spec and thought it might do well over at that new one hour they have in the works." It's amazing what feats an agent can achieve when prodded by the challenge of others. Challenge can be a powerful motivator when passion and enthusiasm fail.

If you call your agent about a project and your agent tells you "you're not right," it might actually mean: *you're not right.* And if you do get in on the audition and you don't get the job, then your agent is hoping that from now on you'll believe *everything* your agent tells you. But, *not right* might also mean your agent couldn't get you in the door, or it could mean that four of those other guys are from your same agency and the agent pushed them first. Or maybe, your agent just doesn't see you the way you think you should be seen. All of the above should be addressed. You can't possibly be right for every role, so it's your responsibility to choose your battles.

> *A word to the wise: if you're going to agent your agent, be as good at it as he or she is and then back it up with good work. Ultimately the work is what counts.*

If your agent can't get you in the door, for a role you're right for and you believe it's worth the battle, then help your agent fight to get you in. Ask if she thinks you should call the casting director—and I guarantee she'll say no. If the agent covering the project is not your point person, solicit the help of your responsible agent. If you're with a small or mid-size agency and the owner or partners of the agency were influential in getting you to sign—even if they don't take on the day-to-day tasks of agenting—call them and solicit their help.

Actors want more auditions so they can get more work. They feel, and rightfully so, "The more auditions I get, the more jobs I'll land." Your agent is doing the same math, but with an eye on diminishing returns. Consider an agent's thoughts: "The more auditions he gets that don't result in jobs—the fewer auditions I will be able to get for him in the future.

Never do the two sides see the same conclusion!

Here's a prime example:

A good friend of mine is married to an actress. He calls to tell me she's left her agent and wants my opinion of the manager she's recently met. As it turns out, the agent she has left is a previous co-worker, a good agent, and a friend of mine. Two days later I happen to speak with the agent and casually mention the actress. I get five minutes of how surprised they were that she left and the chicken way she did it, followed by twenty minutes of rehashing *every single appointment* she had in the one year she was with the agency. "Fifty-four appointments, a handful of callbacks, and not one job." The agent recounted every single one (by the way, computers make this sort of thing easy to do), and they were impressive: films, pilots, soaps, contract, guest-star, recurring roles. All good stuff. Later that night I speak with my-friend-the-husband, and relay my earlier conversation with the agent. He's got a different but no less complete version of those fifty-four appointments. This was his take: First off, callbacks shouldn't count. It's not a new appointment, but an extension of the first appointment and should be gauged in the actor's favor, as in; "Look how many callbacks I got, I should be getting more appointments." Next up, appointments not initiated by the agent don't count. The actress had gotten some of those auditions on her own or through the help of her writer/producer husband. Third, quality. An audition for a small role in a straight-to-video B movie with a bad script (that you go on because your agent talks you into it) is hardly something to brag about. Last, passing on a role or missing an audition *invalidates* the audition. Moreover, *if* on or after the appointment it is determined that *you are not right for the role,* then it's a wasted audition and it's the agent's fault.

Act swiftly and pick your battles prudently. Know your strengths and exploit them, use the path-of-least-resistance and then knock on the doors of resistance. You might not get the audition, but you may be more satisfied with the explanation.

On the third hand (extra hands are very useful in the Hollywood Blame Game): If you have an audition, and the feedback is "we really liked her but she wasn't prepared," and your agent is able to make some excuse about you not getting the material, or having just flown in from New York, and manages to convince the casting director to give you another shot—is that a callback? Your husband writes on a TV show, and your agent calls the casting director on your behalf and mentions your husband's name—did the agent do a good job? If you were offered that small role in a B film—would you take it? If your agent didn't suggest you pass on a project, would you think it's because he wants nothing but the commission and doesn't care about the long-term repercussions to your career? And would you prefer your agent follow the age specifications of a role, or ignore them and concentrate instead on giving you opportunities to play the roles you both know you can play? Being wrong for a role is no crime—but is it better than not being seen at all?

So who's right? It doesn't matter. If you make a decision to leave your agent and you feel justified, well, other than a responsibility to your contract and commissions due, that's enough. (The same holds true for agents, though their contractual obligations end when they fire you.) And though it's true that you will all leave your agents, accumulating ex-agents as quickly as you can is *absolutely* not the goal! You've got a better chance of you and your agent wanting to stay together if you've established good communication early on in the relationship.

Communication makes it harder for you to fire your agent and harder for your agent to fire you when the road gets bumpy. And the road *will* get bumpy. Reach out to your agent before and after auditions, when he is most likely to take your call. Don't just jot down an appointment off your answering machine and follow the instructions, talk to someone at your agency. If you have an audition or a pitch-meeting, your agent *will* get on the phone. When he does, you should have something important to say, and be able to speak in a language your agent can understand. Seek his input, as if you respect his opinion (which, ideally, you should). Talk about the project, the director, the network, the character; make your agent feel like he's part of the process, not just the secretary for your appointments. If you ask personal questions, listen to the answers—maybe even respond—and *then* get to the point of your call. If you have nothing important to say, at least say something clever. If you've read a script and you think you can really sink your teeth into a role, call your agent and say so. If you're pitching the same story idea for the umpteenth time, let your agent know that the pitch is "polished" or "cleaner." Agent your agent: lead her to believe that you think she had the foresight and intuition to know the role (or the opportunity) was perfect for you. *Whenever you can, tell your agent that he or she is good and doing a good job. People–all people–need to feel appreciated.* Some agents quick-talk and jargon-speak. Some whine or "Yes" you to death. If you hear urgency in the voice at the other end, disarm it. If you're getting the brush-off, turn it around–use your charm. After the audition, call your agent. Not all interviews are going to result in you being branded the most brilliant thespian in the world, so when you've had a bad one, be the first to tip off your agent.

RULE 6: If Your Agent Can Trust Your Judgment To Know When An Audition Doesn't Go Well, He's More Likely To Believe You When You Say Your Audition Was Terrific.

Minimize the negative effects of the auditions that don't result in jobs, and maximize every aspect of an audition that turned into a job, or almost into a job. If an agent believes in your talent, hearing a funny story about how you botched an audition can alleviate an otherwise disappointed reaction when hearing it first from the casting director or the producer. But don't botch too often! If it's an important audition, speak with your agent directly, it could give him lead-time to call on your behalf and get you another shot, if war-ranted. In that case, passing a message through the assistant will not do. Calling your agent after each audition to complain about traffic getting across town, how long you waited to be seen, how unprepared you were or how poor-ly you were treated is a waste of everyone's time. Do that too often and you can expect your agent to take your calls less frequently.

If you find your agent represents a long list of actors your type, you need to weigh whether or not those statistics work in your favor. For instance, if the agency is known for having great young men, and you're a young man without any credits, you might get the benefit of the doubt and more opportunities because of the preconceived notion of the agency. It might also mean your agent has a knack for selling your type. But if the agency (based on that same reputation) is flooded with young men and you're not at the top of the list, maybe you'd be better served elsewhere.

The same holds true for writers. Look at your agency, look at your agent. If the only writers working at your agency are working on half-hour soaps, guess where your agent has the best connections? Could you be the first feature film writer to break out of their stable? Yes, potentially, but only if the agent is putting forth extraordinary effort on your behalf and believes that you can help bring the agency to a new level.

If your agent doesn't see you the way you see yourself, something is fundamentally wrong and needs to be fixed. Is it you or them? Are their sights limited or are you oblivious?

Complaining to your friend or spouse about what your agent can't or won't do, can't and won't help. Instead, look for opportunities to agent your agent and get what you need for your career. Agents are tools, like headshots and résumés. Know the strengths of your tools and use them to your benefit.

Agents hate it when you call them about projects—unless you're calling to say

Remember: "Sometimes I sing and dance around the house in my underwear—doesn't make me Madonna. Never will."
–Joan Cusack to Melanie Griffith in Working Girl, *1988*

50

you have a friend who's producing or directing and that friend intends to offer you a particular role or opportunity. Even so, agents are generally still skeptical, because friends tend not to pay friends as well as they do strangers.

If you call about a project and subsequently get the audition, your agent doesn't get the credit because you think, "I only got the audition because I called." Meanwhile, your agent is thinking, "Because he got this audition, now he's going to call about every project." If you call and your agent doesn't get you in, your agent gets blamed and looks bad. Your agent

> **ROLE PLAY**
> Chris Meloni plays a menacing character on the HBO drama series Oz, but as an over-the-top coach and Julia Robert's fiancé, he's demonstrably comedic in The Runaway Bride. *Though not yet a household name or a big ticket movie star— if I were his agent and Chris told me he could play a role—I'd believe him.*

doesn't want to look bad, and your agent doesn't want you to call about every project you think that you're right for, either. Should you stop calling? No. Nope. No way, José.

Call when you've got a good reason...even if that reason is fabricated. Unless you're in box-office league, don't call about the lead in a hundred-million-dollar film. An actor calling to tell an agent (as if it was exclusive knowledge) about something the actor read in the breakdowns or the trades is a waste of time. Assume all agents read the same *Variety* and *Hollywood Reporter,* and make your call with the intention of *discussing* the news—not *breaking* the news.

Some agents love industry gossip, which is not the same as "insider information." *Inside info* is knowing before it's public knowledge that Marcia Shulman is going to take over as Head of Casting for Fox Television. *Gossip* is calling to say you heard that Matthew Perry and Jamie Tarses (the former head of ABC) were making out in a restaurant. Though the latter may be a sure way to get many agents on the phone, I'm inclined to tell you to stay out of it. If your information can lead directly or indirectly to your getting work, share it and remind your agent. Otherwise, engaging in gossip...makes you a gossip.

You want your agent operating from the belief that you are a talented cash cow, not a rumormonger.

If you baby-sit to make extra money and your boss is producing a TV series; that's information your agent can use. If nothing else, your agent will call the casting director and the casting director will run your name past the producer—the odds are in your favor that the producer will have the casting director read you for a role. Producers and directors are inundated with favor-asking; it goes with the territory. To make their own lives easier, they pass the requests to the casting director, who will generally give the actor an appointment. Making this call is always worthwhile; you come a lot closer to getting an audition by calling then by waiting until after the role has been cast to inform your agent that you know the producer.

Nepotism

At one time I represented both of Sean Penn's parents, Eileen Ryan and the late (great) Leo Penn. One afternoon my husband and I visited with Eileen at their home in Malibu and after lunch made our way down a narrow path to the beach. Along the way Eileen pointed out areas where Sean used to play with friends...Charlie Sheen...Emilio Estevez...Rob Lowe. She then remarked about *the coincidence that Sean and his friends all turned out to be actors*. Please! The Malibu waters are infected with acting bugs and, let's face it, the local parents aren't exactly chimney sweeps or postal workers. Nepotism is alive and well in the television and film business, and at some point almost everyone has benefited or suffered from it. For example, I represented Arnold Schwarzenegger's best friend, who played a role in every one of Arnold's flicks. He never had to audition for Arnold's films and in instances where there was no role, Arnold would get him hired as his on-set trainer. He was taking care of his buddy, and insuring that he had a playmate on the set. Though I had nothing to do with creating those opportunities, I did make the deals—and with the support and encouragement of the actor, I made them better than they would have been had they called the actor directly. (I also happily collected the commissions.)

In another instance, Sidney Poitier was directing a movie starring Bill Cosby, titled *GhostDad*. I represented Poitier's daughter Pamela, and at her suggestion, she and I went through normal channels to get her an audition for a role that we determined she was right to play. The casting director agreed and set a time for Pamela to read for the director (her father) and the producers. Soon after, Pamela called to say her father had *cancelled* the audition; he was not going to hire her for that role and reading for it would not help. Eventually (and without my input) she did work on the film, credited in the cast as "the screaming girl" and in the crew as a Production Assistant.

If nepotism is the only reason you get the audition or the opportunity to pitch an idea, do a great job and it won't matter.

For a brief time I informally represented Jason Gould (Barbra Streisand's son). During that time, Ms. Streisand was starring and producing *The Prince of Tides,* and Jason wanted a shot at the role. His mother didn't think he was right for the part, which called for a fifteen-year-old football-playing violinist. Besides, it was too late—Chris O'Donnell (who'd just come off a starring turn opposite Jessica Lange in *Men Don't Leave*), had already won the part. Still, Jason was determined and did everything he could to prepare for the role. He hired a coach for football, and petitioned anyone and everyone for a chance to audition. Eventually nepotism got him a shot, but his talent and hard work landed him the job. Jason was hired. That's the good news. The bad news from my perspective as his agent was that there were no negotiations. In fact, the offer was at scale—not even scale plus ten.

Every actor strives to get to the point in his career when he's no longer required to audition. Auditioning is a grueling task and an awkward circumstance that most would rather avoid. Initially everyone has to do it. It is part of what an actor does. It's part of what a writer does. Even stars will audition, if doing so is the only way to be considered for the role. Madonna reportedly won the role of title character in *Evita* only after writing a long and desperate letter to director Alan Parker, convincing him she was perfect for the part.

Chris Sarandon—ex-husband of Susan, star of The Princess Bride, *and Academy Award® nominee for his feature film debut in* Dog Day Afternoon—*auditioned for a supporting role in* Nothing To Lose *at the behest of producer Martin Bregman. Bregman produced* Dog Day Afternoon, *and is more than familiar with Mr. Sarandon's work. Still, he likes to hear an actor say the words.*

If you're not good at auditioning, two things need to happen fast:
1. You have to get better.
2. Your agent has to get creative.

There are seminars, classes, and books to help you perfect your auditioning skills. This is not one of those books. If you don't audition well, you need to agent your agent, otherwise he or she is going to think and work as if *you can't act.*

RULE 7: It's Great If Your Agent Believes You Can Act; It's Crucial That Your Agent Believes You Can Make Money.

I had a client who was a terrible reader and, had his career depended on auditions, we would never have made any money. He could read, he could act, and he filled a room with his charm and confidence. But he couldn't audition. Or so he convinced me. The truth was, he didn't like to audition (and who really does?) but that's not quite the same as couldn't. Before I realized the truth, he had already convinced me of his talent and ability and had agented me into selling him *anyway*. He exuded the perfect mix of confidence, ego, acerbity and urbane smarts. All characteristics of the roles he was most suited for and most frequently played. In other words, he knew how to cast himself and (at least when he was in my company) he played the role. If he was a goofy knucklehead when he got home, I didn't know about it. When he *was* forced to audition, before the appointment I made an extra effort to sell him. I was more specific about his work and ability, more selective about the roles and projects we sent him out for, and always made sure he wasn't lumped in the middle of a cattle call. If necessary I would send tape first, and whenever possible I tried to arrange meetings rather than readings. He was a moneymaker so we got him in the door creatively, and when we did he landed jobs—until eventually his reputation preceded him. Once his "handicap" became common knowledge, even less was expected of him in an audition! He had a body of work, the wisdom to agent his agent, and the ability to convince directors and producers to hire him. Casting directors who had become accustomed to the drill would try to get him hired from his tape—without auditioning. And if that failed, they assumed the task of massaging the producers before his reading. Most agents with most actors do not go this extra mile.

Only after forging a strong relationship can you expect or even hope to have your agent work that hard. Think about it: unless you're a name actor with a body of work, no agent is going to be excited about the prospect of getting you auditions knowing you stink at auditioning. You can and should expect your agent to create the hype, but I strongly suggest you possess the ability to back-up that hype in a room and in front of a camera. Because agents are just as disappointed when your auditions don't immediately lead to work.

For a very short time I represented a handsome, charismatic Italian actor. I sent him to ABC to meet with a network casting director who was immediately won over by his charm. She arranged a screen test that (if things went well) would result in a holding deal. The actor was given material, a date and a time. When the test date arrived the actor was totally unprepared. He hadn't looked at, much less memorized, the material. He was totally out of his league, nervous, unprepared and unprofessional. When push came to shove, charm and good looks couldn't compensate for his lack of skills. There was no excuse. That episode prompted me to look more closely at his credits, all of which had been embellished. Needless to say, I dropped him as a client.

Reading just for the casting director will never get you the job (see Chapter 4 for more on casting). Your résumé, the casting director's opinion and your agent's fortitude will get you in front of producers quickly without the preliminary audition. When those fail, the agent decides how determinedly and to what extreme they should fight on your behalf. How you agent your agent will directly influence your agent's efforts. Should your agent beg the casting director for a pre-read, and if she does, will the actor agree to it? Should she go over the casting director's head...speak to the director, producer, studio or network? Or, should she just let it go?

Coaxing the casting director into pre-reading an actress who, under ordinary circumstances would not pre-read, is only effective if both the actor and the casting director are open-minded. With any kind of luck, the casting director will be looking forward to the meeting, the actor will welcome the opportunity to open another door, and the agent will get credit for making it happen. Once the decision is made to pre-read, the actor should exercise a little *agenting* as well.

Entering an audition defensively, or with trepidation because you think the casting director doesn't like you, defeats the purpose. Your aim is to get the job. The casting director's goal is to get the project cast, providing not just the best but as many choices as possible to the creator. What can you do? Be confident without being cocky. Sell yourself without making the buyer feel as if you're pushing yourself to be sold. Have fun.

What can your agent do? Keep pushing.

Sue Wohl at Gold/Marshak/Liedtke had been pitching her clients daily on a half-hour pilot for ABC. She'd gotten a number of auditions for other clients, but the casting director would not bring a particular actress to producers. It wasn't because of her résumé, which boasted a long stint on a hit series; it wasn't her age, which was right-on; it was *familiarity*. Though the casting director hadn't been in the same room with this actress in at least ten years (which the agent pointed out), the casting director had formed an opinion (ten years ago) which she now just couldn't shake. It was an opinion of the actor's range, presence, carriage—her mien, if you will. But actors change—if they didn't, we'd only see Julia Roberts as the loveable but flighty *Runaway Bride* and never as the sassy and determined *Erin Brockovich*. Armed with nothing more than belief in her client, familiarity with the project and dogged determination, Sue persisted. Ultimately she persuaded the casting director to open her mind to the possibility that *perhaps* it had been a long time and neither party would suffer by taking ten minutes to get re-acquainted. The actress was everything the agent said she was, and she nailed the audition. If the actress knew that convincing the casting director was going to be an uphill climb, she never let on. She was just there to do her job and enjoy every

> **A NOTE TO WRITERS**
> *Pitching the same story over and over as you go up the ladder from development exec to Sr. VP of Television is draining—for everyone. Most often the first person you pitched to is in every subsequent pitch meeting, which can prove deadly for the comic punches you've strategically placed in the pitch. Try to mix it up, be flexible. Enjoy hearing your story again—if you don't, why should anyone else?*

minute of it. How could you not like her? She didn't win the role, but she tested at the network and both she and Sue changed the mindset of the casting director. Forever? Probably not. But it's more ammunition for the next battle.

All things considered, when you can, read for producers and insist you get the material as far in advance as possible. The producer session may be your only shot. Preparation will increase your chance of winning the role.

If you're a writer, do some homework—know who you're meeting, what they've done, where they've worked. If you have information about what they "think" they're looking for, don't change your pitch to fit their niche. Instead, be aware of how your idea might compliment their needs. Allow the buyers their input and suggestions. If it's one you've already considered, rather than saying, "Yeah, I know," try, "That's exactly what I was thinking!" If it's a new idea that works, tell them you intend to "steal that line" for your next meeting. Get the buyer involved in the process of discovering the potential of your work.

Very rarely will an agent impart material to an actor before the actor has a scheduled audition—in doing so the agent sets himself up for failure if he can't deliver the goods. It never bothered me if an actor wanted to read a script knowing I hadn't secured an audition; I provided the script and left it in the hands of the actor to chose to prepare for it or not. Whereas this challenge made me work harder, it might make your agent insane.

If your agent calls you at 7pm and gives you a 10am audition for a series lead or a feature film, at the very least change the time—ideally change the day. Your work shouldn't suffer because you didn't want to trouble your agent. Who would you rather represent: an actor who is prepared, or one who is available? Sitting through an audition with an unprepared actor is frustrating and wasteful for everyone concerned.

> *Writers, pay attention: practice saying your pitch out loud. Learn how to tell a story and engage your audience. Pitching is performance. If you have a story or a script, know it well or bone-up on your improv skills—because you never know when you might be asked to pitch an idea.*

Luck is that moment when opportunity meets preparation. Auditions are an actor's opportunity and preparation should never be compromised.

RULE 8: Your Agent Is Lying To You About Feedback.

But the lie is not always generated by the agent. Casting directors lie, as do producers, directors and network execs. And just as many actors and writers return from auditions and meetings raving misleadingly about the grand job they've done.

There is a common belief that certain lies, "the little white ones," are necessary and acceptable. I found it necessary to constantly embellish my clients' feedback, sometimes to the client, sometimes to the buyers, but more so to the other agents in the office. A callback became he's down to the wire, or, it's between him and two other guys. Agents need to take every opportunity to use or create feedback to inspire colleagues to work harder for their clients. Agents do it all the time. Sometimes it worked—remember the young actor I mentioned in Chapter One? Because I'd made such a fuss over

> *An actor I know signed with CAA. They hadn't pursued him, the truth was that his responsible agent had moved to CAA and the actor was part of the package. So now he's with a top agency...represented by agents who hadn't chosen to represent him. A week after signing, he got a feature film audition. He walked into the audition and said, "Do me a favor, guys—no matter what you think of my audition, I just got new agents and I need you to tell them I was great." He didn't get the job, but he did get the "feedback." Now that's agenting your agent!*

him at the agency, the other agents were reluctant to release him for fear I might be right about his talent and they might lose a moneymaker. He has since held regular roles on at least two TV series. If I hadn't agented the agents, I would have lost a terrific client.

Another reason agents consciously lie about negative feedback is because not all feedback (even if it is true—and that's subjective at best) is constructive. If it doesn't affect the agent's belief in the client, it might do the actor more harm than good, so what's the use?

I sent an actress to meet the casting director for a small role in a *big* film. The character needed to be beautiful (which she was) because her scene opens the film, whereupon she mutters two lines and *dies*. The movie is about finding her murderer. Initially the client went in to "meet only." The meeting went well. The actress was given the material and told to return the next day, as they intended to put her audition on tape for the director. The next day gave her plenty of time to learn the "scene." After her callback, I phoned the casting director fully expecting an offer. Instead I was told they had taped the scene at least a dozen times, and spent an hour line-reading, then desperately tried to exhume a performance out of the actress, all to no avail. I was not her responsible agent, and despite her agent's protestations to the contrary, I never thought she could act. But she was beautiful, she got meetings, and she had a résumé—so someone at sometime had hired her. Not this time. The feedback I got (and I'm quoting), *"She is the worst actress in the world; no, no, the world is far too limiting—she is in fact the worse actress in the Universe."* Do I go running back to the client with this info? Would hearing this make her a better actress? Was this feedback *constructive*? Let's just say, if you're considering leaving the business because you don't think you're talented and you're looking for a sign, there you have it. Conversely, we've all heard the stories about Fred Astaire's screen test and Lucille Ball's feedback...who are we to judge? I chose not to. "They had stronger choices" was the feedback I offered the client, leaving any further explanation in the capable hands of her responsible agent, who subsequently also chose not to elaborate. In the agent book of lies, I don't think the above even qualifies. In this case omission would not be considered lying: It was true, they *did* have stronger choices; we just didn't tell her that we knew why.

RULE 9: You May Safely Assume That Any Time You Do Not Get A Role, It Is Because There Were "Stronger Choices."

That doesn't necessarily mean you're the worst actor in the history of the universe (besides, by definition there can only be one...and I'm pretty sure she was it). "Stronger choices," means another actor was better suited to the needs of the project, and the purposes of those involved. Agents lie about feedback when they don't have any but the actor needs to hear something. How much stock you choose to put in that feedback (good or bad) is your decision. For my money, the actor's time is better spent honestly assessing his or her own performance, learning what lessons, if any, are to be learned, and moving forward. In this instance the casting director chose not to lie.

Others do. Casting directors are so often bombarded with calls from agents, managers and sometimes actors themselves, begging for feedback—they have to say *something*. Pat answers alleviate the time and effort they might otherwise expend in an effort to satisfy the masses. If an agent or manager is convinced of an actor's talent, the casting director's feedback is of little or no consequence; and I say that knowing that there are exceptions. In those instances the *agent* decides what is constructive and what is not.

I represented an actor who didn't drive and chose instead to bicycle to and from auditions. From Hollywood to Culver City, from Burbank to the Fox lot on Pico. He rode everywhere. I never questioned his talent, and I never thought to question his personal hygiene, either—until, on more than one occasion, his feedback was "he stinks." As it turned out, they meant literally: he stinks!

When actors aren't getting auditions the inclination is to blame the agent. Though never eager to accept that blame, your agent will take credit when you do work. If you're not getting auditions, if your agent can't get you in the door or doesn't put forth the effort on your behalf—there is always something you can do. Something needs to change, and that could be your representation.

A NOTE TO WRITERS

Everyone is an expert when it comes to reading a script or nitpicking a pitch. If a writer had to consider every reader's version of the script ending, the story might never end. Likewise you can't anticipate the mood of a room before you go in and try to "wow" them. The best you can do is be prepared, and put your efforts toward being comfortable in a room. As for the feedback of your written words, listen to the problem rather than concentrating on what the critic thinks is the solution and always consider the source. Let people you respect read your work. And remember, three million flies can't be wrong—if the consensus is "save the brads," consider a page-one rewrite.

4

Hook, Line $ Sinker
- Agents and Casting -

Opinions about casting abound. Enough in fact, that you may be inclined to skip this chapter. Don't. There is still plenty to be said. Books written by casting directors talk about "the process," "what to wear," or "what we look for;" books written by agents do the same, adding "how to submit," "breakdowns," and so on. Nothing I've read conveys my experience; one that I've learned is not the exception. As an agent, I dealt with casting directors who liked me and liked my clients, and I dealt (or tried to deal) with those who didn't. Though the subject of casting directors is invariably raised when agents and actors meet, most agents don't wave a flag calling attention to how hard it is to get Casey Casting to see their clients. It's something you learn only *after* you become a client. However, if the actor has a productive relationship with Casey Casting, that can work to the agent's advantage.

Case in point, I repped an actor who left Triad[1] and signed with me. Triad for a time had done well by him and he had some great fans. One of which was a casting director who hadn't given me the time of day until I signed her "favorite" actor. When I signed him, she took notice of my agency and my other clients. I didn't sign him for that reason, but agents need contacts and good agents take every opportunity to make more. Casting people deal with

[1]Triad was bought by the William Morris Agency in October 1992

agents (like them or not) because agents represent actors. Too often agents get bogged down in the misinterpretation of casting. A casting director's job is to know the talent pool, and to know when and how it changes, because actors change. The agent's job is sign, sell and service clients. Neither you nor your agent should allow casting people to determine your career. Even when casting appears to be working on your behalf, the goal is to cast the project.

Remember: The casting director is not *your agent.*

There are casting directors who can or will try to help you (in the pre-read) be better prepared for the producer session. Sometimes it works and sometimes it backfires. For example, an actor I know very well had an audition to pre-read for a role in the TV movie *Dress Gray*. After the reading, the casting director told the actor that he had "made too much out of the scene." Do it again, she insisted, but remember: "You're just a nice guy, giving them information." Assuming she knew the character best (and against the actor's better judgement), he made the adjustment and was given a callback for the producer and director. Not halfway through the callback the director broke in with, "Wait a minute, hold on, what are you doing?! You're reading this like you're *just a nice guy, giving them information*." Whereupon the actor whipped his attention to the casting director—who remained stoic and silent. The actor didn't get the job, but he did learn the lesson.

> *Master your craft, keep an open mind, be flexible, but follow your instincts. Sound advice for actor and writer alike.*

If agents all did their jobs and casting directors all did theirs, everyone who was right for a role would get an audition, right? Wrong.

After I stopped being an agent, I grabbed a chance to work in casting, seeing it as an opportunity to gain insight from a new perspective. In that capacity I thought I might be able to determine what casting directors did and didn't like, and whether their opinions of me had influenced their opinion of my clients, or my clients' talent. (Maybe I'd learn why some casting directors had to be cajoled, begged, or threatened into reading an actor for a role...and, where, when, and if they lied.) I started from the ground up, working first as an assistant, then an associate, and then from time to time as the sole casting director on multiple independent projects. I learned from the best, and also learned I did not want to live out my days in casting.

Allison Jones is, bar none, one of the top casting directors in Los Angeles. An exceptional judge of talent, she works out of a responsibility to her own taste, the best interest of the project, the desires of the creators and the requirements of the network or studio. A Herculean task. Forthright and forthcoming, she is tough as nails and doesn't suffer fools. If you want her to read your client, you'd best know the role and know your client, because she does. If she thinks your client isn't right, prepare yourself with information to prove her wrong. If you succeed in proving her wrong, she'll be the first to commend you on a job well done.

To the agent who has earned her respect she will give the benefit of the doubt. And, though she may eventually respond to an agent's unwavering passion for a client's ability, she'll laugh in your face if you try to bribe her with box-seat season tickets to the Hollywood Bowl. She is the best in her field and still she is doubted, second-guessed, lied to, harassed and badgered by agents, managers, inexperienced executives, directors, producers, studios and networks. Because that's the job. There are casting directors whose reputations are such that an agent will determine the quality of a project (good or bad) because he or she is attached to cast. Allison Jones is one of these.

I started with Allison, so under her tutelage my standards were set. Like it or not, casting people, like agents, run the gamut, and for every Allison there are four others, struggling along without anything near her depth of professional knowledge. Those are the casting directors who take their opinions from the populace, rather than form opinions of their own. They are master list makers who accumulate names but can't recall credits. Pop culturalists without historic reference. And because of this, rare is the casting director who can get an actor hired. (There are occasions where casting directors have

65

the authority to hire, usually for very small roles.) What they can do, is prevent you from performing for the people who *can* hire you. In short, they come between the actor and the job, and they're not going away.

RULE 10: If You Want Your Agent To Agent The Casting Director, Then You Have To Agent Your Agent.

Give your agent the ammunition he needs to get past the casting director's prejudices. I've seen and heard far too many agents pitch a client to a casting director only to hear the casting director (sometimes me) run a litany of excuses for not seeing the actor. "I know Bob, he's too old, he's not right, he's not funny"...the list goes on and on.

Is it personal? *Everything* is personal. Unfortunately, a bad agent will relay these excuses back to the actor with equal conviction. A good agent, even if they don't know your work, can bluff right through the excuse and get you the audition—maybe not on the first call, and maybe not on all auditions, but they have to want to keep trying. You can influence whether or not your agent continues to try. Give her the tools and be sure she has the information and the desire to sell you. If your agent hasn't seen you in six months, can she honestly tell the producer that you "look great"? Don't waste the time you spend laboring in a comedy at an Equity-Waiver theatre—with the funniest scene in the play—and not tell your agent about it because the rest of the play is dreadful. Your agent doesn't have to see the play, he just has to *sell* how howlingly funny you are in it. Give your agents every soundbite, every morsel of positive feedback, *any* thread of information that can help them sell you.

The agent-casting relationship see-saws between extremes of love and hate. Luckily for most, casting directors are not usually the decision makers and if your agents have been paying attention they've nurtured some additional relationships with directors, producers, a network exec or two (or, better yet, three or four). Your agent must know someone besides the casting directors. If you think your agent is good in a room and you have contacts to offer them, do it. If your agent is only concerned with maintaining a relationship with a casting director, eventually that limited thinking might cut a big swath right through the middle of your agency contracts. Never forget: Your agent works for you. You pay the bills and keep gas in the 740i. If you're right for a role and the casting director is blocking your chance at getting a shot at it and you truly believe it's worth the effort, then your agent should go over the casting director's head. If your agent doesn't already know someone, now is the time to make a new friend and solve a casting problem at the same time. Screaming and threatening has never been my style, though I got an earful while working in casting. If I felt required to go around the casting person, I always let my intentions be known. If I sent a letter with pictures and résumés of my clients to the producer, I always mentioned that the same information had been sent to the casting director—and I never bad-mouthed. Every agent has their own style. Regardless of *how* they do it, sooner or later, it must be done. Going over a casting director's head is an agent's job—your agent will not be the first to attempt such a feat. It's really no big deal, and to some degree, casting directors expect it. They may hate your agent for doing it, and it may fail miserably at the time, but that's the chance you want your agent to take. It's the chance you want your agent to believe is always worth taking. I cannot say this enough: You there, the one with the talent—yeah, you: You must empower your agent with the conviction that you are always worth selling.

> One agent I know is the bane of most casting directors' existence. He knows his clients, familiarizes himself with the projects and immerses himself in matching the two. Passionate to the point of dementia, he demands auditions for clients, and when his demands go unanswered, he knocks down doors. On one pilot in particular, after calling repeatedly to pitch his client, the agent finally called the network ranting and raving about the difficulty he was having in getting his client an audition. The network in turn called the casting director demanding to know why they were being bothered by the agent and instructed her to let the actress audition. The actress read for producers, tested for network, and got the job. From then on when the agent called, the casting director gave the appointments. Like him or not, crazy or otherwise...he and his signature Southern drawl got him the access he needed. On the other hand, I also know of an agent who was banned from a studio for harassing and threatening a casting director.
> The moral: Persistence is good, insanity is not.

If an actor has an audition to read for a director or producer, he is as close as one can get (through normal channels) to securing a job. Likewise for the writer who sits down with the star, the director and/or the executive producer. Reading only for the casting director (or in the writer's case, the development exec) puts you in jeopardy of never meeting the director or producer. Trust me, your agent feels the same way. Agents want you to read for producers. But, they also want you to get appointments. The more you "go out" on auditions, the happier you'll be with your agent. But pleasing the actor while maintaining or creating a working relationship with the casting directors is a tight-rope walk for most agents.

By the time information trickles down to the agent, the chances of hitting the nail on the head by submitting the perfect client every time is, well, nil. An agent trying to sell a client is the second to last person in a long line of telephone, the last being the actor. So many changes and exchanges are made during the process that unless the agent is maintaining almost daily contact, anything can fall through the cracks—even the perfect actor.

> **A NOTE TO WRITERS**
> *If television is your field, this is the time that agents are gathering information. They're drilling the networks about the odds-on favorites for pilot pick-up. They're watching for fat deals with stars attached that might increase the chances of a network order, because right after the announcements staffing season begins.*

Let's assume it's pilot season and a breakdown has been released for a pilot that shoots in five weeks. Your agent has made the necessary submissions, retrieved a script and is now in the process of trying to obtain auditions for as many clients as humanly possible.

Back at the casting office they have or are in the process of receiving written submissions of pictures and résumés. Submissions are opened in order of priority (by agent or agencies) as decided by the casting office. The assistants make piles: 'A', 'B', 'C', 'D', and distribute accordingly. Every casting office I have known follows a similar procedure. The 'A's and 'B's are opened first. The 'C's are opened eventually. The 'D's and below are some-times opened and most times not[2], depending on the casting director.

Don't be alarmed if you think your agent doesn't have the clout to be in the 'A' pile. Piles are decided by the relationships between the agent and the casting office. Where your agent might be an A in one office, that same agent could be a 'D' in another. Rarely do the Big 3 (CAA, ICM, WMA) send submissions at all. In fact, getting some of the larger agencies to submit a picture and résumé is nearly as difficult as getting confirmation that their client will indeed be at the audition.

Stop right here: I know you're trying to assign your agency a letter, but it's not that simple. This is a business of relationships and though the likelihood of The Gersh Agency getting knocked down to a D is unrealistic, it is reasonable to believe that a small agency might be in the A pile. While I owned my agency, I passed Simon Ayer Casting everyday on my way to and from work and I would drop off submissions or just drop in to visit. One evening I noticed three piles of pictures and résumés on Simon's couch, designated A, B and C. My submissions were in the A pile and I asked Simon what that meant...it meant that he liked me.

Seasoned casting directors don't depend on written submissions; they are used primarily as a reference, a tool, a reminder that the actor exists or has changed agents, or is in town and available. If the casting director knows you and likes you or is intent on bringing you in from the get-go, having a picture and résumé in hand is helpful. Managers also submit, which can lead to double submissions. Manager submissions are generally placed in a separate pile and again, if the office has a particular manager with whom they like

[2]D categories are opened most often when there are a number of day player roles to be cast.

to work, those submissions are opened, while the others are not. Within the first two days after a breakdown is released, casting directors can expect roughly 200- 300 packages delivered by messenger and mail. Some offices are meticulous about opening submissions—others are not. *This is why written submissions by your agent are not enough.*

Making Lists for the Network and the Studio

Casting ideas are bantered about long before scripts are released and even before the casting director has been hired. If scripts are available, casting directors have read them and prepared lists of name actors and prominent suggestions, which they pitch (there's that word again) when they interview for the position (that's the casting director's audition). Once the casting director is hired for the job, these lists include names and agents of all the recognized actors, who are available or unavailable, interested or not. Those lists are constantly updated to include every actor who reads for the producers and are continually distributed to the studio, network, producers and directors. It is a tedious task. Very often offers have been made to star names for lead roles even before the casting person is hired.

Fielding Hundreds of Calls

Calls for scripts start immediately, and because only a limited number are available, they're distributed to the larger agencies and the favorites, on a first-come-first-served basis. There is no perfect time to make contact, and smart agents finesse their calls so that the untimely calls are not construed as intrusive. If an agent calls in the middle of a crisis (which for a casting director could mean ten actors have cancelled from the producer session that starts in ten minutes, leaving huge gaps of time between actors), that agent had better have a qualified actor prepared, right and ready to read. If not, the agent should consider saving the pitch for another time. Even a casting assistant will harbor resentment when an agent doesn't take the hint, or worse yet, promises something that can't be delivered.

Calling a casting director after hours, when they're putting together the next casting session, is a good time to grab their attention and maybe land an appointment. As quickly as submissions roll in, the casting director is usually simultaneously setting up pre-reads and producer sessions. Pre-reads are mostly derived from pictures, résumés, and phone pitches, while initial producer sessions are based on the casting director's taste, suggestions and requests from producers and directors, network and studio directives, and all those damn lists. (Being a staple on a network list nearly guarantees you consideration for a part, which is not the same as guaranteeing an audition.) If your agent knows you're on a network list, he or she should use that information to get you an audition. And, since actors are placed on and off those lists so unceremoniously, neither agents nor actors should assume that placement on last year's list has any influence on this year's opinion. Remember, networks, not unlike casting directors, have different tastes, so while you may have done a pilot for ABC last season, that doesn't insure you are on NBC's list this season.

Writers, pay attention...you get listed as well.

A short list *is jargon used by casting directors to agents and often repeated by agents to actors. It means you're on a list, be it the casting director's, the producer's, the network's—doesn't matter. Unless you're of "offer only" status, your name on a* short list *does not guarantee you an audition. Without an audition you cannot win the job.*

Though casting directors wield great power in their ability to say no, as in:
"No, you can't audition."
"No, you can't audition."
"NO, YOU CAN'T AUDITION."

71

> *I was working as a casting associate; the project was a half-hour comedy pilot. Soon after the breakdown was released, I got a call from an agent at an mid-level agency asking for a script. The script was picked up and the next day a pack of pictures and résumés were submitted to our office without any discrimination whatsoever. Literally every client available from this agency, some fitting nothing other than the gender description, was in this packet. One week later the agent calls, hoping for auditions.*
> *"Okay," I say, "pitch me." But he couldn't because he hadn't read the script, and he wasn't even savvy enough to fake it. Another week and or so goes by, and he calls again. This time he wants me to tell him which roles have already been cast, and which of his clients are right for whatever is left.*
> *"Did you read the script?" I ask.*
> *"Part of it."*
> *"Part of it, it's only twenty-two pages of a half-hour sitcom, what part did you read?"*
> *"Oh, come on..." he says, "just tell me if any of my clients are right."*
> *"Why don't you read the script during lunch, call me back and then you can tell me which of your clients is right."*
> *"Okay," he says, but he never called back. And none of his clients auditioned for this pilot.*
> *Three months later, I saw his name in the trades—he'd left that company and was now representing actors at a very prestigious agency.*

An agent's power can prove to be even greater if you can convince him or her to call the people who have the authority to say, "Oh yes, you can."

What your agent has to do (let me repeat: *has* to do), to really get close to hitting the mark, is to first get the information and read the material. Reading material gives experienced agents a chance to be helpful. Casting people are much more responsive to an informed agent asking intelligent questions and making educated suggestions. And there is no excuse for inexperienced agents who don't read everything they can wrap their hands around. And yet I know some successful agents at some major agencies who simply do not read. If this is the case with your agent, then it falls to you to get the information so you can give your agent the ammo he needs to get you the audition.

Sometimes, the material is not available. If your agent hasn't read material, and the casting director hasn't read material, and you won't get a chance to read material, how is this project to be cast? Your agent has to get the information. How? By any means necessary.

How Does Your Agent Get You the Audition?

Every actor, writer, director and musician auditions at some stage and for the majority, at all stages of their career. An agent's ability to secure auditions for a client is of the utmost importance. They cannot do it without *push* and *pull*. Agents and managers fall into four categories. Those with *push*, those with *pull*, those with *both* and those with *neither*. Ideally, you want your agent to have both. (If your agent has neither see Chapter 8.)

Push

Push is the drive an agent must have in their box of tricks when they don't have the muscle and you don't have the name. *Pull* is the agent who has the connections, the power to be heard and the powerful agency behind them. Jennifer Craig at William Morris has *push* and *pull*. She is aggressive, informed, connected and persuasive—when she's working on your behalf. If your agent doesn't have both, one will do. If your agent has neither—get a new agent.

Push is born out of the belief that the client is worth the effort, an awareness of the client's strengths, familiarity with the needs of the project, good instinct, a credible persuasiveness and plain ol' chutzpah. Familiarize yourself with the other clients at your agency; would you like to be counted among them, some of them...none of them? Are they predominantly featured players or guest stars? Are they staff-writers or showrunners? Is your agent equipped to *push* you?

When I worked in casting there was a particular management company that represented a few recognizable names, names known more for celebrity than for thespian feats. Ex-model, ballplayer, wife of rock star, that sort of thing. No matter what the project and with little respect for the demands of the role they *pushed* and *pushed* and *pushed* one particular actress. It *never* resulted in auditions. If the manager had been more selective in his submissions, and had spent time really trying to solve the casting problem rather than just trying to rack up appointments for his clients (especially the actress) then he might have been more successful—at least in our office. We were so accustomed to his inappropriate pitches that we listened with one ear, and rattled off the same response time and again—he's not right, they're not right and *she* is definitely not right. Calls from that office went mostly unreturned and there was never any real consideration on our part—why would there be? The manager never imparted any new information which would lead us to believe that any of their clients, most certainly not that actress, had changed, or grown. Like the little boy who cried wolf—we simply stopped listening. It was empty pushing.

That's *not* the push you want your agent to use.

Pull

Now you're thinking that it's *pull* you want. *Pull* is great. The agent with pull has inside information, access, and the power to open doors. Terrific if they're using it on your behalf, but not if it's used haphazardly.

An actor signed with Triad shortly before they merged with William Morris. After a twenty-minute meeting with about twelve agents, he was onboard. It was pilot season and they bombarded him with appointments, sometimes three or four a day. By the time the scripts arrived the evening before, he barely had time to read them, much less prepare for the next day's auditions. There was no selective process, even the actor knew he was not castable in most of the projects sent his way—but the agents persisted in throwing him against the wall, hoping he would stick. Because the actor was intimidated by the size, the power (and above all) the possible reaction at the agency, he never spoke with an agent. He *never* passed on a project, *never* re-scheduled a time and consequently *never* booked a job. His career, which up until then had clipped along, quickly lost momentum. The agents had used the agency's pull, but not to the client's benefit. It was just silver tongue flattery and muscle. These agents had used their pull as randomly as the manager had used his push and in the end both clients lost out.

While we're on the subject, when I hear "silver tongue" I think car sales-men: fast-talking, glad-handing and duplicitous. Not a great leap from the common depiction of agents. Your agent doesn't have to be Sammy Glick[3] to be good; don't mistake silver tongued for credibly persuasive. If your agent will *easily* sell a lie, it could easily be the lie you buy.

Schmoozing

Agents schmooze; some more than others, some all the time. Larger agencies have more schmoozing power, but they also have more people to schmooze. The *really* big guns employ a full-time concierge who manufactures schmooze; house-seats at the theatre, front-row at the Stones, baskets for birthdays—stars are treated like stars. Mid-size agencies offer their share of perks, but on nowhere near as grand a scale.

> *I represented an actress whose career was on the move.*
> *When she left me (on the advice of a casting director) and*
> *made a lateral move to another agency, I confronted the*
> *casting person. The difference between our two agencies?*
> *"They," he said, "have season tickets to the Dodgers."*

Unfortunately, for the smaller agency running with the Joneses can be pricey, but subtle gestures of appreciation can be equally effective.

The Christmas after opening my agency, Chris Gorman, former VP of casting at CBS (who sadly has since passed away), met with me for the very first time. I brought a book of pictures and résumés of all the clients I believed had

Schmoozing, though an accepted and intrinsic part of this business we call entertainment, is not a substitute for hard work.

---

[3] If you want to see how little agents have changed in fifty years read Bud Shulberg's novel, *What Makes Sammy Run?*

A well-heeled agency represented talented actors, hosted elaborate soirees, sent tony gifts during the holidays, and, after the annual Casting Society of America (CSA) luncheon would have enormous bouquets of flowers delivered to the casting offices that were nominated or had garnered awards that day. They were the darlings of the industry—until clients started complaining about late or lost paychecks. Eventually the gig was up and the Los Angeles partner was found to have been illegally dipping into client funds. SAG pulled the franchise, the agency was disbanded and the party was over.

series potential in the upcoming pilot season. While waiting in the reception area, I was bowled-over by an enormous flower arrangement lavishly displayed on the coffee table in front of me. It was no surprise that a "Happy Holidays" gift note signed CAA popped blatantly from its center.

Unable to compete with that, I instead *replaced* their note with my business card and a greeting from *The Rainford Agency*. Once inside the office, I confessed my sin to Chris who more than appreciated the joke. From that day forward he always took my calls and the doors of CBS casting were open to my clients.

An agency that is respected and connected raises the visibility and prestige of clients and agents. An agency can employ two great agents at top-dollar, then spend less money on junior agents, because the junior agents need the respect and connections that the agency offers. Those junior agents cover the smaller projects. Independent films, non-network series, plays, industrials—whatever the other agents don't want, can't make money from, or have no interest in. *Schmooze them!* These junior agents of today are the hot shots of the future, and besides, some of those small independent films can turn out to be gold (e.g., *Swingers*).

One last story about schmoozing, because it's just too good to leave out—a writer sits in the living room of his second story apartment the day after the movie-of-the-week he wrote has aired on network television. The overnights[4] are

---

[4] Overnights are Nielsen ratings available the morning after a program airs. They determine the number of households watching and the "share" of that viewership attained by each program.

*in and they are more than respectable. The writer is feeling
a little put out because his agent hasn't even called
to say she watched the show. His phone rings.
"Honey, look out the window," says the voice
on the other end.
He peers through the curtains to see his agent
in her car on her cell phone. She slows down and
yells up to him, "The overnights were great!
The show was fabulous! I loved it!"
And she's gone....
Drive-By Schmoozing at its finest.*

Most of the top casting directors have agents, and that agent might be yours as well. Agents consider it a great sales tool to rattle off how many casting directors they represent—but will it really get you a job? No. An audition? Don't depend on it. I worked with a leading film and television casting director who, during pilot season, was offered all the best scripts—both one-hour dramas and half-hour comedies on all networks. Her agent was a top agent at a very reputable mid-sized agency. He negotiated all her deals, but was *never* responsible for getting her any work. Agents do *not* commission casting directors.

It is a courtesy negotiation and in return they may get a nice gift, a nice lunch or a thank you. Though some agents boast about the advantage of *repping* casting directors, the *preferential* treatment an actor should expect from the arrangement is negligible. The agents get their calls returned, but any agent a casting director trusts to negotiate her deals is going to get his calls returned regardless of whether or not he represents the casting director. The inside track, they get that too, but familiarity breeds contempt, or at least compliance, and for the most part I've found agents far *less* aggressive with casting directors they represent.

You've got the audition...now what?

In Front of the Casting Director

Now you go before the casting director and hope his or her bias won't prevent you from getting to the next step. But the casting person is just the beginning of a very long battle, especially in television casting. Getting past the casting director can be the most frustrating of all obstacles. I've seen actors go all the way to the job despite the silent protests of a casting director, and I've sat with my mouth closed when it wasn't my place to say, "Wait what about that last girl...?" Casting directors believe the chance of finding that unknown breakout star in a pre-read is like finding a needle in a haystack. After years of reading and thousands of pre-reads, many are disillusioned and look to the efforts of "others" to call a new face to their attention. ("Others" in this case meaning other casting directors.) Information spreads like wildfire and it's not always because friends are calling friends.

The competition is fierce.

> *We were testing young actors for a pilot at the network; scheduled to test immediately after us was another group of actors for a different project with a different casting director. One of our actors was a find. At the production company's expense we'd flown him in from New York, paid the cost of housing, feeding and delivering him to and from the audition. The network loved him, and thought he was perfect for a different pilot, so he didn't get our job. But before they could make a deal on the other pilot, the waiting casting director got on the phone to a different studio regarding another project she was casting for a competing network. In a matter of minutes, the actor got a call from his manager, left our test, hightailed it across town, met with that studio and had the job that evening. Could happen. Did happen. And a lot of people were furious!*

From the very first producer session, the casting person brings forth the "best choices" for the role. On a TV pilot, the best choice is the actor with network approval. After that, the work begins. *Network approval* means before the creators, the director, and the studio meet the actor, the network suits— the ultimate decision-makers—say: "Okay with us." If only the others were so easily convinced. If only the director didn't need to see more actors; and the creators would accept the fact, that no matter how brilliant they may think their project is, Mark Wahlberg, at this stage of his career, is *not* going to do a sitcom. And if only the studios didn't have to stick in their two cents, slow down the process and then drag their feet making deals. Very few actors are network approved, even in cases where a network has a deal with an actor; they may still require the actor to read or at least meet with the network before they can be hired.

In a business that requires the collaboration of many experts and much expertise, whose whole is the sum of its parts, you'd think there'd be a better understanding or at least appreciation for every cog in the wheel. Not the case. To the wigmaker it's a movie about wigs, to the location manager, it's parking; the caterer, prop guys, set designer, wardrobe—all their needs are immediate and critical. Long before those experts come aboard, the casting has begun. And when it does, the casting director is the eye of the storm, demanding attention to the "most important aspect" of the project: casting. Their intention: get it cast, get it well-cast, get it quickly cast. Their complaints: bad agents, bad material, fickle directors, intrusive executives, lazy business affairs, and no talent! Stop worrying about casting directors—get in front of producers and directors.

In Front of Producers and Directors

Getting in front of the producers/director is achieved by getting past the casting director. Sometimes you pre-read for the casting director who deems you are either right, not-quite-right-but-hirable, or not at all their choice but right to satisfy the wants and needs of the producer, director studio and/or network—so they give you a call-back. Once there, it's your goal to get the job. When you're in the room with the creative team, you are a very specific part of that team, so act like it. Show them your wares, show them your ease, show them that you are prepared. If you have intelligent questions about the project, ask them. They will answer you, *not* the casting director. Even though the casting director is in the room, this is not casting's time. When you walk in the room, appear personable, confident and capable. They *want* you to solve their problem so they can go deal with the network, and the studio, the wardrobe, the editor, and the wigs.

For feature film auditions, the action is in front of the director and producer; that's where you need to be. Unless the role is pivotal, a movie studio will usually defer to the choices of the director and producers. If the role *is* pivotal and the studio is involved, then a screen test will be necessary. This is an important time for your agent to campaign on your behalf. Your agent can and should call directors and producers of influence who have worked with you before and solicit their help in supporting your abilities. It isn't always enough to say, "My client just finished working in a great film," you need proof.

When opportunities arise, seize the moment and work with your agent to get the tools to support your campaign. Stay on top of it. It requires the enthusiasm of your entire team to infuse others with enthusiasm for you.

In Front of the Television Studios

Now that so many studios are subsidizing the cost of a television pilot and a series, they increasingly demand creative input. Actors routinely test more than once to win a role on series. First for the casting director, then maybe two or more times for the producer and/or the director, all of whom are considered Creative People. The next level, the studio, is that netherworld between Heaven and Hell. Studio executives are the go-betweens who understand how to mold a creator's baby into a network darling. The good ones, of which there are few, know instinctively how and when to reel in the creator, and when to do battle with the network. Since I don't personally know any successful actors, writers or directors who have stepped away from their creative positions and into the role of a studio exec, I have to assume that studio execs who are not creators, are, for the most part, former network development execs. Which would account for their familiarity with network likes and dislikes. As for their creative tendencies, the jury is still out. The studio or network exec with a true understanding of the creative process is a rare and precious find. The most popular goal, as far as I've seen, is to protect the studio's interest, and to that end as the actor you are now required to sign series contracts, audition for the studio and then, if they are so inclined, go before the network. This extra step infuriates the casting director, ticks off the agents and worries the actor. Casting directors hate it. Having just spent weeks placating the whims of writer/producer/director—reading and re-reading actor after actor, and at last when the creators are finally willing to accept any one of three choice performers, *in step the suits to muck it up. "She's not pretty enough—I don't like her voice—His neck is too thick—Sorry guys, we're not going to the network,"* and with that, the whole blasted process begins again. The enormity of the task makes casting directors far more receptive to new ideas because they believe, as they so often profess, that the director and producers have seen everybody.

For the agent whose client has been nixed, a pre-network *network* audition that leaves everyone empty-handed is the ultimate let-down...especially after hours and hours of posturing, and oft times painstaking negotiations. On the plus side, these same agents are usually the first to be informed that the role has gone uncast and *that* is valuable information. Yes, your agent may be mourning your loss, but they can't, won't and shouldn't negate an obvious opportunity.

For other agents it's all good. Clients who read and weren't first choice now move up a rung, because the casting director—burdened with the studio and everyone one else breathing fire—has to pore through all those lists again and find the holes. Actors who were out of town, sick, not available or just blindly dismissed will be re-addressed. For the actor who hasn't yet had a shot...this is your chance. If an agent calls a casting director on the heels of a studio or network test, and the show isn't completely cast, the agent stands a good chance of solving the problem. Casting directors are all ears when they feel backed against a wall.

But what about the actor left at the altar—disappointed and humiliated—but mostly in the dark? Assuming the actor did everything she'd done before and didn't tank in the room, what changed? Sometimes nothing. Since you never really know who your biggest allies are—you also never know who voted you down. The power of veto is rampant, nearly everyone has it, some without realizing they have any power at all. Suppose, for instance, after you left the room, a casting assistant inadvertently mumbled, *"I didn't realize she was so tall."* That could be the statement that spreads to a fear, which turns to a panic that knocks you out of the running. No one bothers to ask, *"Tall...in relation to what?"*

One of the top casting directors in her field has a reputation for inadvertently deriding actors at the most inopportune time because they've changed their appearance even slightly before a callback or a network test. She's been known to deliver classic confidence killers like: "Ugh, you cut your hair," or, "Why did you wear those pants?" And then, without waiting for an answer, and while the actor's still reeling from the shock, she walks them into a room filled with network execs.

But take heart, because there *is* something your agent can do. Some agents do it all the time; many agents don't know they can do it and might never know until you tell them. But if you're testing for a pilot...

Agents can get a studio to guarantee that you go to network.

If the studio agrees, you know someone is a fan. In the final negotiations, this is a deal point, and could be a dealbreaker. You still have to read for the studio, but if they axe you, *you don't know it*. The studio alerts the network that they are bringing you in as a contractual obligation. You get to show your wares to the network and again to the studio. If the other actors work with the director, you work with the director. And the truth is, once in front of the network, the playing field is leveled. Anyone can win the job. I've seen it happen repeatedly.

In Front of the Network

Hopefully, your career has or will at some point present you with an opportunity to be in front of the network. The upside is, doing so and being successful can change your life and your bank account dramatically almost overnight. On the other side, the network experience can be so harrowing and unforgiving that once subjected to it, the actor, though forever prepared for anything short of public flogging, can get stuck in the fear. It shouldn't be hard to imagine sitting in a waiting room with at least three other actors all competing for the same role. But now the stakes are higher; now it's win or lose. Fifteen executives sit just inside the door to your left and through the paper-thin walls you can hear them roaring with laughter at every single line the actor delivers—the same lines you're poised to bring to life immediately after he walks out. Pressure, eh?

In you go, and it is as if the jokes have become eulogies—the roars are reduced to polite smiles and your dreams of paying off your credit card debt are dashed. Were you that awful/was he that good? You'll never know. But if you get that far in the casting process, give yourself a little credit. In the network, all bets are off. Favorites walk in the door and lose the role, while underdogs emerge triumphant.

I worked on a pilot where the female lead was down to two women, although four were testing at the network. No one expected the other two to be a factor, but the networks generally frown upon gathering so many executives together in one place at one time to make a decision between only two options for a lead role. From the casting director's point of view this makes sense. If given only two choices, the network can't help but think there's someone else out there—at least two more.

By the end of the session, it's decided that Actress A had won the part. She was hired. Four days before shooting Actress A was fired and a desperate search began for her replacement. In a three day spree, no fewer than seventy-five actresses, some who'd been seen before, others who had been adamantly refused, traipsed before the Powers That Be.

Ultimately Actress B, who lost the role originally, was re-tested and this time emerged triumphant. Shooting had already begun before she was hired. One network exec commented that the first hiring was the result of the network being overly excited by Actress A's recent appearance in a hit summer movie. It's not exactly what I remember, but that notion seemed acceptable to the others and so they ran with it—and eventually probably believed it.

I have to hand it to the networks, though. In the past few years they've gotten better at publicly disguising their favoritism. When I was an agent, I frequently escorted my actors to their network tests. It can be intimidating to the seasoned professional, let alone the novice. Hours of waiting, thinking, thinking, waiting. So I would go as a show of support, as a diversion—and it didn't hurt to look over the revised contracts, which actors are required to sign before they test. One teenaged client of mine (testing for the first time) spent an hour and a half waiting to go in. There were two others testing for the same role and they read, then read again and were excitedly asked to wait. Finally they read my client. She was in and out, and on her heels was the casting director. "Lisa," she said "You were great, thanks; you can go home." She then turned excitedly to Maria and Rhonda: "Great job, let's go over the next scene before you go back in...." Lisa cried all the way back to my office, and later that day when the official news arrived, I was told she was too mature.

Did I believe it? Didn't matter, it was all the information I was going to get.

On another occasion four guys zipped up to the network for a last minute call on a role that was to start right away. All four actors know that one of them will emerge triumphant and be ushered off to wardrobe immediately. The four go in, the four come out. They all wait, No.4 gets called back in, the other three nod knowingly. No.4 comes out and all are thanked and politely released by the casting director who instructs them to check with their agents. The actors pile on to the elevator and just as the door is closing, No.4 realizes—Oops, he left his wallet in the office—and jumps off the elevator. Guess who got the job. (Incidentally the "wallet trick" was the brainchild of a network executive.)

What can you do in front of the network to gain your invitation to the party? Let's safely assume you've got the material and the character down. They're looking at your *presence*. They're looking for what makes you pop, on and off the screen. The air-of-ease that says, "I'm comfortable but not complacent, I'm glad I'm here, and I'm happy to meet all you nice folks. See you at the top." (Sense your carriage, be comfortable in your skin—own the whole package.)

If it's a comedy, they want to feel your sense of humor before you walk in the room—know that you're easy to listen to and funny—*inherently* funny. The network *wants* to be impressed. The director and producers *want* you to make them look smart *("Please, at least one of you, win this role")*. Don't choke. Just as they are proficient in their expertise, you are proficient in yours. The actor is just one cog in the wheel, albeit a very important cog—show them that the casting dilemma is solved so they can move on to dealing with those damn wigs.

One actor I know always has a gimmick
when he goes to network...
I wouldn't be the first to say he's arrogant and
obnoxious, but he's also talented, funny and memorable.
On one occasion (late to a network test), he came
fumbling in, disconcerted and full of snappy repartee
about the screw-ups that caused his tardiness.
Exactly something the character—in this script—might do.
Everyone laughed from the moment he entered the room,
and he was funny. If he had a strategy (and I'm not saying
he did...), it was executed with brilliance. The only thing
left to do was say the lines—he'd already won over the
room, and convinced everyone that he was the guy.

The network is not always right. There are plenty of stories of mis casting. I know an actor with only passable talent who works constantly. In auditions he appears to be confident, breezy and in control. I know him to personally be passive, soft and nondescript. But, that's why they have thirty-two flavors, right?

Don't rely on the career and status of your current fans to sustain you throughout your career. Especially those of a casting director. You can be the darling of the casting office today, and three months later they stop bringing you in. Nothing is more frustrating to an actor than not being considered for a role by a friend. If you're always working on a casting director's co-star parts, when is that casting director going to bring you in for the series lead?

Probably never. (At least, not without being agented.)

> **A NOTE TO WRITERS**
> *Writers can also be the darlings of a network. One TV comedy writer I know got a laugh every time he opened his mouth; the one-liners just never stopped. Everyone from the production company to the network loved him. During the most serious of meetings, it was acceptable for him to crack a joke because it was expected of him. He couldn't help it, he was always thinking, always writing—but I have to tell you in truth— he wasn't always funny.*

Many actors find it difficult to say no when a casting director requests a favor. It has been my experience that casting favors are never returned. Casting directors never ask favors like, "Hey, would you mind reading for this lead role in a Spielberg film?" *That's* a favor your agent can get behind. More often it's, "I have this role, it's only three lines, but I need a *really* good actor." If you grant that favor, expect the return favor (if you get one at all) to be of equal caliber. There are graceful ways for both agents and actors to *pass* and to *accept* work, use them. Get your agent to do the talking. Casting directors who bring you in all the time might expect you in after your career has moved forward. It's your agent's job to diplomatically not burn your bridges. But your agent needs reminders.

If you find yourself in an uncomfortable situation where you need to say no— be sure your agent and manager don't put the onus entirely on you.

5

Card Sharks
- Agents and the Deals They Make -

Negotiating and re-negotiating—when all is said and done, this is the true test of an agent. Contracts, small print, screen credit, dollars, test-option deals, re-location, residuals, foreign rights, favored-nation and morality clauses, even trailers. The deal may be in the agent's hands, but truth is, it's your butt on the line and you'd better know if your agent is rocking the boat or selling you up the river. Just because agents can get you an audition or a meeting doesn't qualify them to make your deal. While your agent is negotiating on your behalf, instill him with confidence, and encourage him to mind the fine points. Many agents fizzle out after the monies have been decided. Don't let this happen.

The trick is to inspire your agent—agents are keen on telling clients about a brilliant deal point they single-handedly conjured out of thin air. I once made a deal for a client to do a small role on a film. The money was low, but the client needed the work, so I orchestrated the deal as if the client was taking a huge cut in pay *only* because the actor loved the project and wanted to work with the director. In the deal, I stipulated that the production company would have three dozen roses delivered to the client's dressing room on the first day of shooting. Silly? Maybe. But my client felt appreciated rather than desperate. That small gesture led my client to believe that I was a good negotiator. It shouldn't have. *Clever* shouldn't replace negotiation skills and attention to detail. Don't ever let your agent's flair leave you unaware!

Negotiating and deal making should not mean lying!

If you hear your agent on the phone telling out-and-out lies to get you a better deal (i.e., making up quotes), you may think, "Hey, he's doing his job," but keep in mind that he's probably lying to you as well.

A junior agent who worked in my office received an offer for a client to star in a low-budget film. The agent had virtually *no* contract experience, so I insisted that every dealpoint had to get my approval. The negotiations went along uneventfully, until one major deal point brought everything to a screeching halt. I called the casting office to intervene, but as far as they were concerned, the terms had been agreed upon and the deal was done. Because the agent *insisted* the casting office was lying, and because he also *swore* to me that he had *not* accepted the terms, *nor* closed the deal—I fought for the contract change, and eventually reached an agreement with the casting director.

Six months later, I discovered the truth—the agent had lied. He *had* closed the deal, and he told the casting office that I knew the deal was closed. A cardinal rule of agenting is: once the deal is closed—the deal is closed. Blaming me and the casting office took the onus and responsibility off of him.

That's why you don't want your agent to close a deal without your okay. And before you give the okay, you need to be sure you understand the pros and the cons of each deal. Good deals can still be flawed. What you *don't* get can be just as important as what you *do* get.

Every deal is unique. Deal points are determined by the savvy of the agent, the demand for the talent, the passion for the project, the willingness of both parties to make a deal, and the client's understanding of the business. There are "industry norms," of course, but don't assume that a writer or actor with few or no credits must accept whatever is offered. Question your agent.

Even agents without any qualifications to do so make deals every day. The goal most often being: make money, keep the client. I learned dealmaking from listening to and asking questions of other agents, studying contracts, hiring lawyers, referring to the SAG books[1], calling friends in Business Affairs at major studios—and, of course trial and error. I wanted to learn as much as I could from every situation and to make sound deals. You want your agent to treat your deal like it's brand new, and at the same time you need to be sure that she can and will make as sweet a deal for you as she did her other client. You decide the deal your agent will make; you give your agent the ability to negotiate better terms. Your power to say yes or no is the ultimate decision-maker. Yes, you want better terms, but if your agent can't sell those better terms to the buyer, then you're both going to lose.

When I first opened my agency I had the good fortune to rep an actor named Juney Smith. I was a young agent and he believed in my abilities and stroked my ego like no client had done before or probably since. A talented actor and a terrific salesperson, he would have made a great agent. Always upbeat, positive and full of energy, he worked at his craft and agented me as his agent. Juney landed a lead role in the feature film *Good Morning, Vietnam* and spent eight weeks in Thailand working opposite Robin Williams. (Incidentally, I had negotiated an additional first-class round-trip ticket for Juney, which he graciously offered to me, but at the time leaving for Thailand would have left my agency agent-less, so I was forced to decline.) We spoke regularly while he was away and the experience for him could not have been better. Robin Williams played a DJ and Juney was his "engineer," the guy who spins the records and who Robin's character spoke to and played to behind the glass partition. When the project wrapped and Juney returned, you could have lit all of Los Angeles with his energy and enthusiasm. "This movie is going to be huge," he said (it was), "...and the offers of work will be non-stop." This role, in this film, was going to catapult Juney to the next level—and I was going with him. Now, as I've said, Juney was an enthusiastic guy, and his excitement was contagious. Three weeks before the Los Angeles screening, a Business Affairs exec at Paramount called my office and made an offer to Juney Smith

---

[1] The SAG books referred to are the *Codified Basic Agreement for Independent Producers* and the *Independent Television Agreement*.

for the TV series of *Good Morning, Vietnam*. But the offer was well below industry standard, so I jotted down the numbers and informed my client. Juney didn't have recent TV pilot or series quotes, but he did have a good body of work. Moreover, he pitched his performance, and the intrinsic value of his character in the series, to me with credible conviction. *His* agenting prompted *my* response to Business Affairs. I let them know that I felt the offer was insulting, that I believed they low-balled me because I was a small agency and that I was certain their offer would not have been presented to William Morris or ICM. More importantly, until they put something more substantial on the table, I would not take this offer to my client. The exec had not seen the movie (neither had I, at this point) so I pitched her everything Juney had pitched to me, with confidence and passion. Ultimately we got a very lucrative deal, and Juney publicly gave me all the credit. When I saw the movie, I realized I'd been agented somewhat, because editing had reduced his role and screen time—but for those few weeks before I saw the film I pitched Juney feverishly. Would we have gotten as grand a deal had he not agented me? I'd like to think yes, but there's no guarantee.

> *The gift of a good negotiator is knowledge of the product and the climate of the business. You need information and the ability to sell the terms of the deal. There is no room for fear.*

I am not a good liar, but I can sell anything I believe in. If I don't believe in it but I'm *obligated* to sell, I present a sound argument. If I can't sell the product with conviction, I can sell the argument. That's just me; every agent has their own way of negotiating. Some bully, some plead, some reason, some bluff, some demand and threaten, some act (?) crazy, and some roll over—but everybody compromises. Watching an agent roll over is most disturbing.

As an executive producer, I hired a friend (who had previously been a client) to work as an actor in a pilot. My offer wasn't insulting, but it wasn't great. I tried to find an amount that could be justified to the studio and worthwhile to the performer. Because my friend's present agent knew my past history with the client, the offer was accepted without question. On a different project, as a casting director, I was authorized to offer an actor $600 for a day role on a feature film, but was told I could go as high as $2000 if the agent *pushed* for more. The actor had a higher quote but I began the negotiation as follows:

Even if the compromise is something you are willing to give up from the start, an agent should present the compromise as a compromise, not as a given.

Me: I can offer you $600 for the day.
Agent: Okay.
Me: You don't want any more?
Agent: Of course I do.
Me: Then why don't you ask me for more?
Agent: Can I have more?
Me: How much?
Agent: Can I get $1000.00 for the day?
Me: Okay.

Should the agent have stopped there? It depends on the uniqueness of the situation and the particulars of the project. There is no blanket yes or no answer. But if your agent never gets you a raise, or can't ever seem to make a deal beyond the original offer, be afraid.

Early on as an agent...I believed the casting directors when they said, "I only have $800 for the role." Were they lying? Not completely, but a more accurate translation might be: "I only have the authority to offer $800 on this role, any more would require someone else's okay."

In feature films, most casting directors are given a loose budget with which to guide their spending. Depending on the actor, his or her credits, and the role and prestige of the film, this amount should be considered a starting place. As a casting director, if you're told you have $2000.00 a week for the role of "Paul" and $5,000 a week for the comparable role of "Julie," one might consider there is $7,000 a week allotted for both roles—therein lies the wiggle room. The money can be divvied up creatively. For an agent, the difference in commission between $2000 and $2500 is only $50, and to some, hardly worth the fight. But for the actor or writer, a raise, even a meager one, can be significantly and emotionally gratifying. (Not to mention that even a nominal raise can give the client a sense of progress.)

> **A NOTE TO WRITERS**
> *A call comes in from your lit agent. The production company that optioned your script wants you to do a "small polish on a few characters" so they can make offers to star names. They don't want to call it a re-write, because that would mean they have to pay you. Will you do them this favor? You want your script made into a film, and you want that star name attached— but for free? Isn't this the same production company that just a week ago wouldn't contract transportation for you and a guest to the premiere?*

Agents don't set out to make bad deals, but bad deals are made all the time. The small print, the details, the minutiae will all bite you in the butt at some point if you're not careful. When it does, actors and writers often suffer "amnesia," and are unable to recall that they okayed the particulars of a deal that included things like *free re-writes, standard accommodations*, or *overtime buy-outs*. Bad deals get okayed because the clients are either mislead or uninformed about the nature of the business, and the consequences of the deal points. Or, because the client, the agent (or both) are too eager to make a deal.

Oh, and about that dressing room you think doesn't matter because at least it means you're working...you're wrong. Everything matters....

Say you've just landed your first (or even third) opportunity to test for a television pilot. Let's call the series *Buddies.* It's an ensemble cast with four series regular roles. You want the job. Three days before you read for the network, your agent starts hammering out the deal. All you're thinking about is landing the job. The day before the test, your agent calls to say the producers won't guarantee that your dressing room is equal to the three other leads, none of which have been cast. Everything else is set, money, billing, episode guarantees.

My money says the unseasoned performer will tell the agent to agree to the terms. The smart agent knows that if you get this job, and it's a hit, when you get on that set and you're the only actor in a *tiny* dressing room...you won't blame yourself. You'll blame your agent.

RULE 11: It's Your Agent's Job To Play The Bad Guy.

I was less than enthused to be negotiating a Canadian TV series with a Canadian production company with little regard for SAG rules[2]. Negligible money and difficult working conditions left only perks for dealbreakers—and we had quite a few. The client would have to be away from his family, so we needed a minimum number of guaranteed roundtrip first-class tickets, a house, a family gym membership, and a car. My client was adamant about a late-model Chevy Suburban 4-wheel drive SUV (it snows a lot in Canada and he was a big guy). Negotiations for the vehicle dragged on, but eventually we got what we needed and closed the deal. Once on the set, the executive producer took the client aside and asked if he'd "mind" driving a rental car instead of the agreed upon SUV. "No problem," said the client, "the car never mattered to *me*—I'd ride a bicycle to work...but my agent is tough as nails, and a real pain-in-the-ass." Then he called me. The SUV was delivered as promised.

---

[2] Canada is not governed by the SAG rules and regulations.

GOOD COP/BAD COP
Unless there is a manager, the only cop other than the agent is the actor. Actors should always play good cop. Because if the agent blames negotiations on the actor...who gets punished on the set?

Negotiating for money is like playing blackjack in Vegas. It's not the dealer's money, and has no effect on the dealer's personal life, but more often than not you're still sitting in front of a dealer who *wants* to beat you. And you still have to play by the rules. My strictest rule was no out-and-out lying. That meant no reneging on deals, no unethical agenting, and no falsifying quotes.

If your agent can't be creative with your quotes, help him.

QUOTES
An actor's quote refers to money the actor has received in the past for work in a comparable medium. A feature film quote will not satisfy a TV pilot deal. Whether Business Affairs applies the quote (i.e., it's very high and you didn't get the job, so they argue it's not really a quote) or the agent dismisses it (i.e., it's really low and you didn't get the job, so it shouldn't "count"). Quotes should be considered just a starting place for negotiations.

As an agent I always gave an accurate quote—and working in casting confirmed what I always believed: *all quotes are verified.* The casting office *always* calls the production or Business Affairs office from whence the quote originates and verifies its legitimacy. Knowing that, some agents still lie. You may think that's a quality you should appreciate in an agent—after all, he or she is trying to get you more money—but it isn't. Once the negotiators discover they've been lied to, deal-making gets personal.

While working in casting I was asked to verify a pilot quote on an actor. The negotiations had begun, and the quote was very high, but we were prepared to pay. When we verified that the actor's actual quote was far below the figure we'd been given, the deal changed significantly.

RULE 12: Quotes Are Not The Gospel.

In the long run, don't worry about your quote. Consider it the least amount of money you can earn, not the most. Remember, quotes should be considered a starting place for negotiations—an ice-breaker. If your agent can't be creative with your quotes...help them. I don't believe Robert De Niro has a quote for a half-hour series—but that's not going to hurt his negotiating power if he should decide to do a sitcom. If a deal is less than favorable, an agent may insist it be a "no quote" deal. Which simply means if someone calls Business Affairs and asks to verify a quote, "no quote" is the response. Agents can also increase an actor's quote by playing with the numbers. Let's say the agent makes a deal at $5000.00 a week for four weeks of work. That equals a total of $20,000. Without changing the dollars, the agent could make the following deal instead: $20,000.00 for two weeks, plus two free consecutive weeks. That would increase the actor's *weekly quote* from 5,000 to 10Gs. (Notice that I added the term "consecutive"—*that's* the detail. Get your agent to be specific.)

Dealbreakers...

As the name suggests, a dealbreaker is a deal point that is considered *non-negotiable* by either party, and unless it is satisfied, a dealbreaker is a deal killer. Dealbreaker does *not* mean, "I really want this deal point but if I don't get it I'll still take the job." Don't bluff about a dealbreaker. Bluffing is inherently a very tricky practice (especially when you're gambling with a person's livelihood.) If you and your agent decide that the *whole* deal is not worth the sum of its parts, and you are considering passing on a deal, know this: the possibility of the deal going away *forever* genuinely exists. Complicating matters is the fact that sometimes a deal *has* to be passed on before it can move forward. The risk is still real. Calling someone else's bluff is equally risky and can be outright disastrous if the call is wrong.

An actress gets an offer for a half-hour sitcom of $10 grand a week, guaranteed seven out of thirteen episodes, with a $5000.00 relocation fee from Los Angeles to New York. The role is minor, but the show is guaranteed on-air, and a major star is attached. The agent asks for $25,000, plus all-shows produced[3] and $10,000.00 for the move. The studio responds: $15 grand, all-shows produced, with $5,000 to move, take it or leave it. With the client's consent, the agent turns down the deal. The actress calls their bluff, but the studio isn't bluffing, and they move on to their second choice. Desperate now—the actress phones the producer/star, blames the agent for her decision, and pleads for the job. They agree to hire her, but the deal is changed. No more $15,000; now she's back to $10,000 with the original seven episode guarantee and no relocation fee at all. She accepts the deal and moves herself to New York.

• • •

In a different example, I negotiated a deal with a studio whose top executive repeatedly informed me, from the onset of negotiations, the amount of money he "would not under any circumstances pay." And that's exactly where we made the deal.

Agents, good agents, get a sense, a feel, for a negotiation and for the person with whom they are negotiating. Dealmaking will volley back and forth between the buyer and the seller, right up until someone says, "That's it, take it or leave it." That doesn't mean your agent should wait to hear *take it or leave it* before he or she considers closing a deal, but it does mean your agent should pay attention to those words, and then respond to them appropriately.

Regardless of how much you may or may not trust your agent, ask directly: "Before I sign, are there any deal points in today's contract that will make me want to fire you tomorrow?"

That will give 'em something to think about.

Making a bad deal can cost an agent the client and hurt the agent's reputation. That's why most of the large agencies have in-house attorneys who pore over long-form contracts *for months* before they're given to you to sign. Don't be fooled—these attorneys are not concerned with your dressing room; their sole interest is ensuring the contract's language protects the agency's interest—one of which is you. It's the agent's job to *sell and service* the client. Before the agency attorneys even see the contract, the broad strokes of the deal are

---

[3] All shows produced entitles the actor a *guaranteed* payment for all episodes produced, regardless of whether or not the actor performs in the episode.

in place and particulars have been addressed and agreed upon. The agency attorney gets a copy of the agent's booking slip and *then* tackles the language of the agreement. As your career progresses and your deals get more complicated, incorporating the skills of an entertainment attorney before your deal is made is simply common sense.

> **A WORD ABOUT ATTORNEYS**
> Attorneys: The good ones—like John Sloss, Tom Fox, Jacqueline Eckhouse and Jay Froberg—are brilliant with contract detail, and equally passionate and knowledgeable about the art of the industry and the clients they represent. If you are inclined to hire an attorney, find one who cares enough to successfully blend the artistry of show with the pragmatism of business.

6

The Early Bird Gets the Worm
- Agents and Work -

If you "hang-in" long enough, will you eventually make it? One way or another, something's gotta give. And when it does, the relationship between you and your agent will change. Agents are always waxing poetic about how they launched someone's career only to be scorned and forgotten when the hard work finally paid off. There is some truth to this in the sense that agents don't make money unless *you* make money, but they *spend* money every day on behalf of their clients. Messengers, phone calls, stamps, lunches, resumes, breakdowns, copying—it adds up fast. Not to mention things like overhead, salaries, office space, lights, phones, electricity and letterhead. More importantly, agents think they work harder than you do because they make the calls, sell the goods and fight the fight. The actor, on the other hand, "merely" has to convince a bunch of strangers to trust him or her to bring to life a two-million dollar TV show or 50 million dollar feature film. And the writer? Sure, the writer wrote the script, but the agent had to compete to get someone with power to read it.

An agency with 100 clients may have five who pay the bills, which means the desire (need) to sign clients who work is genuine. On the upside, every day there is the potential to represent a big box-office draw, television star, or in-demand writer—and in doing so earn great sums of money, not to mention perks and prestige. If your agent thinks you have talent and believes that he or she can earn great sums of money selling that talent, what *else* might motivate that agent to get you work? Loyalty. Loyalty equals a long-term guaranteed income to your agent, and loyalty means the agent can attract other talent of equal caliber (which may lead to even *larger* sums of money). Loyalty means recognition. Being the agent who first signed Tom Cruise or Quentin Tarantino might impress the novice, but don't buy into the hype. If your agent *still* represents Cruise, or if they signed Leonardo DiCaprio *and* Heather Graham before Tom left, then they can get some mileage out of it; otherwise it's just a good story. Yes, I was the first agent to sign Jada Pinkett, and she did become a recognizable name in television and film while with me, but she has been with several agents since and I'm sure they *all* take responsibility for her career...as long as it's going strong.

For the time—regardless of how long—you and your agent are together, your agent needs to believe you are there for the long haul. Agents will put forth more effort toward clients they believe they can keep. If you were an agent and had to choose between two people with similar earning potential and comparable talent, you'd want to represent the person you believed would stay with you after "making it."

A word to the wise...don't lay the "I'll never leave you" syrup on too heavily. Or make promises you can't (or don't intend) to keep. Agents, like elephants, never forget.

> *I once represented an actress who had every reason to believe she was going to be successful. She had the chops and an agent who was getting her auditions. Between declarations of being eternally indebted to me, were her constant proclamations that as soon as "we" got a series, she was going to buy me a desperately needed new office chair. I wasn't working for the chair, but the thought was touching and sincere, so why not? She hadn't earned the agency a dime in the first year and a half that we worked together, though she'd been out plenty (more than fifty auditions). Still, I didn't give up on her; I believed her desire to land a series went beyond the obvious and had something to do with wanting to give back. Of course, by now you realize that she did get the series and I didn't get the office chair. Well, not entirely true. That Christmas she did present me with a chair. A miniature dollhouse furniture chair. Cute, yes, but I wanted—and had earned—the stupid promised chair. Would I continue to work for her? Of course. But would I go that extra mile? That, I couldn't promise.*

Agents Are Gamblers

It would stand to reason that larger agencies, rather than smaller agencies, would be more likely to take chances with newcomers, since they're assured the bills will be paid by their star clients or other investments. Instead, the opposite is true. Large agencies have money and manpower; star names give them cachet and prestige. They don't need to invest in rookies—why should they, when they can leave the developing to the small fry, and pluck the winners out when they're in full bloom?

Though all agents are gamblers, ironically, the smaller the agency, the bigger the gamble. Small agencies don't have the muscle to draw big names. They constantly need to look for talent they can develop, and hope that once it's developed the client lingers around long enough to move the agency's visibility up a rung or two. But that takes time—and money. And for every novice who blossoms into a working professional, there are dozens more who fade off into the horizon. That said, I still believe that when an actor, writer, musician, director, comedian or any type of artist, wholly invests their time, effort, heart and soul into their craft and their career, and those efforts are matched by an agent who is equally invested—eventually *something* has to give. Hopefully it will give in the form of work.

Working *in* your chosen profession is not the only bona fide validation that you are a member of that profession. You cannot always control when you work "in" your business, but you can always control when you work "at" it. The person waiting tables, hoping to be discovered, is a waiter. But the person waiting tables, taking acting classes, and auditioning, is an actor. Witness the new trend in the literary field: on any given day you can whip through the trades and read about some young literary, development or production assistant who has sold their first screenplay. Coincidence? No. Using your contacts and the readily available information from your day job to push yourself toward your ultimate goal is cost- and time-effective. And since most performers can't dictate when they get paid to work in their field, generating income from other sources can keep the dream alive. Working or not, if you don't take an interest in who represents you, you move further away from controlling when you get paid to work. This isn't easy. Every degree of your working and not working influences your agent's behavior. When you are working, you need to influence your agent to continue the effort—to create more and greater opportunities, to strike while the iron is hot. This is also a time when an agent's shortcomings become most apparent, i.e., an inability or unwillingness to capitalize on opportunity.

If you're not working, keeping your agent enthused and passionate is a challenge and requirement. Do not let the fact that you're not working lead to self-doubt or worry about your agent dropping you. You have to communicate with your agent. No matter how difficult, once the communication stops you've lost them. Establish communication with your agent before and after auditions (but not to the point of nausea). If you get a job, that's great, because...

Agents Need Something To Talk About And Work Goes A Long Way

Witness the hype-life of a guest-star spot on *The Practice*. The actor lands the job the first week in September, but doesn't work until the third week. The first two weeks, the agent hypes the actor as having "just landed," the role. The next week, the actor "is working on" an episode of *The Practice.* It's an auspicious gig, in that the show is a critically acclaimed, Emmy-winning, Nielsen-scoring slam-dunk. For the next few weeks after the episode wraps, the actor "just finished working" on the episode. Once the air date is determined, "he's got an upcoming episode." Then there's the actual air date, followed by roughly three weeks of "his episode just aired." Because the show has cachet and is still on the air, working on it is a coup, regardless of when the work was done. Pitching the fact that your client worked on *Seinfeld* won't have the same effect, because the show is over and done and there's no way for an agent to claim that an actor *just finished* working on it. But a spot on

Seinfeld is still effective for the agent trying to convince a buyer that a client is funny. Guest-starring on *Seinfeld,* no matter how "straight" the role was, helps an agent pitch the client as comedic, even without tape. (Incidentally, landing a job on either show lends credibility to two claims: First, that the actor is able to act. And second, that the actor is hirable.)

As for the writer; he or she "just pitched" an idea to a studio and is working on the second draft of a script. "USA Films loved the pitch...I need to quickly finish this draft because they're anxious to read it," sounds a whole lot better than, "USA Films didn't buy the pitch, so I have to write a script instead." If your agent can use a four-month old guest-star spot or a three-year old script to excite a buyer, then you can find something to excite your agent. The possibilities of work, pending work, past work—use them. Give your agent the hook that they need to embellish and sell, and every opportunity they need to do so. Be mindful of the agent who relaxes when you work. Keep your agent rolling while you're on a roll. Actors audition better when they're working so don't "book out" because you're shooting a movie, an episodic or commercial. Don't assume that because you're rehearsing a play in New York, you cannot audition for a job in Los Angeles. If the agent can get you an audition, everyone will try to work around your schedule. Get as many auditions and meetings as you can while you are working. The less available you are—the more valuable you become.

RULE 13: An Agent's Response To An Actor's Needs Is Directly Related To The Amount Of Revenue That Actor Generates For The Agent And Agency.

If Mel Gibson is feeling less than enthusiastic about his film options, it's guaranteed that an army of agents are losing sleep over his dissatisfaction and the impending doom that would result from his leaving the agency.

If you earn $200,000 dollars a year as an actor doing television and film, that generates $20,000 dollars for the agency. Now say that for the past six

> **RUN FOR YOUR MONEY**
> *I worked for a mid-size agency in the mid '80s (before cell-phones) that represented a strong list of working actors. One moneymaker stood out among the rest, primarily because he generated most of the income that kept the doors open. He was the only client the agency needed to stay afloat. Instructions were clear— if that client calls—put him through. But I have to admit—it still surprised me to see the agency owner race out of the bathroom, down the stairs and into his office, just to schedule a lunch with Mr. Moneymaker.*

months you've been out of work and are pissed off that your agents aren't busting their tails to get you more auditions. Your commissions cover the cost of their lunches for a year, but you are not their top priority. The actor who hasn't worked in three weeks, but who earns $450,000 for a movie of the week, only needs to do two MOWs a year to eclipse your earning potential. That's $90,000 a year in commission, and it only takes the MOW actor two jobs. The actor earning $50,000 dollars per episode on a television series might shoot up to twenty-two episodes a year. That's $110,000.00 in commission. That could cover the salary *and* expenses of a mid-level agent. Which seems like a lot of money, but pales in comparison to the agency that doesn't commission the client because they have a profit-participation in the TV series.

Feeling a little left out? Don't. The beauty of this business is its refusal to conform to rules. Think of potential as your upper hand. The actor earning fifty-thousand dollars a week on a series is usually stuck on that series, at least for a while. Very few are willing to relinquish that steady paycheck for the unknown. You, however, have the power of potential.

Convince your agent that you can earn some serious bucks and eventually they will believe it. How do you get your agent to respond to your lack of work with enough enthusiasm to get you working? That requires some pretty fancy agenting. The agent needs to believe you can, you should, and that, if you leave and go to a different agency—you *will* get work. Don't think that because you're not yet a star, your agent would not second-guess your departure. Years after I stopped agenting, the pit in my gut was palpable when I witnessed other agents reaping benefits from the hard work I'd done on a client's behalf. Especially if the actor left me, or was forced to leave because I failed to rally the support of the other agents. Agents think, "I begged that director to hire her, and now she's in all his movies." If your agent really believes you are talented, and that with his help you have made headway in your career, unless you're a total pain in the ass it will bother him if you leave. But, if your agent did not make money and never really believed in your talent, your leaving will only bother him when you become successful—so go ahead, become *really* successful; you deserve it.

I read an article in the Los Angeles Times *about an actress discussing her career. For over ten years she said she'd been working in the business as a steadily rising star. She'd gotten the house in Hollywood Hills, the designer gowns, the fancy cars, the private trainers and so on. But then the work stopped.*

I knew this actress and her career all too well, having represented her for many years. The picture she painted was not at all my recollection. Yes, commercially she had worked all the time, and she constantly worked in theatre—good theatre. But whatever magic transpired on stage fell through the cracks on television and film. I believed she was a good actress who would work, but selling her was never easy. Eventually she fired me, and because she did, I kept an eye on her career, looking for signs that someone else would be able to do for her what I had not. I didn't see signs of her career moving forward—until she married a well-established, Emmy award-winning actor on a highly acclaimed television series. And while it was true that she had the house and the gowns, etc., when the marriage fell apart, many of those perks dissolved along with it.

RULE 14: Agent Complacency Is a Career Killer.

Complacency can set in at any point in a career. It can occur when an actor or writer begins working steadily or when you suddenly become the hot new star lighting the world on fire. Either way it's a killer. If you're plugging along, making a living but finding that you're always working for the same casting director, the same studio, the same production company or the same network, be afraid. They will use you until they use you up, and when they're through, then what? If you regularly work for Viacom, someone needs to introduce you to Disney. If Fox is your network, concentrate your efforts on meeting the folks at Warner Bros. Diversify. If, as an actor, you test for two pilots at ABC, even if you don't get the job, you need to be on NBC's radar. The writer who finds himself making unspeakable money re-writing and doctoring someone else's scripts needs to take the time to generate his own original work or become resigned to a career as a script doctor.

When you're on hiatus from your television series, invest in your career *before* they cancel your show. Because eventually your show will end, and once it's over you are just another out-of-work actor or writer who used to be on a series.

An actor stars on a popular series for five years. Six months before his contract ends, his agents, his manager, his publicists, everyone, knows the actor's intent to leave the show, but—to do what? Two commissions and one monthly fee have been spent on advisors, negotiators and spin-doctors, but no one executes a game plan. So what happens? First he's waiting for offers, and before too long, he's back to waiting for auditions.

Think like an agent. Who is more desirable—the actor *on* a hit series, or the actor who *used to be on* a hit series? The writer with a viable script, or the writer with the good idea? No agent waits until quitting his job to put out feelers for their next job. So why should you? Use your opportunities to create the next opportunity. Otherwise another five years will fly by and those years on a series will become just another credit on your resume.

Don't Let Your Agent Wait Until the Job Is Done to Start the Work

Let's say things give in your favor and you find yourself not just working, but quickly shooting to "star" status. Hold on tight. Good agents know how to take advantage of the inherent liberties of success, and pave the way for a first-rate, long-term career. Too many others are happy to ride the wave—the work is behind them (if they did any work at all) and now they can sit back, field offers and count money. Agents take their cues from you. They signed you, they sold you, and now they will service you. Maybe. Show indifference toward your career and so will everyone else. *Don't do it.* There is no better time to pave the way for more work than while you are working. Exercise control. All of your agenting skills will need to be called to the task. People who met you before you were hot and who wouldn't give you the time of day then, will meet you now and tell you they always knew you'd make it. Don't hold a grudge. Make friends, even if you can't stand the sight of your co-star and the executive producer is a greedy toad. Leave resentment at home. Encourage your agent to set her sights high. Have a game plan, and don't wait to execute it. Use your time in the spotlight to establish the career you want *after* the project is history. Take the media, the celebrity, the money, and the ass-kissing all in stride. The stakes get higher with greater visibility; there's more to lose, and more to consider. Creative control, money, lifestyle and the often denied—but inevitable—plateau.

Success is not trouble-free.

Can you be "on top of the world" without being a jerk? I think so, but the land mines are everywhere. People will come at you like never before, asking for more, demanding more and flattering you more than you ever imagined. Agents, managers, publicists, lawyers, business managers, stockbrokers, investors, family, friends and strangers.

An actor I know is the star of a series. He regularly receives mail—registered, Fed-Ex'ed, certified—requesting his help financially. One woman wrote asking him to save her home from foreclosure by purchasing the property outright and quit-claiming it back to her! She even included preliminary paperwork and detailed information! She sighted his reported salary, noting he had more than enough money to live comfortably and save her home.

A client of mine was not yet eighteen when she started to earn a living as an actress. She'd put forth a lot of effort on her own behalf and at her own expense. She wasn't on a series for more than two weeks when the calls flooded in—old friends, new friends and family members, asking for money, cars and handouts. At the start of a promising career, when all her hard work was just beginning to pay off, she should have been jumping for joy. Instead, she was curled up on my living room couch crying over the pain of resentment. Her story isn't unusual. No matter how long and hard you may have struggled, if you're not struggling now—at least, not financially—you will be resented for your success. There's nothing you can do, there is no compromise to make. You can't control how your success changes your friends' behavior, but you should control how it changes your own. Chances are, if you were a poor jerk *then*, success will only make you a rich jerk *now*.

Getting Fired

If you think not getting work affects your agent's enthusiasm for your career, wait until you get *fired!* I think every actor, at some point in his or her career, will be fired. What I've learned is this: When an agent is given the news of the client's impending doom—an immediate opinion is formed, but that opinion is not (and may never be) expressed to the client. I've also learned that an opinion can be changed. Depending on the magnitude of the job and its potential domino effect, immediate and appropriate efforts are put forth on the client's behalf. But first, the agent has to tell the client, comfort the client, and dissect every moment leading up to the dismissal. Information is essential, and your agent has to acquire a satisfying explanation or accept the fact that, sooner or later, when you're feeling better again, you're going to leave the agency. By any definition, and for whatever reason, being fired is difficult. Experience has taught me that unless you're witness to the pre-firing conversations, you may never know the real reason "why."

Once the powers that be decide to let you go, before they leave that room and make public their decision, they will have agreed upon the company line. Only those who *need* to know (and there are very few), are ever privy to the true reason. Sometimes the true reason has nothing at all to do with the talent. A bad script can get a good actor fired. On the other hand, if you're the writer of that bad script and that script really isn't bad—firing you might be the only way to keep a difficult star onboard. Knowing you've been fired over the dreaded *creative differences* doesn't ease the pain, and rarely satisfies anyone. But knowing that you will still get paid can help take some of the sting out of it.

> *The creator and executive producer of a popular television series was fired from his own show. I know two very prolific writer/producers who have been fired almost as often as they've been hired...but they keep getting hired. Sometimes leaving your own creation seems a better option than taking part in its bastardization. Even if that's not true, the industry will readily accept it.*

Come On Down

The step down, the end of the series, the three bad films. Growing up, growing older, fatter, thinner, tired or just plain out of style. No more money, lots more pride. The inevitable and the unenviable return to auditioning. What's the agent thinking? Well, with pre-conceived ideas about you and what you can and cannot do, you'll be surprised.

Typecasting

Typecasting is the double-edged sword of careers and no one typecasts more often or with more skill than casting directors, agents and, if they're not careful, actors themselves. Fitting a type is a great way to get a foot in the door when you're trying to get your SAG card or build an early career. Initially, the more specific the character, the easier the sell. If I represent a 6' Nordic blond, bodybuilder-power lifter-martial artist who is fluent in five languages, when a role calls for an Arnold type, he's the guy I know I can sell. But let's say my guy is also a father, husband and damn good actor. The truth is, whether or not he possesses the chops to play the role, if casting called for an overworked dad trying to buy a Christmas toy for his young son, my guy would never get a shot...unless he's Arnold Schwarzenegger in *Jingle All The Way*.

Once you've been hired as a "type," getting your next gig playing the same "type" is easier. Then it gets really easy, and before you know it, that's *all* you ever play. Don't disregard this path-of-least-resistance, just remember there is a risk in never breaking out of the mold that has served you so well in the past. If you are working, find opportunities to play roles against type. You may have to accept smaller roles or less pay, but consider that a reinvestment in your career. If the project and the work is good, it's well worth your while. Keep track of how often your short-term choices facilitate your long-term goals, and be sure your agent is willing and able to navigate the same roads.

> **A NOTE TO WRITERS**
> *The example earlier in the book of the young writer who posed as a younger writer underscores the fact that writers are also not immune to ageism.*

People change and careers change; it's a fact of life and a fact of the business. No one stays on top forever; actors re-invent themselves all the time.

How silly '70s heartthrobs Redford, Eastwood and Beatty would look if they were still trying to play young leading men—they would look like caricatures of their former selves. With the help of some very talented creative people, John Travolta has repeatedly re-invented himself, and you have to hand it to William Shatner for his willingness to play his acting style as a cultural phenomena. From the standpoint of a global entertainer, no one surprises her public more often than Madonna. And who can ignore Britney Spears' segue from squeaky clean to just obscene?

But not all performers are receptive to change. Two actresses, both nearing their fifties, were television stars and household names twenty-five years ago. One easily and graciously slipped into the natural role of playing the wife or mother. She's had no problem stepping back and letting a younger generation take the spotlight and she works all the time. The other actress looks in the mirror and sees only who she used to be, refusing to age in either in real life or on film. In her world, starring on her own series in the '80s guaranteed her TV Q for life, so when her agent suggests a series with an ensemble cast, she changes agents. Needless to say, she cycles herself through agents and *still* doesn't get the ingenue roles she craves.

Take chances. Don't be afraid to fail. Failure can be freeing and strong relationships are forged when both parties take risks and fail or succeed together—as partners.

Change is the only guarantee. Go with it. Be aware of who you are and who others perceive you to be. If you and/or your agent are "livin' in oblivion," your dreams of a comeback are greatly diminished. In instances where it is necessary and advantageous, be willing to read for people who "already know you." Insist on it, because old celluloid and videotape can be killers. Acting styles change, but you won't convince anyone that *you've* changed if you were saying DY-NO-MITE! the last time they saw you work. People see you on late night cable or a Blockbuster rental and they think you still look and act that way. You don't and *you shouldn't.* Typecasting can be your friend or your enemy. You choose.

Chapter Two's story of Chris Sarandon auditioning for Martin Bregman should also mention that Sarandon came in with no chip and no attitude. In return, Bregman treated him with the respect and dignity deserved by an Oscar® nominated actor. There's a technical term for someone like Mr. Sarandon: "a sweetheart." Get a chip on your shoulder or sport an over-blown ego, and there's a technical term for you, too: "pain in the ass." Be a sweetheart and people will work with you because they want to, not because they have to.

The Comeback

Resurrecting careers from bad choices and dealing with career lapses, caused by outside forces or inner demons, is an everyday fact of life in this business we call show. It is as much your agent's problem as it is yours, and your agent should deal with it—because the more trouble you cause today, the more damage control your agent has to deploy tomorrow. I know an agent who continually turned a blind eye to his client's drug and alcohol abuse. The actor was a moneymaker so the agent didn't want to rock the boat. No one seemed to notice that the offers had dwindled down from bad films to bad videos. No one cared that the actor actually had talent and potential and could have been something more than a pathetic waste of videotape. The actor was the

A young TV star has a "little problem" with drugs, and on more than one occasion the actor has overdosed. During the crisis, the actor's live-in companion made two phone calls. The first call to an ambulance, the second to the actor's agent. Before the ambulance even arrives, the agent is controlling the damage. By the time the agent was through, even the actor believed "exhaustion" had landed him in the emergency room.

112

agent's golden goose, and nobody wants to kill the money source. Instead, agent and client together conspired to kill a career.

The Agent Who Protects You From Rumors and From the Truth Is Not Always Your Ally

If you had problems in the past and now they are behind you—congratulations! If you still have an agent or just signed with a new one, even better.

I've checked clients into rehab and personally vouched for them with producers. Sometimes I've been burned, sometimes not—the key is if you align yourself with an agent or manager and desire from that relationship a confidante or babysitter, try to find someone who shows an interest in keeping you alive, not just keeping you working. Look for someone who believes in you and in your talent. Don't be coy about your past—don't romanticize it, but don't deny it either—chances are, you have fewer secrets than you think. Imperfection makes you human, and in this business there are plenty of other people battling demons. Besides, America loves rooting for the underdog—can you spell *Rocky?*

7

Alpha Dog
- Agents and Power -
(And a word about assistants)

It's a commonly accepted theory that knowledge is power. Knowledge is only valuable if you use it carefully, and it proves most valuable when you use it to your own benefit. From casting assistant to network head, this is a collaborative business, with only a few individuals having the power to say *yes*. Unless you are an independent, self-financing, self-distributing filmmaker, most *yes's* are determined by committee. So, while one hungers for the *yes*, one must constantly battle the influence of *no*.

"No," even at the lowest level, can thwart your efforts to move ahead. But take heart, *no* can be fluid. People in this business move fast...up and down, back and forth, in and out of power. The miscreant who passed on your script last week may be out of a job by now, so go ahead change the title on that cover sheet and send that little gem over to his replacement. The trainee in the mailroom this morning may well be the powerbroker in the conference room by lunch. If you treat everyone with respect, eventually you will save yourself from some, if not several, brushes with humiliation.

There is the celebrated story of Jay Kantor, a mailroom clerk at MCA (a talent agency in the '40s) who—as the story goes—was sent to the airport to pick up Marlon Brando. When the two returned to the agency, Brando insisted Kantor become his agent. Years later, his story was the basis for *The Famous Teddy Z.*, a short-lived television series about the agency biz.

Though creative careers can move swiftly, stories of instant discovery and success are not always as they seem to be Yes, Steven Spielberg offered Gwyneth Paltrow the role of young Wendy in his feature film *Hook* while she stood in line to see a movie, but it was not the Hollywood discovery one might be inclined to believe. The Spielbergs and Paltrows are long-time family friends and in fact both families were at that screening together. You may be unemployed today and at the top of *People* magazine's list of the 100 sexiest people tomorrow—but that doesn't mean you haven't been laboring away at your dream for fifteen years. It's the way of life in this business; sometimes it falls in your favor, sometimes not, but there's always tomorrow. And because there's always tomorrow, it will serve you well to familiarize yourself with the constantly shifting concept of Hollywood Power.

> *Christine Elise came to my agency for representation in 1987. She'd sent me her picture and resume on the advice of an actor in her drama class. When she arrived, there were two other women in the meeting. One was a talent agent who had just begun working with me, and the other was a friend. We three took the meeting, quickly introducing ourselves by first name and jumping right in. Christine was certain that the other two (who seemed older, less animated and more serious) were the "powers," so she directed her intentions toward them. She was never rude, but certainly went to no great effort to impress me. At the end of our meeting, I said, "Okay, let's do it." Now she was flummoxed. First, she was certain I had no authority to make that decision and secondly, if it turned out I did have the authority, then who were those other people?*

Unlike other corporate businesses, in Hollywood, one's *title* is not necessarily synonymous with one's *power*. It's a business where people often fail *up* rather than *out*, and promotions fill vacancies rather than needs. In Hollywood the old school rule of working your way up and paying your dues just doesn't hold true. The hot young kid with nothing more than a quick repartee, a shiny sports car and a crisp-collared shirt might be your next powerbroker. I was twenty-four when I started my own agency and *never* would have taken on the endeavor at that age when I lived and worked in New York. In Los Angeles, twenty-four seemed like now or never time. I didn't think I was too young because the town didn't think I was too young, or at least they didn't say so publicly.

Except one agent who did. After excitedly announcing that I'd opened my own shop, he slapped me down with a snide remark about the "lack of qualifications" for agents and agencies. His rudeness inspired my ambition; I made a mental note not to become a mediocre agent and moved on. When you're twenty-four, you can afford to look the future in the face and say, "HA!"

Assistants to Agents and Managers

My first job in the agency business was as an assistant, an often unenviable but always active position. Assistants, especially agent assistants, see and hear everything. If casting assistants are the gatekeepers, then an agent's assistant is the palace guard. They witness the humor and the disgust, they hear the tantrums and demands of agents and clients. They are extremely loyal and keenly aware of when to keep their mouths shut.

If you're on the phone with your agent, assume an assistant is also on the line. Staying on the line while the agent conducts business saves the agent the hassle of having to repeat instructions. The assistant hears the agent make a lunch date, and puts it in the calendar. If the agent says, "I'll send the script," by the time the agent is off the phone, the assistant is licking the stamp. The good ones really are that good. And the better they are, the more duties they're assigned.

They jot down the names of clients next to character descriptions in the breakdowns, and later that morning they pull your picture. They read your script and very often write your coverage. They know when to put a call through and how to put a call off. They make calls on the agent's behalf, and

A young actress arrives, portfolio in hand, for her 11 A.M. interview with a prospective agent. The agent introduces himself and invites her into his office where the two talk behind closed doors for hours. Phones are ringing off the hook, but the agent's intercom is ignored. Eventually the assistant taps on the door with an important message. The door, though locked, is shut improperly and swings open to reveal the agent and the actress—both buck-naked on the couch. The lovers are startled. The assistant, mortified, returns to her desk and resumes her duties. The agent later apologizes and the assistant keeps the story to herself for years. For years—right up until the time she writes this book.

they speak with everyone. If you sense that your agent's assistant is movin' and shakin', make an effort to make an alliance with him or her. The assistant's opinion of you will influence the agent's opinion—if it doesn't, chances are that the assistant will soon have her own desk, and you'll have your next agent.

I don't know any assistants who aspire to be assistants. They take the job because it pays (sort of) and places them amidst the action. At some point an assistant naturally progresses to the next level or has to make a definitive decision to move up or out. Many of the larger agencies have agent training programs, which literally start in the mailroom. I know lawyers who have chucked their profession to sort mail at a talent agency. Yes, really!

Casting Assistants

They answer the phone, but unlike agents' assistants, casting assistants don't stay on the line. Too many phones are ringing and casting directors have no interest in training their assistants to do their job. Assistants, interns, coordinators...they all open pictures and resumes, and if you don't get through to the casting director, the assistant can color your message and invoke their own opinions. They can lose your agent's package or tell you there are no more scripts available. If they're setting up sessions, they can make it difficult to re-schedule an actor or not schedule you at all. Worse then that, they can take any of these traits and expand upon them as they rise from assistant to associate and from associate to say, Head of Casting. If your agent is intimidated or thwarted in their efforts by the casting assistant, getting through to the boss could be difficult. And let's face it—if the assistant can bully your agent, how can your agent ever expect to make an impact on the casting director?

On the other hand, some assistants are extremely helpful. They tend to see the showcases and plays. They watch television and see actors' tapes. They have information that agents need, especially when the casting director doesn't return calls. They have opinions and whenever possible, depending on who they work for, they try to get actors auditions. The majority like actors, were actors or want to be actors. Unfortunately, too many of them take their gatekeeper position far too seriously.

In Production...

Various levels of development titles exist. Somewhere between executive assistant and development assistant—all the way up the ladder to President of Entertainment—lie the Directors of Development, the Creative Executives and about a gazillion managers, VPs and Senior VPs.

The Hollywood Creative Directory is a great source for discerning the hierarchy of a company. Producers, studios, networks, television shows and staff are all listed— with credits. It's printed three times a year (an example that shows just how fluid the Hollywood power structure is) and is an excellent reference.

The fact is, today's development executive is tomorrow's network head. That annoying, prickly casting assistant could prevent you from getting an audition, and likewise the barely-out-of-college agent's assistant has the ability to *pass* on your script. In the same sense, you, the struggling and unemployed artist, could find yourself a mega-star, or at least working steadily, and well-respected overnight. That's what keeps the Hollywood dream alive.

Television and Film

In television, Executive Producers are the big shots. They are the showrunners upon whose shoulders fall the burden of "making it happen."

They oversee and orchestrate the physical production and creative aspect of a show, answering to and battling with the studio and the network. There are very few non-writing showrunners, so from this seat the tone of the working environment and the core of the show is established. If you step on the set of *Boston Public*, a David Kelley Production, you know instantly that the professionalism, respect and creative excellence starts at the top and trickles down to the very last production assistant. It makes a difference. A *strong* showrunner multi-tasks, delegates fairly and makes quick and informed decisions, all without compromising the creative integrity of the show. A *powerful* showrunner does all of the above with little or no interference from the network.

There are creative producers and physical production producers, but both share in some form of producer credit. A staff writer might get supervising producer credit, while a production manager might see "Produced By." I knew a writer/creator who, whenever he had a show in production, always credited his longtime secretary as an associate producer.

The following is a list of just the producer credits pulled from the debut (1989) season of The Simpsons:

Larina Adamson (producer)	*Conan O'Brien (producer)*
Sherry Argaman (animation producer)	*Bill Oakley (executive producer)*
Lolee Aries (animation producer)	*Carolyn Omine (producer)*
Joseph A. Boucher (producer)	*Margot Pipkin (producer)*
James L. Brooks (executive producer)	*Richard Raynis (producer)*
David X. Cohen (producer) (as David S. Cohen)	*Mike Reiss (executive producer)*
Jonathan Collier (producer)	*David Richardson (supervising producer)*
Gabor Csupo (executive producer)	*Jace Richdale (co-executive producer)*
Greg Daniels (co-producer)	*Phil Roman (executive animation producer)*
Paul Germain (co-producer)	*David Sachs (producer)*
Matt Groening (executive producer)	*Richard Sakai (producer)*
Al Jean (executive producer)	*Bill Schultz (producer)*
Ken Keeler (producer)	*Mike Scully (producer)*
Harold Kimmel (supervising producer)	*David Silverman (producer)*
Jay Kogen (supervising producer)	*Sam Simon (executive producer)*
Colin A.B.V. Lewis (producer)	*Denise Sirkot (producer)*
Jeff Martin (producer)	*John Swartzwelder (producer)*
Ian Maxtone-Graham (co-executive producer)	*Ken Tsumura (co-producer)*
J. Michael Mendel (producer)	*Jon Vitti (producer)*
George Meyer (executive producer)	*Michael Wolf (producer)*
David Mirkin (executive producer)	*Wallace Wolodarsky (supervising producer)*
Frank Mula (supervising producer)	

In the world of feature film, producers are the decision makers, while line producers control the physical production. Executive producer credit is not reserved for anyone in particular. It is commonly given to line producers, and to people who, though they may have been instrumental in putting together the deal, are often no longer even associated with the film by the time it's released. As a vanity credit, executive producer sounds important and so it is given to stars and their managers, or used to appease a person or persons who either contractually or conceptually believe they contributed to the development of the film. But, make no mistake, a feature film's *producer*(s) collect the Oscar® come Academy Award® time, while television's Emmy® goes home with the *executive producer*.

There is a great deal of controversy regarding film credits. The credit "A Film By," has become a touchstone for directors, which is alarming to writers and infuriating to the Writers Guild. Equally dissatisfying is the role of and respect for the writer during both the production and post-production of a film. Writers have been banned from the sets of *their own* movies, and are generally never invited to the editing bay.

There is an age-old dispute about who wields the power in Hollywood. Whether it's the writer whose creation is born of a thought, the actor who breathes life and emotion into those words, or the director whose vision unites the two, it is always the talent who wields the power. Unfortunately, the art of exercising their power is lost to most artists—and that's why agents and the like are still in business.

8

Ebb and Flow
- Changing Agents -

There are four ways to change agents.
1. Get Fired.
2. Fire Them.
3. Leave the Business (you or your agent).
4. Fizzle Out.

At one-shop agencies, firing a client is *never* easy to do. When you are the owner and sole agent, there is no one else to blame. "*I* love you...but the other agents don't support me," doesn't fly, because you are the *only* agent and making *all* the decisions. Firing someone you have grown to dislike is easier than firing a person you like but can't sell. I had clients I liked both personally and professionally, but that didn't negate the fact that neither of us was doing the other any good. On occasions when I tried to agent them into leaving me, most didn't. They weren't happy with their careers—but they were even less happy to look for a new agent. For them, the security of the known was better than the risk of the unknown. If your agent says, "I love you, but..." or, if they "understand if you want to leave," what they really mean is, "Please, please leave me. Relieve me of this burden and find yourself another agent." Start looking. Don't wait for your agent to drop you, or to never drop you.

For the actor or writer who is getting shots and getting close to turning the corner to success, this rule does *not* apply. Agents never drop those clients. In fact, they don't understand *at all* when those clients want to leave. Agents only drop the clients who make their lives miserable, clients whose commissions are not worth the effort the agency has to put forth to service, and the clients they can't sell. They also fire deadwood. *Webster's Dictionary* defines deadwood as "something that is not useful, unsalable stock, redundant employees, or useless information." Ouch.

> **A NOTE TO WRITERS**
> *As a rule, agents don't let on that they dislike your material unless they're pretty certain they won't mind losing you as a client. That doesn't mean agents can't constructively critique or express their tastes and opinions, but if in doing so there is no attempt to reassure you that they believe in your writing, appreciate your talent, and want to work on your behalf—then there's a good chance they don't care if you leave.*
> *If that's the case, it's past time for you to scout for new representation.*

There are some very tough lessons learned by representing actors when you're less than enthused to be doing so. I did it both in my own shop and at other agencies. At my own agency, I had a policy of never representing couples, born out of an experience I'd had at another agency years before. In that instance both actors were very talented, sported impressive resumes and shared a home. As the years went by, work was noticeably more frequent for him than it was for her. And that made calling the house a *nightmare*. If he had an audition, she demanded to know why she didn't have an audition for the same project. After all, if there's a role for a guy in his thirties there's usually a role for a thirty-year-old woman as well—but in televisionland, she played older than he did and no one wanted to tell her. She would read his scripts and badger the agents to get her in on any female role in the project. If she didn't crash his auditions, she'd cross-examine him when he got home about the types of women he'd seen in the waiting room. Collectively, she made everyone's life hell. I swore I'd left that scenario behind when I opened my own shop. And then I got agented...

This time, *she* was a favorite client, and I was more convinced than anyone of her talent and inimitability, even before seeing her perform. If she was right for a part, I got her an audition. Selling her was a snap.

He was her live-in boyfriend—handsome, smart and probably very talented, but representing him was never my idea.

Immediately after she signed with me, her career hit a fast track and I looked good. The more *I* worked, the more *she* worked. Our friendship grew and her importance as a long term moneymaking client increased. The pressure was on, and my client was determined. She flattered, challenged, pleaded, argued. Eventually I gave in (knowing I was doomed). For a year or so, both he and I suffered through the hardships of reality. I submitted him and I pitched him but I couldn't and I didn't sell him—of course I could *never* drop him.

On occasion, when I took the fall and offered to let him fire me because I knew I wasn't getting him out, he wouldn't take the bait.

Instead his resentment grew. It would seem unfair to say that his dissatisfaction with me influenced the demise of my relationship with her, but it did. Their relationship was strained, our friendship was

> *Take the bait. Fire your agent, or at the very least consider the offering as a free pass to meet other agents.*

strained, and calling the house with appointments and jobs for her and having to speak to him didn't help. The professional relationship and personal friendship between she and I ended when she fired the agency. But he never left...he just...fizzled out. One evening, my assistant left his photos in an envelope outside the office (per request), and the next day they were gone. Soon thereafter he quit the business.

Choose the agent who is right for you, not the agent who is right for your best friend or neighbor. I was her agent, and would have been better able to service him had I not represented him. Had he signed with a different agent, I could have helped him agent his agent, and he definitely could have helped me. Before I took him on, he kept my client in check. He pointed out the number of auditions she was getting and reminded her of the money she was beginning to earn. When our relationship changed, he became determined to find fault with my agenting skills and I can't say that I blame him.

An agent doesn't need a reason to fire an actor. At my own agency choosing whom I represented was a luxury and deciding whom to drop was a chore. At other agencies the determination to release a client, and when to do it, is *personal, political,* and *financial.*

If an agent suggests in a staff meeting that "we have too many clients," out come the client lists and the cutting begins. Back and forth go negotiations, arguments and compromises, with responsible agents spinning tales of close auditions and pending jobs in a desperate attempt to save favorite clients from the axe. Meanwhile, other agents are poised to cut clients by recalling and exaggerating tough sells and low bookings. In a room filled with agents all agenting each other, the atmosphere is testy at best. Eventually a number is reached and the agents disperse to make the calls, each blaming the others for the cut.

Agencies do need to drop clients, if only to make room for new clients—because agencies always need to sign new talent (see Chapter One). And when they do sign new talent, client lists need to be pared down or more agents need to be hired. Paring down is cost-effective while increasing overhead is not. Every agency routinely "cleans house" once or twice a year, and this is when the big cuts happen. Twenty or thirty clients can be released from an agency under the pretense of streamlining and staying manageable, but in no time that number creeps right back up. *Because agencies* always *need to sign clients.*

If you find yourself on the receiving end of an agency house-cleaning, take heart. It doesn't have to be a bad thing, but it should be a wake-up call that something has to change. A clean slate is advancement in an otherwise

> **A NOTE TO WRITERS**
> *Agents sign writers and drop writers just as frequently as they do actors. Unless you're generating new material or working constantly, your agent will tire of talking about and pitching the same material. This is particularly true of agents whose sales base is narrow. If your agent's strongest relationships are always with the same group of buyers, once that group has been exhausted, your agent has nothing new to say or sell. That's when you are in danger of being considered deadwood. Take your work elsewhere—no matter what your agent claims, he or she didn't show it to everyone. Remember Chapter Seven: Yesterday's "everyone" is never the same as today's "everyone."*

stagnant career, so seize the opportunity to start a new relationship. Force activity. Think of it this way: it was time to make a change *because your representation was no longer working* on your behalf.

And while you'll be best served believing in the above, that isn't what you want to sell to prospective agents. When you're out looking for a new agent, remember that what you sell depends upon who you're meeting. If it's an agency of similar status to the agent you're with now or just left, tell them *too many projects were falling through the cracks*. Tell them you *missed job opportunities because someone wasn't paying attention.* Let them know you have fans who call on you all the time, but that you weren't meeting any new people. *Do not* go into detail. You're not there to bad-mouth your previous agent, you're there to excite your future agent.

If the agency is smaller than the agency you're leaving, tell them what they would tell you: *You're tired of the big agency rhetoric,* and you think you need a boutique. *Do not* tell them your agency dropped you. *Do not* say your agency couldn't get you appointments. *Do not* tell them you didn't book jobs. Instead, imply that the agency didn't know how to sell you. Ask them what roles *they* see you playing. If the answer coincides with what you think and how you want to be sold, say, "Exactly! That's what I've been telling my agents; that's where I get the job!" Sell yourself. Give the agents the impression that you're about to get a lot of work, and need someone to negotiate your deals. If what they have in mind for you isn't what you had in mind for yourself, take a mental note—are either one of you wrong?

Six of us sat down with an actor to talk about representation. He'd worked quite a bit, been on a series, had a recognizable name, and currently starred in B-movies. Though he was easily pitchable for television, most people knew his work and were, like me, less than impressed. Granted, I'd seen only one of his movies, but he was flat-out bad in it; the thought of repping him scared me. During the meeting he spoke about leaving the lousy movies in the past, moving into legitimacy and long-term career building; money, he said, was not an issue. He wanted to do theatre (hmmm) and small roles in quality projects... and so we signed him. Two weeks later I pitched my heart out and got him the most incredible opportunity to audition for an Off-Broadway show. He responded as if I was nuts—he had no intention of even entertaining the notion of performing on stage. Turns out another B movie was in the works. (Surprise.)

Agents drop clients because (a) they're not making money, (b) the agent has lost interest or (c) life is just too damn short. I once represented an actor whom I think maybe half the town has represented at some point or another. He's a brilliant artist, and a royal pain in the butt. His faxes, calls and letters constantly bombard agents, managers, casting people, directors and producers. He'd send a twenty-five page fax to each and every agent at the agency, *from Europe*, outlining his disappointment with his representation, listing projects he should have auditioned for or should now be considered for, or just plain venting. The fax would arrive in the middle of the night, and then the very next morning he'd call each agent to discuss their participation and hear their reactions, then demand to know how they intended to fix the problems. All the while he's working for twelve weeks on a mini-series. Working for him was difficult and negotiating his deals was nearly hopeless—but he *worked*. He hounded everyone, from network heads to casting assistants, and required more agenting skills on a daily basis than any novice or the most outrageous out-of-control star. Ultimately, he also recognized loyalty and was as quick to go to bat for an agent, or an agent's efforts on his behalf, as he was quick to tell you to go to Hell. I liked and respected him, but I personally think that if he pulled back just a *teensy* bit, he would probably work even more.

Is he worth the effort? Maybe not to everyone, but I can name three good agencies right now that could plow right through his idiosyncrasies and make money—smaller agents with excellent taste, an off-beat sensibility and a need for working, established name actors, no matter how trying those actors may be. For me, he was entertaining, and though I don't think I would have stopped him if he wanted to leave, I never felt a burning need to drop him, either. Last I heard he had a personal manager, a business manager, and a lawyer—but no agent.

On the other hand, I once represented an actor who had previously worked on a long-running television series, before moving to a secluded farm in a small California town. In his first audition ever, with no formal training, he won the role and the series ran for many years, not including spin-offs. We signed him to the agency after lengthy career discussions. He needed work immediately, and within two weeks I was negotiating a deal for a three-year term on a soap opera. Initially, he was anxious to accept anything—but that enthusiasm soon wore off and he decided that he was only willing to commit for two years, and needed much more money. I did it. I got him a great deal. Three days later, he changed his mind again. He would only agree to commit to one year and needed an even bigger episode guarantee. Everyone's patience was being tested, but the producers finally agreed and the deal was closed. The contracts arrived, were reviewed and Fed-Ex'ed to the client for signature. Instead, he phoned to say he would only sign the deal if the soap agreed to allow him to work on the series for two weeks and see if he liked the people!! That was it, the deal was off and I was left holding the bag. His behavior was unprofessional, erratic and maddening *but we didn't drop him.* At that point his earning potential and recognizable name still outweighed his otherwise unacceptable actions. Many months later he followed me to my own agency and his behavior became more and more outrageous. The final straw came in the form of a slanderous, threatening, slurred message on my home machine. I fired the client immediately and notified SAG. I drew the line because life is too short to waste on abusive clients.

Determining when it's time to fire your agent can be tricky, but *how* to officially fire your agent is defined by the individual Guild rules. An actor or writer can release an agent at any time—it's the money (past, present and future) that gets tied up. At one time or another every agent has represented series actors whose commissions belong to a previous agent. For smaller agencies, having a television name on your list can attract other names and increase your earning potential. If the agent is fortunate enough to get a chance to renegotiate the monies, the new salary improvements are commissionable by that agent.

> *Writers and Artists Agency represents James Gandolfini (aka Tony Soprano on the hit HBO series* The Sopranos*). Since the show's success, the agency has signed at least four other actors from the series. When an agency represents the star of a show, they inherently have more access, and that includes access to the cast. Actors assume that the agency is privy to more information, and can do more for them, when they represent the Star.*

Ultimately for me, representing talent I believed in and could sell was my focus, and I didn't see a downside to representing someone on a series, even if I didn't collect a commission from that series. Whether you earn money from the performer or not, representing an actor on a series has its perks. You get access, you get prestige, and it can generate good publicity and word-of-mouth. That doesn't mean that a writer or actor should sign with an agency just because they represent an actor on a series, because you may not reap the benefits you expect.

For instance: An actor I know recently fit the very specific criteria for a recurring character on a television series. A shoo-in for the role, he had the added advantage (or so he thought) of being repped by an agent who also repped a series regular on the show. The actor hounded the agent to "get him an audition," but it never happened. Eventually the actor was led to believe (based on a cryptic conversation with the agent), that the series actor was "difficult" and had burned too many bridges with the production and casting offices—for which the agency was being punished. The actor was satisfied and happy to repeat the story of the "difficult" actor. I don't buy it. It sounds more likely to me that those bridges were burned by the agent, or maybe that they'd never been built in the first place.

When do you leave your agents? I think you know, but for purposes of being clear and putting myself on the line, I'll spell it out.

If you haven't heard from your agent in months, something's wrong.

Just because your agent doesn't have anything for you, doesn't mean he or she shouldn't be in contact. I once worked at an agency where we implemented a policy of calling every client every week. The list of roughly 140 names was divided alphabetically and rotated between the four agents. Some of the clients heard from the agents on a daily basis. Some *still* never heard from the agents. Their names were either skipped over, or called when the agent hoped they wouldn't be home. They'd leave the message "just checking in" (*not* a message saying, "call me back"), and then move on down the list. One agent never even made the calls, she just assumed another agent would get to the client the following week. You can tell if your agency has a similar policy. There's something in the voice of an agent that says, "I'm just doing my job, I'm just servicing my client."

Regardless of the intention, there is no excuse for not speaking with your agent...except maybe Elizabeth's: "An agent named Michael signed me after watching a scene I'd done in class. He was really nice, about thirty, a normal kind of guy. I didn't get out a lot, but he kept in touch, until one day I just stopped hearing from him. A couple of weeks later, I'm watching the news, half asleep in front of the TV, and I hear a familiar voice. I look up to see *my agent on national television with a caption below his name reading 'UFO ABDUCTEE'*. All I could think was, 'Oh my God, that's my f*cking agent! A UFO abducted my agent!' I turned up the sound in time to hear him say, 'he wasn't sure where they had taken him, but he'd been gone a long time....' No *wonder* I hadn't been getting out!"

A writer I know signed with a boutique lit agency. About two weeks into the relationship, he learned that the agent regularly skips out of town on Thursday evenings to avoid Friday traffic as she heads to her weekend home. Another month goes by and the client realizes that the agent isn't ever available in the office until Tuesday of each week—though she's "avail if necessary" by cell phone. The writer nicknames the agency "Three Day Lit" and shrugs it off. Before too long, an e-mail arrives from the agent (without any pretense of apology) notifying clients that the agency will close entirely for a couple of weeks—smack at the start of staffing season! As the agent put it in her email: they had expected a writers strike and so made other plans!

If You Haven't Heard From Your Agent in Months... Shame on You

It really is a two-way street. If an agent doesn't hear from you, he will assume you've lost interest or moved on. Your pictures are pulled from the files to make room for others and unless you are specifically right for a role, or someone is searching for *you*, the agency will quietly cease to represent you.

If Your Agent Can't Get You to the Next Level in Your Career

Being with a small agency does not preclude an actor or writer from getting a big job. Regardless of size, an agency determines its own reputation, its caliber of performers, and its areas of expertise. I had a small agency; my clients did guest-star work and occasionally the less-experienced ones co-starred, just to get their feet wet. We didn't submit our clients for smaller roles in television. For feature films, we adjusted to the need and career of the actor, accounting for the quality of the project. In other words, "Yeah, it's a cop, but it's a cop who works ten weeks on *Lethal Weapon*, and you just got your SAG card."

A client in his early twenties stopped by the office to drop off pictures. I couldn't help but notice he'd put on at least fifty pounds since I'd last seen him, and no longer bore any resemblance to the 200 pictures I now held in my hand. "Look," I said, "if you want work as a young leading man, you're gonna have to lose the weight; either that, or get new headshots and consider a career as a character actor." He left the agency to think about it—and never came back. Never. We called, we wrote, we sent carrier pigeons. Nothing. He simply vanished, leaving his pictures and resumes behind

Other agencies make a living supplying day-players for both features and television. If you're with a day-player agency that can't get you seen for roles of any greater significance and you're ready to tackle those bigger roles, start looking for representation elsewhere. If, however, your "day-player agency" is knocking down doors for you and creating greater opportunities—take the time to consider whether you're better suited to being a big fish in a small pond or a small fish in a big one.

Some actors believe that if you're unhappy; move. Others believe that you should stick with what you have and what you know, and fear the unknown. That's ridiculous. *You should fear nothing.* Every situation is unique, and while there are clearly instances where moving will be your only choice and staying put is detrimental, I'm from the school of "if it *is* broken— fix it, and ideally, fix it fast." An actor I know has been with roughly fifteen agencies and a half a dozen managers in the past ten years, including me. We were very good friends, and as a client he was exposed to more information than most other actors at the agency. That didn't stop him from eventually firing me. Prematurely (I believe). When he moved, it was laterally, meaning to an agency with no more clout that mine. He was neither a big fish in their small pond, nor a small fish in their big pond. He was just another fish. I would have advised him to stay with me until a move was *necessary*, or at least until he was able to make a significant move.

RUMOR HAS IT...
Darryl Marshak represented a young Leonardo DiCaprio when he landed a star-turning role in What's Eating Gilbert Grape. *Darryl bet his client $100 that he would be nominated for an Oscar® for the role—and that upon doing so, DiCaprio would leave him for CAA.*
Later that year, Darryl got $100.

Guess who got DiCaprio?

All careers ebb and flow. The actor I spoke of has signed with some pretty terrific agents at agencies more far "powerful" than mine was. He is talented...but he still hasn't mastered the art of agenting his agent.

Actors leave agents because they don't get enough auditions, they don't get enough work, they don't like their deals, or they don't like or believe the advice given by their agents. And actors leave if they feel their agency is too big or too small, if their manager wants them to move or if another agent successfully steals them away.

As of May 2001, Gold/Marshak/Liedtke & Associates and Creative Artists Agency were hammering out a pact that would allow CAA to package G/M/L clients. CAA would commission the package and Gold/Marshak/Liedtke would continue to commission their clients. Moreover, CAA would agree not to steal G/M/L clients.

Writers, directors, comedians, newscasters, dancers, and stylists—*everyone* leaves their agent eventually. It was rumored that when Robert Redford moved to CAA from the William Morris Agency, CAA cut their commission from 10 to 5 percent.[1] For a box-office star, that could represent huge savings in agency fees. Is it worth the move? For Redford, maybe it was.

> *Remember: agenting your agent does not mean alienating him or her to the point where your decision to leave will be a relief.*

If you can't wait to fire your agent as soon as you get that series or sell that script, start looking for a new agent *now*, or change your attitude about the agency. Wanting to leave your agent means you're dissatisfied and it's easier to be dissatisfied with your agent than it is to be dissatisfied with yourself. Complaining and complacency are boring. There is no logic in waiting until you get a job to fire an agent you think isn't capable of getting you an audition. If your agent can't get you an audition, how are you going to get that series that will let you fire the agent? The chances of someone ringing your doorbell and asking to buy your script or offering to put you in a series are

---

[1]Taken from *The Agency* © 1995, written by Frank Rose.

slim. You and your script have to be sold. Someone has to do the selling. If you're less than happy with an agent's negotiating skills, and you do get a shot at that series or an offer on that script, you sure as hell don't want to let that agent make the deal. If you hire a lawyer to negotiate the terms, the lawyer will get a 5 percent commission, and you're *still* obliged to commission 10 percent to the agent.

The bottom line: Don't complain about your agent, fix it or move on. Jumping from agency to agency for the same reason time and again will do you a disservice if you don't take the time to examine your responsibility in the relationship.

By the way, if your agency relationship fizzles out, as it did with my weight-challenged client, don't be passive. Go get your belongings and close that door—open the next. Whenever you have the ability to exercise control over your career, take advantage of it. Confidence in your own decisions can only help you—in every aspect of your career *and* your life.

9

Outsmarting the Fox
– Agent Your Agent –

As if actors and writers don't have enough to concern themselves with, adding the responsibility of keeping an agent enthused can be daunting. But agenting your agent doesn't have to be a difficult task. It's not a secret formula or magic potion. It's business, it's common sense, and it's not really that tough to do. Corporations spend millions of dollars every year on seminars, retreats and lectures designed to teach employers how to get the most out of their employees. In this case, you are the corporation, and your agent, manager or publicist is your sales team.

Cheerlead your sales reps and help them to be successful in your mutual endeavor: the procurement of work. Don't turn your career over to fickle or biased "handlers." Stay involved and protect your most important assets—*you and your talent.*

Following is a list of eight easy ways to agent your agent. Following each is an explanation of why your agent does what he or she does and why you should do it too. Incorporate your agent's marketing skills and habits into your "business" and strengthen your bottom line.

Eight Easy Ways to Agent Your Agent

1. **Appear to be busy, even if you're not. Better yet, *be* busy.**

   Why Agents Do It: Your agent is always "busy." Agents are allegedly the source of work, and of all *information*. They are your link to every aspect of the industry. Appearing to be busy even when he's not supports the perception that your agent is always working. I know an actor-turned-writer who presented his lit agent with a feature film script, and after three weeks wondered why the agent hadn't yet given him notes on it. A few days later the agent called to say she hadn't read his script yet, but could swear she kept turning on the television and seeing him in a commercial. Yes, it was him in the spot, but he was hugely disappointed to learn that his agent had time to watch television but not time to read his script. Common sense dictates that if your *agent* isn't busy...chances are you won't be, either.

   Why You Should Do It: Working for someone who doesn't work for themselves isn't motivating. I have a client who *never* stops working, and who constantly creates his own opportunities. His talent and enthusiasm for his craft inspires me to work harder on his behalf. His habits keep me equally attentive of his career. If your agent believes you are busy and that you are determined to succeed, she will be more determined to reap the benefits when you do.

2. **Whenever you feasibly can, take credit for something.**

   Why Agents Do It: I once worked at an agency where one agent in particular had the good fortune of answering the call whenever a virtual "done deal" came through. In other words, a producer would call the agency to offer Suzy Star six weeks on their movie. This agent would arbitrarily pick up the phone, take the offer and do the deal. Then she'd call Suzy with a story that always ran something like, "Suzy baby, I've been working on this project for three weeks but I didn't want to tell you until it came through! I just got you a six-week gig on the next Davey Director film!" Initiating work was not this agent's forte, but she had a real flair for taking credit. It happened so often that the other agents started calling those deals by her last name, in and out of the office. (By now the term should be common industry slang!)

Why You Should Do It: If it's true it ain't bragging. Taking credit for your own successes gives others a sense of your accomplishments and serves to remind you of your own abilities. If you've earned it, own it. Last time I checked, wallowing in what you haven't done was no springboard to empowerment. Keep your accomplishments in the forefront, where they can serve as the groundwork for your potential.

3. Call your agents during off-hours, and they might just answer the phone.

Why Agents Do It: Agents answer the phone because their assistants have gone home or have yet to arrive, and because they don't really expect you to be calling. If they're in the office and the phone rings after hours, it might be a casting call, or it could be a date—and generally nobody wants to risk missing either one.

Why You Should Do It: Talking to your agent without the interruption of "more important" calls allows you to be more casual in your approach. You can use his tone of voice to sense whether he is running out the door or just fiddling through paperwork. (If it's paperwork, there's more time for chit-chat). If it's evening and you call about a specific project, let your agent know you'll gladly fax, e-mail or call and remind his assistant because it's late and you don't expect him to write anything down. If it's early morning, again offer to fax or email. Always follow up either with the assistant or with the agent himself. If it's with the assistant, phrasing is important. Something like "Did Alan Agent and Casey Casting have a chance to speak?" is more productive than, "Hi, I'm just checking in, what's going on with that project?" The difference here is that if you don't speak with the agent (and he might not take the call if he can't answer your question) your message needs to read: "Did you speak to Casey Casting?" If the answer is yes, you should get a return call with updated information. If the answer is no, the agent now has a physical note to remind him to *make that call*. The "just checking in, what's going on" version gives the assistant license to say "no update" and this time the agent's message will read: Cary Client called—"*just checking in.*"

4. **When you call, have something *for* them rather than always needing something *from* them.**
   Why Agents Do It: If all agents ever did was *ask* for things, they would eventually stop getting people on the phone. Calling to offer rather than ask helps take a relationship one step further, to break it out of its mold and broaden the boundaries. Some agencies offer tickets to sporting events, screening invites or theatre comps. As an agent, I found that calling a casting director when she wasn't working, with information about an upcoming film or pilot that didn't yet have a casting director on board, was a nice change for both of us. And, it works.
   Why You Should Do It: Agents suspect that when you call, it is specifically for your own needs. Usually, they're right. But, it's a huge boost to your agent's ego if you call to tell her that you met an actor on a new series who doesn't have an agent yet, so you recommended yours.

   Remember, inquiring about a project is not a sin, it's just a matter of presentation. Instead of "I," trying saying, "we." Instead of "you" try saying "us."

For example: A month ago you read for *West Wing*; you didn't land the job, but you went to the wire and the feedback was great. You see a breakdown and there's a perfect role for you in an upcoming episode. Your instinct is to call your agent and tell (or ask) her to "get you in there." You can get at least the same, and hopefully a better result by calling your agent and saying, "Let's strike while the iron is still hot; I think this role of Larry Lawyer is one we can land—what do you think?"

See the difference?

5. **Visit your agent when you look and feel terrific, not when you feel depressed and dumpy—and always have somewhere else to go.**
Why Agents Do It: If you want to be on top of your game, you have to look and feel good. I once had an assistant who did great work but when anyone called or asked, "How are you?" they got an earful of complaints and miseries. It was a total enthusiasm killer and eventually she had to go. Agents know that you don't want to hear how tired, depressed or overwhelmed they have been for the past two months. They also know how important it is for clients to believe that the agent is always ready willing and able to do battle on their behalf. Agents like to be indispensable; it's no secret that some of those "can't wait" cell phone calls beckoning them away in the middle of a meeting are staged.
Why You Should Do It: When you stop by your agent's office, whether to pick up a check or drop off a headshot, they get to see you in the flesh, which is what they peddle. Inspire them when you step through the doorway and they'll think, "Hey, she could be the lead in that

> **A NOTE TO WRITERS**
> *It's also important for you to stop in and visit your agency. They sell your scripts, but they sell you as well. It doesn't hurt to show your face once in awhile and have a conversation (not necessarily about the business) that can serve to remind them why they signed this bright, articulate, and personable writer—whom they have the good fortune to represent.*

series," as opposed to, "I can't take another five-minutes in her presence without wanting to hide under my desk." This doesn't mean you can't voice disappointment or lodge a complaint, but the goal is to benefit, not belabor. Don't linger in your agent's office past the point of comfort. He or she needs to get back to work and you need to "have a life" (or at least pretend you do). Be reachable, but fill your days with places to go and people to see, *please.* Don't let your agent think that you're sitting home idly waiting for the phone to ring.

6. Highlight the positives and play down the negatives *before* passing the information on to your agent.
Why Agents Do It: Agents deal with rejected actors and writers on a daily basis. Odds are, they're more often relating bad news then good. So, like publicists, they need to spin information to be the least damaging and the most advantageous. If an agent can't deliver some form of positive news, they will have failed and the client may seek new representation.

"You were fired," is easier to swallow if the agent adds "because they cut the role down to nothing and didn't want to waste you." Massage that with "this is good news because..." throw in a little "you still get paid," and all of a sudden your agent looks like a hero.
Why You Should Do It: Because agents are fickle and easily influenced by what they hear, see and read; rare is the agent who trusts his own judgement explicitly. (Remember the agent in Chapter One who said, "I think I liked it more than I thought"?) You need to be your agent's strongest influence: mold his opinion. Take the negatives lightly and so will your agent. Concentrate on the positives and he will too.

7. **Read the trades, go to the movies, go to the theatre and watch those new television movies.**

Why Agents Do It: Agents read the trades because the trades are the bibles of the industry. They go to movies and watch television because it's entertaining and they can still call it work. They also need to know what's going in their world. And that world is everything from the morning chat shows to the primetime line up and through late night TV. They read scripts because they have to read scripts. In Los Angeles, most agents only set foot in a theatre to appease a client, or to sign new actors. Next time you're at an Equity-waiver play and the person sitting in front of you falls asleep, check to see if a packet of headshots is sitting on his lap—if so, chances are he's an agent.

Why You Should Do It: If you want to agent your agent, you need to familiarize yourself with the sources of information. Speak the language, know what they know, read what they read. Film and television is your world—if you want to be in it, you need to know it. NBC's *Providence* is not the same as HBO's *The Sopranos,* and whether you intend to write an episode or land a guest star spot, if you can't (in one viewing) see how they differ, then you're in the wrong business. The necessity and significance of reading scripts can not be emphasized enough, but I'm sure I don't need to tell *you* that. For the performer, theatre is educational, and the work of other artists can be arousing and inspiring. Not to mention that those are your comrades on stage; support them if you expect their support in return.

8. **Be determined, be accessible, and be fun to have around.**

Why Agents Do It: Agents are salesmen, and salesmen are doomed without determination. If your agent is determined to get you in front of Danny Director, that tenacity will eventually pay off.

Likewise an agent will use that same verve to win a client from a rival agency. In his book, *The Agency: William Morris and the Hidden Story of Show Business,* Frank Rose describes Michael Ovitz's determination thusly:

"With Ovitz, it was always a hunger. Once he'd made contact, Ovitz seemed to call every day: Have you seen this script? Why haven't they told you about this property? Relentless, insinuating, planting the seed...." Determination is an absolute necessity for success.

Believe it or not, agents have to be accessible. You never know when a name actor might be poised to get a new agent. Or how quickly the tiniest spark of trouble can ignite into flames of catastrophe. Cell phones/faxes/emails/private jets—agents can be 100 places at once and still appear to be giving every client undivided attention. When there is success to be shared and opportunity to be gained, agents are everywhere—at the very least, they should be entertaining.

Why You Should Do It: Determination, appropriately defined as a "firmness of purpose or character," is the foundation for success in any endeavor. Let's face it, in this business (*especially* in this business) you have to believe in yourself every single day, and more so on the days when no one else does. You have to *know* that you are talented—even when a network says your not. Be determined, but not bullheaded. Stay accessible and open to change, suggestion, and direction in your business dealings and in your craft. Doing so leaves you free to move about personally and professionally in the restive waters of "the biz." But accessible also means available. I once represented a very beautiful actress, married to the son of a very famous actor. I'd get her a meeting and she'd cancel it for golf lessons. She would blow off appointments for movie-star dinner parties, or arrive at auditions unprepared because she "just flew in" from Hawaii. She wasn't determined and certainly wasn't available. Eventually I caught on—she *wasn't* an actress. She *was* (and may still be) a very beautiful woman married to the son of a famous actor.

On the sound stage, in the green room, two months on location, twelve hours a day, twenty-two weeks a year—have fun! You're working in your chosen field and living out your dream, so lighten up. Being pleasant to work with helps everyone. The reports of discord between Bruce Willis and Cybill Shepherd on the set of *Moonlighting* are legendary. Just as legendary is the fact that everyone loved Bruce. He ate with the crew and asked about their families; he was the brunt and the instigator of numerous practical jokes, and he still got the work done. If you're fun to work with and fun to be around, you'll be fun to *work with again*.

Friends used to call Mark Ruffalo "the hardest working guy in Los Angeles." Seven days a week he bartended, rehearsed, took acting classes, built sets, understudied and auditioned—he was always in one play and rehearsing another. He was so talented on stage that people who had *never even seen him perform* would rave confidently about his performance. For years conventional television and film work eluded him; and though his means of support in those times wasn't acting, he never stopped working as an actor. Eventually the agents and managers came, and soon after came the movies and offers of work. Work begets work.

Remember: you didn't become an actor to get an agent.

Seven Lies Your Agent Has Already Told You

1. We only have (blank #) clients.
2. Everybody has the same deal.
3. You were submitted...(The writer's version—"I sent your script").
4. I think there's an offer out on that role. (The writer's version—They're "not looking for new material").
5. We have no one else like you at the agency.
6. I have a call in....
7. I didn't get the message (at which point the agent shouts to his assistant, *without* covering the phone), "You didn't tell me Andy Actor called!"

Five Signs You Need a New Agent

1. Your agent won't return your calls.
2. Six months; no meetings (and there isn't a strike).
3. Your checks are arriving weeks after they are due, or are missing altogether.
4. You're starring in a play at a reputable theatre, garnering terrific reviews... and no one from the agency attends. (The writer's version—You wrote the play.)
5. Whether you're a writer or an actor, if you discover that your agent has been abducted by a UFO...*you need a new agent.*

Agents lie and that's just the way it is so don't set your agent up for the easy answer, re-phrase your questions so the old fibs won't fly.

Warning

There are more than a few suggestions throughout this book, that when exercised, may cause your agent to blurt out, "Really? Well if Nancy Rainford is so damn smart, let *her* represent you."

Pissing off your agent and dividing camps is not my intention—quite the opposite. This book is about teaching you the language, skills, and rules of the game. If you're looking for easy answers and already have piles of "how to" books stacked neatly beside your bed, throw this one on the heap and turn off the light. Until *you* make the decision and put forth the effort to navigate your career, no book will be able to help you.

If you've learned something in these few pages (and I hope you have), don't *tell* it...*use* it. That will make us *both* look good!

10

Your Questions, My Answers
- FAQs -

The following is a sample of questions and answers obtained through a questionnaire distributed throughout Hollywood via the Internet, acting classes, casting offices, writing groups and personal friends. I asked, "What do you want to know about agents?" If your question doesn't appear in this section, read the book, and see if isn't covered in previous chapters. I don't answer questions about how to act or how to write—while I do have opinions on both topics, I leave those skills in others' capable hands. I will say that you will be a better actor if you act and a better writer if you write. There are no stupid questions; the ones I have answered here are just the most frequently asked— by both novices and veterans, working and non-working.

Q. What can I do in an agent's office to get them to sign me?
A. The question of what we can *do* to get someone else to *want* us permeates every aspect of almost everyone's life. While attending an open house at a private elementary school in North Hollywood, I was surprised to learn that nearly half of the two hundred parents of prospective students had already paid the $100 application fee—before ever setting foot on the campus. There were roughly fifteen spots open for new kindergarten students and the hosts of the open house did their best to "sell" each and every parent on the merits of their school. So successful and orchestrated was the pitch that parents

began frantically asking what the school was looking for, as if they could somehow mold their *child* into the perfect candidate. What all agents (and apparently all private schools) want, is for *you* to want *them*. And to that end, they will always show themselves in the best possible light. Before you ask, "How can I get an agent to want to sign me?" ask yourself, "Why do I want to sign with this agent?" And then remember: one man's roof is another man's floor. Agents know what they can sell. The minute you walk in the door and the small talk begins, the agent is thinking—and not necessarily in any particular order:

- Do I like you?
- Do I think you're talented?
- Do I need your type?
- Is there a role for you today?
- Can I sell you? And if so, who can help me?
- What is your hook? (The hook is what an agent uses to sell your wares. If they can't sell you, why represent you?)

The one thing you should do in a meeting is present yourself accurately. If you think your casting is young, urban-hip, don't go to a meeting in a Brooks Brothers suit. What you present needs to coincide with you, albeit the best of who you are. I'll never forget the day that Lucy, a just-out-of-college actress, came to my office in a pink Peter Pan collared short-sleeved blouse and a sensible skirt. She was adorable, but restrained, and I was hoping to find an interesting young actress emerge from beneath the carefully tailored façade. So I asked, in my best non-threatening manner, "Do you always dress like this?" "Oh, no," she laughed; someone had advised her to dress conservatively when meeting agents. Our meeting ended with my request that she return the next day, dressed to have lunch with a friend. The next day, back she came...as the young college graduate who could still play fifteen. Not because she dressed like a fifteen-year-old, but because she dressed the way she felt most comfortable, and therefore she presented herself more confidently.

I signed her, and she went on to appear as a series regular on *Doogie Houser, M.D.* If something about her hadn't struck me, I might never have brought her back. And had I been in more of hurry that day, this story might not exist—but something clicked and I had the time; it does happen. It also happens that an actor can walk in your office handsome, talented and castable—and *still* be the last person on earth you would ever represent. I was excited to set a meeting with a very striking actor, who at the time was dating a very successful television actress. But when he walked into my office, demanded to see my client list and haughtily rattled off his credentials, never even bothering to remove his sunglasses, all bets were off. He was probably talented, was definitely well-trained, was obviously worldly and smart as a whip—but perched demonstrably upon his shoulder was a chip the size of Connecticut. No, thank you. I don't know what he was thinking, but the little bubble over my head was saying "Run! This is the most arrogant non-working actor you have ever met! No one will ever hire him twice!" He might have thought he was the best thing since Olivier, and maybe he was, but I wasn't willing to put forth the effort and eventually pay the price of having to put up with him. Meeting with him was a chore, the thought of *working* for him was unimaginable. Still, I sold him on the agency. Not because I had any desire to sign him, but because I wanted him to and believed that he should *want* to sign with me. I sold him on the agency because that's what agents *do*.

On the other hand, I remember a young female writer who presented herself so ideally that I was certain she was talented and I eagerly anticipated selling her talent and working on her behalf. Until I actually read her scripts. *Ugh*. They were *awful*. Boring, amateurish, poorly structured and every one of them was too long.

Don't concern yourself with agents. Yes, some agents are powerful enough to open doors and get you opportunities, but no amount of prepping, primping or saying the right thing can guarantee that an agent will want to sign you. And if an agent isn't interested, you don't *want* him to represent you. Period.

If you are hell-bent on changing an agent's mind or feel the agent is on the fence about taking you on—they say they have too many clients, or too many actors your type—maybe all they require is a little agenting to close the deal. Go back to Chapter One, and re-read the section on using your resources, but keep in mind that when an agent is truly interested, having too many clients, or too many actors of your type, is not a deterrent. Agents don't like to say no. They want you to want them, regardless of whether or not they intend to sign you. You, desiring them, is in their best interest. Because the artist is the agent's reputation.

Q. I need a new agent. Do I have to leave my old one before I start looking? What if they hear about it on the street?
A. I had a client who was a good friend and got a good number of auditions but very little work. Eventually (through the agency's introduction), she became friendly with a casting director who was determined to move her to another agency. At the time she was living with the man who had been instrumental in getting me to sign her. The casting director was calling her house, setting meetings, and yapping in her ear—but my client *never* told me. She didn't tell me because she wasn't sure the new agency would sign her, and she didn't want to be left without an agent. The agency she was interviewing represented my husband, so I knew them well. Within days I got calls from the agency letting me know that she was unhappy and they had been solicited to meet with her. Her boyfriend called me too; he neither approved nor trusted the casting director's motives and felt an allegiance to me since I had signed her on his recommendation. I called the actress and dropped her from the agency. Why?

- Because we had a relationship outside the office.
- Because she never voiced any dissatisfaction to me.
- Because life is just too short.

On another occasion, an actress I had represented for some time met a top director who arranged for her to meet with his agents at CAA. The actress called in tears and in an understandable dilemma. She *had* to take that meeting, and we both hoped they *would* and *wouldn't* sign her. Together we decided that, regardless of the outcome, she would always have a home with me. Ultimately they didn't sign her and I continued to represent her until years later when she felt her career needed a change. Again, I supported her and after a short while she returned. Handling a situation with honesty and grace can save you a lot of heartache down the line.

Every situation is different. How and when you tell your agent you're leaving depends chiefly on your relationship. Unless some horrific event has come between the two of you, talk to your agent if you're unhappy—*before* you take the meetings. That way you can honestly say you haven't met other agents rather than lie, possibly get caught, and look bad in the process. If you both agree to give it another try, give it a time frame and stick to it. If you have a manager, he or she should do your bidding. Of course, as I have suggested in earlier chapters, if you have no real relationship with your agent and your agent displays a blatant disinterest in you and your work—you need to find a new agent right away. If you meet with agents and your current agents give you grief, tell them exactly why you were seeking new representation. If they want to salvage the relationship, they will.

Q. I'm not happy with my agent, but I'm not ready to leave. Can I make the situation better?
A. Of course you can make it better, but *how* you do that depends on why you're not ready to leave, and why you're unhappy. Yes, you may be a good actor, but are you giving your agent more than that to sell? Are you selling yourself? Let's assume your reason for being unhappy is the obvious: You don't get enough auditions. How many do you think you should be getting? Sit down with your agent and ask "Are you happy with the number of auditions I've had this past year?" It could be that your agent is just as frustrated. Find

out. If all you can expect to get from your agent is all you have gotten thus far, then stop expecting more and make a decision. Ask yourself "Is this enough? Is there more I can do, or do I have to leave?"

Q. Do my checks have to go to my agent?

A. This is an agent's nightmare. Most agents hate it when actors and writers get paid directly on a job, that's why they have you sign pay authorizations that direct your checks to the agency. Otherwise they have to chase *you* for the money. Agents worry that a client will be less likely to pay up once the check is in hand, and chasing clients for money is never fun.

Let's say you earn $5000,00 for the week. $1800 is taken in taxes; minus the $500 you owe the agent and let's say $750.00 for the manager. That leaves you a whopping $1950.00—assuming you don't have a lawyer and a business manager as well. With the check in hand, giving up the $1250.00 in commission isn't easy for some, and agents would rather not wait.

> A writer I know picked up a long awaited check from the production company that had optioned her screenplay. Her agent—having refused to pressure the production company for payment—didn't catch the irony of his willingness to immediately dispatch a messenger (to the writer's home) to retrieve the agency commission.

Unfortunately, over the years a small number of otherwise reputable agencies have been caught misappropriating client funds—which makes everyone want to get their checks at home. Money is not the only thing at stake. I've heard stories of a well-known manager whose financial reputation was questionable. In debt up to his nose, his personal and business credit was shot; on occasion he even used the names and social security numbers of clients to rent apartments and lease office equipment! While this is certainly an unusual case, if you plan to sign papers with a manager or agent, be sure they are of good standing and *always* pay attention to your finances. When I opened my agency, I hired a business management company to set up my office and accounts—but I never gave them access to the money. Some years later my files were returned to me (long after I'd stopped using them), the company had gone out of business because the heads of this fancy Century City firm had been bilking clients for years. Decide where you are comfortable with your finances and make the appropriate arrangements.

By the way, unless you have negotiated for less, the standard commission due all franchised agents is 10 percent of the gross, including monies for overtime. Agents do not get a percentage of reimbursement for car fare, meal penalties or wardrobe. If you have any questions about what to pay your agent, ask your agent or call your Guild. Generally speaking, reading a contract before you sign it is a good rule of thumb.

Q. I am in the process of looking for new representation. I have decided to try a mass mailing to boutique agencies. What do you write as a cover letter to get them to interview you? Do you keep your current agency listed on your resume?

A. Mass mailings are never my first choice. Your money and time are better spent talking with friends and peers and asking them for referrals. Better still, ask those friends and peers to make calls on your behalf. If you get a lead, follow through. If you're asked to send a picture and resume, send one, along with a short note reminding him or her that the submission had been requested. If asked for a script or writing sample, submit one after registering it with the Writers Guild. Follow up with a phone call in a week or so.

Unless your last agent will impress your next agent, do not keep your current agency listed on your resume. The prospective agent will form an immediate opinion of who you are and what you can do based on who you were with—save that stuff for the meeting.

> **A NOTE TO WRITERS**
> *If you want your material returned to you, put that request in your letter, along with a self-addressed, stamped envelope. Don't expect agents to keep your script. A young writer once sent me two television spec scripts and a feature film script...but no return envelope. I read one script, sensed we were not a match, wrote an explanatory note and two weeks later spoke with the writer personally and wished him well. There was no mention of returning the material, so it was recycled. Three weeks later I got a call asking me to return the scripts, which the writer now desperately needed.*

Q. How does a talented actress with no television credits, few films but lots of Off-Off Broadway get an agent?
A. Read the book, read the question above, then stop worrying about what you're up against. You're in the entertainment business with all that that implies. Off-Off Broadway is nothing to sneer at, list it first on your resume and don't date the plays. Act as if you're an undiscovered talent with something to offer and others will eventually believe you. On a personal note, if you have friends and family who are in the business, ask them to make calls on your behalf. Use your resources.

Q. What is the formal rule for signing with more than one agency?
A. Assuming you're a SAG member and the agencies are signatory to the Guild, you can have an agent in different states or in different countries. You can also sign with different agents to cover different aspects of your career (i.e., commercials, legit, literary, television and feature work). Before you sign, find out how and where the agent expects to cover you.

Q. In one sentence, what does it mean when an agent tells you they already have someone like you?
A. It means they already represent an actor who requires work to sell and that work has yet to pay off. (Of course, that person might also be your age and similarly cast, if they could get a job.)

Q. When I have an excellent relationship with a casting director, and there is an appropriate part in a film that he or she is casting, why won't my agent make the necessary phone calls?
A. Who told you the agent didn't make the call? It could be that the agent's call wasn't returned. Follow-up. If your relationship with the casting director is as strong as you think, pick up the phone and call the casting director yourself. Say that your agent made you call because she is convinced you're right for the role, and you've read the material and have to agree. Remember too: sometimes familiarity doesn't work to your advantage.

Q. What type of writing samples do agents require?

A. Most writers are signed based upon specs. Either you've written a spec feature, or a spec episode of a popular television series. Spec implies that it is speculative—no one has paid you to write it, you've written it on your own volition. At the first signs of *Sex In The City* or *West Wing* becoming a hit, the town was inundated with those specs. There comes a point in a series career, no matter how successful the series continues to be, when writers should stop writing those specs. Usually somewhere after the second or third season, enough is enough. Agents are sick of reading yet another bad (or even good) *Seinfeld* episode. Don't forget that the agents already represent clients writing series specs. If you have an agent and your agent asks you for a new spec, she will usually tell you what shows she thinks you should write. It should also be mentioned that it is never the agent's intention to send your spec to the show you've written. In other words, if you write a spec *Friends* episode, you do so to show that you can (a) write in a half-hour television format, (b) capture the tone of the show and its characters, and (c) write dialogue, an interesting story and comedy with a beginning, middle and end.

The fact of the matter is that by the end of the second season a successful show is so set in its ways and clear in its own voice that a novice writer has to be a total stand-out to make the team. Writing the individual voices for each character to satisfy the opinion of the people who *created* and who *continue to create* those characters on a daily basis is difficult at best.

Regardless of the spec you choose to write, be sure it's written in the specific form of the show. Is it in two acts or three, does it have a teaser or not? Present an agent with a script out of form, and judgement will be passed long before that teaser is read.

Q. Should I write what my agents tell me to write or what I want to write?

A. This is a great question! On the one hand, you have to rely on your agent to know the trends of the business—what's selling versus what's not—and to share that information with you. Right after the success of *Scream,* the teen horror genre came back with a vengeance. That doesn't mean you should throw out your romantic comedy and switch gears. One agent decided his client needed to write a new spec script specifically geared toward what the studios were desperately looking to buy. What he wanted from the writer, and persuaded him to write, was a spec buddy-comedy action-adventure written for two hot stars. With the agent's strict guidance (and heavy influence) the writer delivered a first-draft, a re-write and ultimately a polished script that satisfied all of the agent's criteria. As promised, the agent quickly sent the script to the needy buyers, but *no one bought it*. The unanimous feedback was that the script is "too derivative."

If agents were writers, they wouldn't need you.

Should you write what you want? Absolutely, but keep in mind that what you write may or may not be timely. Write what you know is always appropriate advice. If you want to increase your chances of selling what you write, appeal to a wide audience—and agent your agent.

If you have questions or want more information on
How To Agent Your Agent
E-mail to: **info@howtoagentyouragent.com**

Appendix

SAG Franchised Talent Agents

5 STAR TALENT AGENCY
2312 Janet Lee Drive
La Crescenta, CA 91214
(818) 249-4241

A S A
4430 Fountain Avenue, Suite #A
Hollywood, CA 90029
(323) 662-9787

ABOUT ARTISTS AGENCY INC.
355 Lexington Avenue, 17th Floor
New York, NY 10017
(212) 490-7191

ABOVE THE LINE AGENCY
9200 Sunset Boulvard, Suite 804
West Hollywood, CA 90069
(310) 859-6115

ABRAMS ARTISTS AGENCY INC.
9200 Sunset Blvd, Suite 1130
Los Angeles, CA 90069
(310) 859-0625

ABRAMS ARTISTS AGENCY LTD.
275 Seventh Avenue, 26th Floor
New York, NY 10001
(646) 486-46000

ABRAMS-RUBALOFF & LAWRENCE
8075 West Third Street, Suite 303
Los Angeles, CA 90048
(323) 935-1700

ACCESS TALENT INC.
37 East 28 Street, Suite 500
New York, NY 10016
(212) 684-7795

ACME TALENT & LITERARY AGENCY
875 Avenue of the Americas, Suite 2108
New York, NY 10001
(212) 328-0387

ACME TALENT & LITERARY TALENT AGENCY
4727 Wilshire Blvd, Suite 333
Los Angeles, CA 90010
(323) 954-2263

ACTION TALENT AGENCY
2530 East Broadway Blvd., Suite H
Tucson, AZ 85716-5334
(520) 881-6535

ACTIVENTERTAINMENT TALENT AGENCY
325 S Robertson Blvd, Suite A
Beverly Hills, CA 90211
(310) 289-8200

ACTOR AND OTHERS TALENT AGENCY
6676 Memphis-Arlington Road
Bartlett, TN 38135
(901) 385-7885

ACTORS ETC
2620 Fountainview, Suite #210
Houston, TX 77057
(713) 785-4495

ACTORS GROUP
603 Stewart Street, Suite 214
Seattle, WA 98121
(206) 624-9465

ADAMS LTD., BRET
448 West 44th Street
New York, NY 10036
(212) 765-5630

ADR MODEL & TALENT AGENCY
419 Waiakamilo Road, Suite #204-205
Honolulu, HI 96817
(808) 842-1313

ADVANTAGE MODELS & TALENT
4825 Trousdale Drive, Suite 230
Nashville, TN 37220
(615) 833-3005

AFFILIATED MODELS INC.
1680 Crooks Road, Suite #200
Troy, MI 48084
(248) 244-8770

AFFINITY MODEL & TALENT AGENCY
873-B Sutter Street
San Francisco, CA 94109
(415) 788-9998

AGENCY 2 MODEL & TALENT AGENCY
1717 Kettner Boulevard, Suite #200
San Diego, CA 92101
(619) 645-7744

AGENCY FOR PERFORMING ARTS
9200 Sunset Blvd, Suite 900
Los Angeles, CA 90069
(310) 888-4200

AGENCY, THE
1800 Avenue of the Stars, Suite #1114
Los Angeles, CA 90067
(310) 551-3000

AGENCY WEST ENTERTAINMENT TALENT AGENCY
6255 W Sunset Blvd, Suite 908
Hollywood, CA 90028
(323) 468-9470

AGENTS FOR THE ARTS INC.
203 West 23rd Street, 3rd Floor
New York, NY 10011
(212) 229-2562

AIMEE ENTERTAINMENT
15840 Ventura Blvd., Suite 215
Encino, CA 91436
(818) 783-9115

AKA TALENT AGENCY
6310 San Vicente Blvd., Suite 200
Los Angeles, CA 90048
(323) 965-5600

ALEXA MODEL & TALENT
4100 W Kennedy Blvd., Suite 228
Tampa, FL 33609
(813) 289-8020

ALLEN TALENT AGENCY
3832 Wilshire Blvd., 2nd Floor
Los Angeles, CA 90010
(213) 605-1110

ALLIANCE TALENT GROUP INC.
1940 Harrison Street, Suite 300
Hollywood, FL 33020
(954) 927-0072

SAG FRANCHISED TALENT AGENTS

ALLURE MODELS AND TALENT AGENCY
5556 Centinela Avenue
Los Angeles, CA 90066
(310) 306-1150

ALVARADO REY AGENCY
8455 Beverly Boulevard, Suite 410
Los Angeles, CA 90048
(323) 655-7978

AMATO THEATRICAL ENTERPRISE, MICHAEL
1650 Broadway, Suite 307
New York, NY 10019
(212) 247-4456

AMATRUDA BENSON & ASSOC.
TALENT AGENCY
9107 Wilshire Blvd., Suite 500
Beverly Hills, CA 90210
(310) 276-1851

AMBASSADOR TALENT AGENTS
333 N. Michigan Ave., Suite 910
Chicago, IL 60601
(312) 641-3491

AMERICAN INTERNATIONAL TALENT
303 West 42nd Street, Suite #608
New York, NY 10036
(212) 245-8888

AMSEL EISENSTADT & FRAZIER
5757 Wilshire Blvd, Suite #510
Los Angeles, CA 90036
(323) 939-1188

ANDERSON AGENCY, BEVERLY
1501 Broadway, Suite 2008
New York, NY 10036
(212) 944-7773

ANDREADIS TALENT AGENCY INC.
119 West 57th Street, Suite # 813
New York, NY 10019
(212) 315-0303

ANN WRIGHT REPRESENTATIVES INC.
165 West 46th Street
New York, NY 10036
(212) 764-6770

APPLAUSE TALENT AGENCY
225 San Pedro NE
Albuquerque, NM 87108
(505) 262-9733

ARCIERI & ASSOCIATES INC.
305 Madison Avenue, Suite 2315
New York, NY 10165
(212) 286-1700

ARIA MODEL & TALENT MGMT.
1017 W Washington Street, #2C
Chicago, IL 60607
(312) 243-9400

ARTHUR ARTHUR INC.
6542 U.S. Highway 41 North, Suite 203A
Apollo Beach, FL 33572
(813) 0645-9700

ARTIST MANAGEMENT AGENCY
1800 E Garry St, Suite 101
Santa Ana, CA 92705
(949) 261-7557

ARTIST MANAGEMENT TALENT AGENCY
835 Fifth Avenue, Suite #411
San Diego, CA 92101
(619) 233-6655

ARTIST'S AGENCY INC.
230 West 55th Street, Suite 29D
New York, NY 10019
(212) 245-6960

ARTISTS AGENCY
1180 S Beverly Dr, Suite 301
Los Angeles, CA 90035
(310) 277-7779

161

ARTISTS & AUDIENCE ENTERTAINMENT
4 Charles Coleman Blvd.
Pawling, NY 12564
(845) 586-1452

ARTISTS GROUP EAST
1650 Broadway, Suite 711
New York, NY 10019
(212) 586-1452

ARTISTS GROUP LTD.
10100 Santa Monica Blvd., Suite 2490
Los Angeles, CA 90067
(310) 552-1100

ASKINS, DENNISE
55 N. 3rd Street
Philadelphia, PA 19106
(215) 925-7795

ASSOCIATED BOOKING CORPORATION
1995 Broadway
New York, NY 10023
(212) 874-2400

ASTOR AGENCY, RICHARD
250 West 57th Street, Suite 2014
New York, NY 10107
(212) 581-1970

ATLANTA MODELS & TALENT INC.
2970 Peachtree Road NW, Suite #660
Atlanta, GA 30305
(404) 261-9627

ATLAS TALENT AGENCY INC.
36 West 44th Street, Suite #1000
New York, NY 10036
(212) 730-4500

AUSTIN AGENCY, THE
6715 Hollywood Blvd, Suite 204
Hollywood, CA 90028
(323) 957-4444

AW/ATLANTA
887 West Marietta Street, Suite #N-101
Atlanta, GA 30318
(404) 876-8555

AYRES TALENT AGENCY
1826 14th Street, Suite 101
Santa Monica, CA 90404
(310) 452-0208

AZUREE TALENT INC.
140 N Orlando Ave #120
Winter Park, FL 32789
(407) 629-5025

BADGLEY CONNOR TALENT AGENCY
9229 Sunset Boulevard, Suite 311
Los Angeles, CA 90069
(310) 278-9313

BAIER-KLEINMAN INTERNATIONAL
3575 Cahuenga Blvd. West, Suite 500
Los Angeles, CA 90068
(323) 874-9800

BAKER & ROWLEY TALENT AGENCY INC.
1327 W. Washington, Suite 5-C
Chicago, IL 60607-1914
(312) 850-4700

BALDWIN TALENT, DONNA
2150 W. 29th Avenue, Suite #200
Denver, CO 80211
(303) 561-1199

BALDWIN TALENT, INC.
8055 West Manchester Ave, Suite 550
Playa Del Rey, CA 90293
(310) 827-2422

BALL, BOBBY TALENT AGENCY
4342 Lankershim Blvd.
Universal City, CA 91602
(818) 506-8188

SAG Franchised Talent Agents

BARBARA HOGENSON AGENCY
165 West End Avenue, Suite 19C
New York, NY 10023
(212) 874-8084

BARBIZON AGENCY
7535 E Hampden #108
Denver, CO 80231
(303) 337-6952

BARON ENTERTAINMENT INC.
5757 Wilshire Blvd, Suite 659
Los Angeles, CA 90036
(323) 936-7600

BARRY HAFT BROWN ARTISTS
165 West 46th Street, Suite 908
New York, NY 10036
(212) 869-9310

BASKOW, J & ASSOCIATES
2948 E. Russell Rd.
Las Vegas, NV 89120
(702) 733-7818

BAUMAN REDANTY & SHAUL
TALENT AGENCY
5757 Wilshire Blvd, Suite #473
Los Angeles, CA 90036
(323) 857-6666

BAUMAN REDANTY & SHAUL
TALENT AGENCY
250 West 57th Street, Suite 2223
New York, NY 10107
(212) 757-0098

BEILIN AGENCY, PETER
230 Park Avenue, Suite 1223
New York, NY 10169
(212) 949-9119

BELL, SANDI TALENT AGENCY
2582 S. Maguire Road, Suite 171
Ocoee, FL 34761
(407) 445-9221

BENZ MODEL-TALENT AGENCY
1320 6th Avenue East
Tampa, FL 33605
(813) 242-4400

BERG TALENT & MODEL AGENCY
15908 Eagle River Way
Tampa, FL 33624
(813) 877-5533

BERMAN BOALS & FLYNN INC.
208 West 30th Street, Suite 401
New York, NY 10001
(212) 868-1068

BERNARD LIEBHABER AGENCY
352 Seventh Avenue
New York, NY 10001
(212) 631-7561

BERZON, MARIAN TALENT AGENCY
336 East 17th Street
Costa Mesa, CA 92627
(949) 631-5936

BEST MODELS & TALENT INC.
4270 Cameron Street, Suite 6
Las Vegas, NV 89103
(702) 889-2900

BETHEL AGENCY
311 West 43rd Street, Suite 602
New York, NY 10036
(212) 664-0455

BICOASTAL TALENT INC.
8380 Melrose Ave, Suite 204
West Hollywood, CA 90069
(323) 512-7755

BIG MOUTH TALENT
935 W. Chestnut, Suite 415
Chicago, IL 60622
(312) 421-4400

BLACK AGENCY, ROBERT
4300 N. Miller Road, No. 202
Scottsdale, AZ 85251
(480) 966-2537

BLACK, BONNIE TALENT AGENCY
5318 Wilkinson Ave #A
Valley Village, CA 91607
(818) 753-5424

BLAKE AGENCY, THE
1327 Ocean Avenue, Suite J
Santa Monica, CA 90401
(310) 899-9898

BLOC TALENT AGENCY INC.
5225 Wilshire Blvd, Suite 311
Los Angeles, CA 90036
(323) 954-7730

BOCA TALENT AND MODEL AGENCY
829 SE 9th Street
Deerfield Beach, FL 33441
(954) 428-4677

BOOM MODELS & TALENT
2325 3rd Street, Suite #223
San Francisco, CA 94107
(415) 626-6591

BORDEN & ASSOCIATES, TED
2434 Adina Drive NE, Suite B
Atlanta, GA 30324
(404) 266-0664

BRAND MODEL AND TALENT
1520 Brookhollow, Suite 39
Santa Ana, CA 92705
(714) 850-1158

**BRANDON'S COMMERCIALS
UNLIMITED S.W.**
8383 Wilshire Boulevard, Suite 850
Beverly Hills, CA 90211
(323) 655-0069

BRANDT COMPANY TALENT AGENCY
15159 Greenleaf Street
Sherman Oaks, CA 91403
(818) 783-7747

BRESLER, KELLY & ASSOCIATES
11500 W. Olympic Blvd., Suite 510
Los Angeles, CA 90064
(310) 479-5611

BREVARD TALENT GROUP INC.
906 Pinetree Drive
Indian Harbour Beach, FL 32937
(321) 773-1355

BRUCE LEVY AGENCY
311 West 43rd Street, Suite 602
New York, NY 10036
(212) 563-7079

BUCHWALD & ASSOC, DON
10 East 44th Street
New York, NY 10017
(212) 867-1070

BUCHWALD & ASSOCIATES, DON
6500 Wilshire Blvd., Suite 2200
Los Angeles, CA 90048
(323) 655-7400

BUCHWALD TALENT GROUP LLC
6300 Wilshire Blvd, Suite 910
Los Angeles, CA 90048
(323) 852-9555

BULLOCK AGENCY, THE
5200 Baltimore Avenue, Suite 102
Hyattsville, MD 20781
(301) 498-9308

BURNS AGENCY, THE
3800 Bretton Woods Road
Decatur, GA 30032
(404) 299-8114

SAG Franchised Talent Agents

BURTON AGENCY, IRIS
1450 Belfast Drive
Los Angeles, CA 90069
(310) 288-0121

C LA VIE TALENT
7507 Sunset Boulevard, Suite #201
Los Angeles, CA 90046
(323) 969-0541

CAMERON & ASSOCIATES, BARBARA
8369 Sausalito Avenue, Suite A
West Hills, CA 91304
(818) 888-6107

CAMPBELL AGENCY, THE
3906 Lemmon Avenue, Suite 200
Dallas, TX 75219
(214) 522-8991

CAMPBELL, CASSANDRA
MODELS & TALENT
1617 El Centro Ave, Suite 19
Los Angeles, CA 90028
(323) 467-1949

CAREER ARTISTS INTERNATIONAL
11030 Ventura Blvd, Suite #3
Studio City, CA 91604
(818) 980-1315

CARLSON-MENASHE AGENCY
149 Fifth Avenue, Suite #1204
New York, NY 10010
(212) 228-8826

CARROLL AGENCY, WILLIAM
139 N San Fernando Rd, Suite A
Burbank, CA 91502
(818) 848-9948

CARRY COMPANY
49 West 46th Street, Fourth Floor
New York, NY 10036
(212) 768-2793

CARSON ORGANIZATION LTD., THE
240 West 44th Street
Penthouse 12
New York, NY 10036
(212) 221-1517

CARSON/ADLER AGENCY INC.
250 West 57th Street, Suite #808
New York, NY 10107
(212) 307-1882

CASTLE-HILL TALENT AGENCY
1101 S Orlando Avenue
Los Angeles, CA 90035
(323) 653-3535

CAVALERI & ASSOCIATES
178 S Victory Blvd, Suite #205
Burbank, CA 91502
(818) 955-9300

CENTRAL FLORIDA TALENT INC.
2601 Wells Avenue, Suite 181
Fern Park, FL 32730
(407) 830-9226

CHAMPAGNE/TROTT LTD. TALENT AGENCY
9250 Wilshire Blvd., Suite 303
Beverly Hills, CA 90212
(310) 275-0067

CHARLES AGENCY, THE
11950 Ventura Blvd., Suite 3
Studio City, CA 91604
(818) 761-2224

CHASIN AGENCY, THE
8899 Beverly Blvd., Suite #716
Los Angeles, CA 90048
(310) 278-7505

CHATEAU BILLINGS TALENT AGENCY
5657 Wilshire Blvd., Suite 200
Los Angeles, CA 90036
(323) 965-5432

CHRISTENSEN GROUP, THE
235 Coastline Road
Sanford, FL 32771
(407) 302-2272

CHRISTOPHER GROUP, TORY
6381 Hollywood Blvd, Suite 600
Hollywood, CA 90028
(323) 469-6906

CIMARRON TALENT AGENCY
10605 Casador Del Oso NE
Albuquerque, NM 87111
(505) 292-2314

CINEMA TALENT AGENCY
2609 Wyoming Avenue, Suite A
Burbank, CA 91505
(818) 845-3816

CIRCLE TALENT ASSOCIATES
433 N. Camden Drive, Suite #400
Beverly Hills, CA 90210
(310) 285-1585

CL INC.
843 N. Sycamore Avenue
Los Angeles, CA 90038
(323) 461-3971

CLARK COMPANYM W RANDOLPH
13415 Ventura Blvd., Suite 3
Sherman Oaks, CA 91423
(818) 385-0583

CLASSIC MODEL & TALENT MANAGEMENT INC.
213 West 35th Street, 10th Floor
New York, NY 10001
(908) 766-6663

CLASSIC MODELS LTD.
3305 Spring Mountain Rd., Suite 12
Las Vegas, NV 89102
(702) 367-1444

CLER MODELING, COLLEEN
178 S Victory, Suite #108
Burbank, CA 91502
(818) 841-7943

COAST TO COAST TALENT GROUP INC.
3350 Barham Blvd.
Los Angeles, CA 90068
(323) 845-9200

COCONUT GROVE TALENT AGENCY
3525 Vista Court
Coconut Grove, FL 33133
(305) 858-3002

COLEMAN-ROSENBERG
155 E. 55th Street, Apt. 5D
New York, NY 10022-4039
(212) 838-0734

COLLEEN BELL MODELING & TALENT AGENCY
14205 SE 36th St. #100
Bellevue, WA 98006
(425) 649-1111

COLLINS, MARY AGENT C. TALENT
2909 Cole Avenue, Suite #250
Dallas, TX 75204-1307
(214) 871-8900

COLOURS MODEL & TALENT MANAGEMENT AGENCY
8344 1/2 West Third Street
Los Angeles, CA 90048
(323) 658-7072

COMMERCIAL TALENT AGENCY
9157 Sunset Blvd, Suite 215
West Hollywood, CA 90069
(310) 247-1431

CONTEMPORARY ARTISTS LTD.
1317 Fifth Street, Suite 200
Santa Monica, CA 90401
(310) 395-1800

SAG Franchised Talent Agents

COPPAGE COMPANY, THE
5411 Camellia Ave
North Hollywood, CA 91601
(818) 980-8806

CORALIE JR. THEATRICAL AGENCY
4789 Vineland Avenue, Suite #100
North Hollywood, CA 91602
(818) 766-9501

CORNERSTONE TALENT AGENCY
132 West 22nd Street, 4th floor
New York, NY 10011
(212) 807-8344

COSDEN AGENCY, THE
129 W Wilson Street, Suite 202
Costa Mesa, CA 92627
(323) 874-7200

CREATIVE ARTISTS AGENCY INC.
3310 West End Avenue, 5th Floor
Nashville, TN 37203
(615) 383-8787

CREATIVE ARTISTS AGENCY LLC
9830 Wilshire Blvd
Beverly Hills, CA 90212
(310) 288-4545

CULBERTSON ARGAZZI GROUP TALENT AGENCY
8430 Santa Monica Blvd, Suite 210
West Hollywood, CA 90069
(323) 650-9454

CUNNINGHAM ESCOTT & DIPENE
10635 Santa Monica Blvd., Suite 130
Los Angeles, CA 90025
(310) 475-2111

CUNNINGHAM-ESCOTT-DIPENE
257 Park Avenue South, Suite 900
New York, NY 10010
(212) 477-1666

CUSICK'S TALENT MANAGEMENT
1009 N.W. Hoyt Street, Suite 100
Portland, OR 97209
(503) 274-8555

D S ENTERTAINMENT
4741 Trousdale Drive, Suite 108
Nashville, TN 37220
(615) 331-6264

DADE/SCHULTZ ASSOCIATES
6442 Coldwater Canyon, Suite 206
Valley Glen, CA 91606
(818) 760-3100

DAN AGENCY MODELS & TALENT
209 10th Avenue South, Suite 301
Nashville, TN 37203
(615) 244-3266

DANGERFIELD AGENCY, THE
4053 Radford Ave, Suite C
Studio City, CA 91604
(818) 766-7717

DANI'S AGENCY
One East Camelback Road, Suite 550
Phoenix, AZ 85012
(602) 263-1918

DAWSON AGENCY, KIM
700 Tower North
2710 N. Stemmons Freeway
Dallas, TX 75207
(214) 630-5161

DDK TALENT REPRESENTATIVES
3800 Barham Blvd, Suite #303
Los Angeles, CA 90068
(310) 274-9356

DELL TALENT, MARLA
2124 Union Street
San Francisco, CA 94123
(415) 563-9213

DIAMOND AGENCY INC. THE
The Historic District
204 W. Bay Avenue
Longwood, FL 32750
(407) 830-4040

DICCE TALENT AGENCY INC., GINGER
56 West 45th Street, Suite 1100
New York, NY 10036
(212) 869-9650

DIMENSIONS 3 MODELING
5205 S Orange Avenue, Suite 209
Orlando, FL 32809
(407) 851-2575

DIVERSE TALENT GROUP INC.
1875 Century Park East, Suite 2250
Los Angeles, CA 90067
(310) 201-6565

DOCHERTY INC.
109 Market Street
Pittsburgh, PA 15222
(412) 765-1400

DORFMAN, CRAIG S & ASSOCIATES
6100 Wilshire Blvd, Suite 310
Los Angeles, CA 90048
(323) 937-8600

**DOUGLAS, GORMAN, ROTHACKER &
WILHELM, INC.**
1501 Broadway, Suite 703
New York, NY 10036
(212) 382-2000

DRAGON TALENT INC.
8444 Wilshire Blvd, Penthouse Suite
Los Angeles, CA 90211
(323) 653-0366

DRAMATIC ARTISTS AGENCY INC.
50 - 16th Avenue
Kirkland, WA 98033
(425) 827-4147

DUVA-FLACK ASSOCIATES INC.
200 West 57th Street, Suite 1008
New York, NY 10019
(212) 957-9600

E T A INC.
7558 S Chicago Ave
Chicago, IL 60619
(773) 752-3955

EASTERN TALENT ALLIANCE INC.
1501 Broadway, Suite 404
New York, NY 10036
(212) 840-6868

EATON AGENCY INC.
3636 High Street N E
Albuquerque, NM 87107
(505) 344-3149

EBS LOS ANGELES
3000 W Olympic Blvd, Suite 1435
Santa Monica, CA 90404
(310) 449-4065

**EDWARDS & ASSOCIATES LLC.
TALENT AGENCY**
5455 Wilshire Blvd., Suite 1614
Los Angeles, CA 90036
(323) 964-0000

EISEN ASSOCIATES, DULCINA
154 East 61st Street
New York, NY 10021
(212) 355-6617

ELEGANCE TALENT AGENCY
2763 State Street
Carlsbad, CA 92008
(760) 434-3397

ELITE MODEL MANAGEMENT CORP/ATLANTA
1708 Peachtree Street NW, Suite #210
Atlanta, GA 30309
(404) 872-7444

SAG Franchised Talent Agents

ELITE OF LOS ANGELES TALENT AGENCY
345 N. Maple Drive, Suite #397
Beverly Hills, CA 90210
(310) 274-9395

ELLECHANTE TALENT AGENCY
274 Spazier Avenue
Burbank, CA 91502
(818) 557-3025

ELLIS TALENT GROUP
14241 Ventura Blvd., Suite 207
Sherman Oaks, CA 91423
(818) 501-7447

ENCORE TALENT AGENCY INC.
700 North Sacramento Blvd., Suite 221
Chicago, IL 60612
(773) 638-7300

ENDEAVOR AGENCY LLC
23 Watts Street, 6th Floor
New York, NY 10013
(212) 625-2500

ENDEAVOR TALENT AGENCY LLC
9701 Wilshire Blvd., 10th Floor
Beverly Hills, CA 90212
(310) 248-2000

ENVY MODEL & TALENT AGENCY
2121 Industrial Road, Loft 211
Las Vegas, NV 89102
(702) 878-7368

**EPSTEIN-WYCKOFF-CORSA-ROSS &
ASSOCIATES**
280 S. Beverly Drive, Suite #400
Beverly Hills, CA 90212
(310) 278-7222

**EPSTEIN/WYCKOFF/CORSA/ROSS &
ASSOCIATES**
311 West 43rd Street, Suite 401
New York, NY 10036
(212) 586-9110

EQUINOX MODELS AND TALENT
8961 Sunset Blvd, Penthouse Suite
West Hollywood, CA 90069
(310) 274-5088

ERHART TALENT INC.
037 S.W. Hamilton Street
Portland, OR 97201
(503) 243-6362

EVOLVE TALENT
3435 Wilshire Blvd, Suite 2700
Los Angeles, CA 90010
(213) 251-1734

EXPRESSIONS MODELING & TALENT
110 Church Street
Philadelphia, PA 19106
(215) 923-4420

FAMOUS FACES ENT CO
2013 Harding St
Hollywood, FL 33020
(954) 922-0700

**FERRAR MEDIA ASSOCIATES
TALENT AGENCY**
8430 Santa Monica Blvd, Suite 220
Los Angeles, CA 90069
(323) 654-2601

FILM ARTISTS ASSOCIATES
13563 1/2 Ventura Blvd., 2nd Floor
Sherman Oaks, CA 91423
(818) 386-9669

FILM THEATRE ACTORS XCHNGE
3145 Geary Blvd., Suite 735
San Francisco, CA 94118
(415) 379-9308

FLAUNT MODEL MANAGEMENT INC.
114 East 32nd Street, Suite 501
New York, NY 10016
(212) 679-9011

FLICK EAST & WEST TALENTS INC.
9057 Nemo Street, Suite #A
West Hollywood, CA 90069
(310) 271-9111

FLORIDA STARS MODEL & TALENT
225 West University Avenue, Suite A
Gainesville, FL 32601
(352) 338-1086

FLYTRAP INC., THE TALENT AGENCY
900 East 1st. Street, Suite 314
Los Angeles, CA 90012
(213) 300-3344

FONTAINE AGENCY/HERO TALENT AGENCY
205 South Beverly Drive, Suite 212
Beverly Hills, CA 90212
(310) 275-4620

FORD TALENT GROUP INC.
641 West Lake Street, Suite 402
Chicago, IL 60661
(312) 707-9000

FOSI'S TALENT AGENCY
2777 N Campbell Avenue #209
Tucson, AZ 85719
(520) 795-3534

FOXX, GWYN TALENT AGENCY
6269 Selma Ave, Suite 18
Los Angeles, CA 90028
(323) 467-7711

FREED, BARRY COMPANY
2040 Avenue of the Stars, Suite 400
Los Angeles, CA 90067
(310) 277-1260

FRESH FACES AGENCY INC.
2911 Carnation Avenue
Baldwin, NY 11510
(516) 223-0034

FRIES, ALICE AGENCY
1927 Vista Del Mar Avenue
Los Angeles, CA 90068
(323) 464-1404

FRONTIER BOOKING INTERNATIONAL
1560 Broadway, Suite 1110
New York, NY 10036
(212) 221-0220

G V A TALENT AGENCY INC.
9229 Sunset Blvd., Suite 320
Los Angeles, CA 90069
(310) 278-1310

G WILLIAMS
525 S. 4th Street #364
Philadelphia, PA 19147
(215) 627-9533

GAGE GROUP INC.
9255 Sunset Boulevard, Suite #515
Los Angeles, CA 90069
(818) 905-3800

GAGE GROUP INC., THE
315 West 57th Street, Suite 4H
New York, NY 10019
(212) 541-5250

GARBER AGENCY
2 Pennsylvania Plaza, Suite 1910
New York, NY 10121
(212) 292-4910

GARRICK INTERNATIONAL, DALE
8831 Sunset Boulevard, Suite #402
Los Angeles, CA 90069
(310) 657-2661

GEDDES AGENCY
1633 N. Halsted Street, Suite 400
Chicago, IL 60614
(312) 787-8333

SAG FRANCHISED TALENT AGENTS

GEDDES AGENCY, THE
8430 Santa Monica Blvd., #200
West Hollywood, CA 90069
(323) 848-2700

GELFF AGENCY, LAYA
16133 Ventura Boulevard, Suite #700
Encino, CA 91436
(818) 996-3100

GENERATION MODEL & TALENT AGENCY
340 Brannan Street, Suite 302
San Francisco, CA 94107
(415) 777-9099

GENERATION TV LLC
20 West 20th Street, Suite 1008
New York, NY 10011
(646) 230-9491

GENESIS MODELS AND TALENT INC.
1465 Northside Drive, Suite #120
Atlanta, GA 30318
(404) 350-9212

GERARD TALENT AGENCY, PAUL
11712 Moorpark Street, Suite 112
Studio City, CA 91604
(818) 769-7015

GERLER, DON AGENCY
3349 Cahuenga Blvd. West, Suite #1
Los Angeles, CA 90068
(323) 850-7386

GERSH AGENCY NEW YORK, INC.
130 West 42nd Street, Suite 2400
New York, NY 10036
(212) 997-1818

GERSH AGENCY, THE
232 N Canon Drive
Beverly Hills, CA 90210
(310) 274-6611

GOLD/LIEDTKE & ASSOCIATES
3500 West Olive Avenue, Suite 1400
Burbank, CA 91505
(818) 972-4300

GOLDNADEL INC.
234 Fifth Avenue
New York, NY 10001
(212) 532-2202

GOODMAN, VERONICA AGENCY
605 West Route 70, #1
Cherry Hills, NJ 08002
(856) 795-3133

GORDON, MICHELLE & ASSOCIATES
260 S. Beverly Drive, Suite 308
Beverly Hills, CA 90212
(310) 246-9930

GRA/GORDON RAEL AGENCY LLC
9242 Beverly Blvd, 3rd Floor
Beverly Hills, CA 90210
(310) 246-7715

GRANT, SAVIC, KOPALOFF AND ASSOCIATES
6399 Wilshire Blvd., Suite 414
Los Angeles, CA 90048
(323) 782-1854

GREEN AGENCY INC.
1329 Alton Road
Miami Beach, FL 33139
(305) 532-9225

GREENE, ANDERSON ENTERTAINMENT INC.
1210 Washington Avenue, Suite 245
Miami Beach, FL 33139
(305) 674-9881

GREENE & ASSOCIATES
526 N Larchmont Blvd, Suite 201
Los Angeles, CA 90004
(323) 960-1333

HADLEY ENTERPRISES, LTD., PEGGY
250 West 57th Street, Suite 2317
New York, NY 10107
(212) 246-2166

HALLIDAY, BUZZ & ASSOCIATES
8899 Beverly Blvd, Suite 715
Los Angeles, CA 90048
(310) 275-6028

HALPERN & ASSOCIATES
12304 Santa Monica Blvd., Suite 104
Los Angeles, CA 90025
(310) 571-4488

HAMIL AGENCY, NEAL
7887 San Felipe, Suite 204
Houston, TX 77063
(713) 789-1335

HAMILBURG AGENCY, MITCHELL J.
8671 Wilshire Blvd, Suite 500
Beverly Hills, CA 90211
(310) 657-1501

HAMILTON, SHIRLEY
333 E Ontario, Suite B
Chicago, IL 60611
(312) 787-4700

HANNS WOLTERS INTERNATIONAL INC.
10 West 37th Street
New York, NY 10018
(212) 714-0100

HARDEN-CURTIS ASSOCIATES
850 Seventh Ave, Suite 405
New York, NY 10019
(212) 977-8502

HART & ASSOCIATES, VAUGHN D.
8899 Beverly Blvd., Suite #815
Los Angeles, CA 90048
(310) 273-7887

HARTIG-HILEPO AGENCY, LTD.
156 Fifth Avenue, Suite 820
New York, NY 10010
(212) 929-1772

HECHT AGENCY, BEVERLY
12001 Ventura Place, Suite 320
Studio City, CA 91604
(818) 505-1192

HENDERSON/HOGAN AGENCY INC.
850 Seventh Avenue, Suite 1003
New York, NY 10019
(212) 765-5190

HENDERSON/HOGAN/MCCABE, LLC
247 S Beverly Dr, Suite 102
Beverly Hills, CA 90212
(310) 274-7815

HERVEY/GRIMES TALENT AGENCY
10561 Missouri, #2
Los Angeles, CA 90025
(310) 475-2010

HOFF, DANIEL AGENCY
1800 N. Highland Avenue, Suite #300
Los Angeles, CA 90028
(323) 962-6643

HOLLANDER TALENT GROUP INC.
14011 Ventura Blvd, Suite 202
Sherman Oaks, CA 91423
(818) 382-9800

HORNE AGENCY INC., THE
4420 West Lovers Lane
Dallas, TX 75209
(214) 350-9220

**HOUSE OF REPRESENTATIVES
TALENT AGENCY**
400 S Beverly Drive, Suite 101
Beverly Hills, CA 90212
(310) 772-0772

SAG FRANCHISED TALENT AGENTS

HOWARD TALENT WEST
10657 Riverside Drive
Toluca Lake, CA 91602
(818) 766-5300

HURT AGENCY INC., THE
400 N New York Avenue, Suite #207
Winter Park, FL 32789
(407) 740-5700

HWA TALENT REPRESENTATIVES INC.
3500 W. Olive Ave., Suite 1400
Burbank, CA 91505
(818) 972-4310

HWA TALENT REPRESENTATIVES
220 East 23rd Street, Suite 400
New York, NY 10010
(212) 889-0800

I GROUP, LLC, THE
29540 Southfield Rd., Suite #200
Southfield, MI 48076
(248) 552-8842

ICON TALENT AGENCY
1717 W Magnolia Blvd, Suite 100
Burbank, CA 91505
(818) 526-1444

IDENTITY TALENT AGENCY
2050 South Bundy Drive, Suite 200
Los Angeles, CA 90025
(310) 882-6070

IFA TALENT AGENCY
8730 Sunset Blvd., Suite 490
Los Angeles, CA 90069
(310) 659-5522

INGBER & ASSOCIATES
274 Madison Avenue, Suite 1104
New York, NY 10016
(212) 889-9450

**INNOVATIVE ARTISTS TALENT &
LITERARY AGENCY**
141 5th Avenue
New York, NY 10011
(212) 253-6900

**INNOVATIVE ARTISTS COMM &
VOICE OVER**
1505 10th Street
Santa Monica, CA 90401
(310) 656-0400

INNOVATIVE ARTISTS TALENT & LITERARY
1505 Tenth Street
Santa Monica, CA 90401
(310) 656-0400

**INNOVATIVE ARTISTS
YOUNG TALENT DIVISION**
1505 Tenth Street
Santa Monica, CA 90401
(310) 656-0400

INTERNATIONAL ARTISTS GROUP INC.
2121 North Bayshore Drive, Suite 2E
Miami, FL 33137
(305) 576-0001

INTERNATIONAL CREATIVE MANAGEMENT
8942 Wilshire Blvd.
Beverly Hills, CA 90211
(310) 550-4000

INTERNATIONAL CREATIVE MANAGEMENT
40 West 57th Street
New York, NY 10019
(212) 556-5600

J E TALENT, LLC.
323 Geary, Suite 302
San Francisco, CA 94102
(415) 395-9475

JACK TALENT, LINDA
230 East Ohio Street, Suite #200
Chicago, IL 60611
(312) 587-1155

JACKSON ARTISTS
7251 Lowell Dr #200
Overland Park, KS 66204
(913) 384-6688

JAY AGENCY, GEORGE
6269 Selma Avenue, Suite 15
Hollywood, CA 90028
(323) 466-6665

JET SET TALENT AGENCY
2160 Avenida De La Playa
La Jolla, CA 92037
(858) 551-9393

JOHNSON SUSAN TALENT AGENCY, THE
13321 Ventura Blvd., Suite C-1
Sherman Oaks, CA 91423
(818) 986-2205

**JORDAN, GILL & DORNBAUM
TALENT AGENCY**
150 Fifth Avenue, Suite 308
New York, NY 10010
(212) 463-8455

JS REPRESENTS TALENT AGENCY
936 1/2 North La Jolla Avenue
Los Angeles, CA 90046
(323) 462-3246

KAPLAN-STAHLER-GUMER, THE
8383 Wilshire Blvd #923
Beverly Hills, CA 90211
(323) 653-4483

KAZARIAN/SPENCER & ASSOCIATES
11365 Ventura Blvd, Suite 100
Studio City, CA 91604
(818) 769-9111

KELLY KELLY ENTERPRISES INC.
10945 State Bridge Rd., Suite 401-316
Alpharetta, GA 30022
(770) 664-2410

KEMP, SHARON TALENT AGENCY
447 S. Robertson Blvd., Suite 204
Beverly Hills, CA 90211
(310) 858-7200

KENNEDY MODELS & TALENT, GLYN
975 Hunter Hill Dr.
Roswell, GA 30075-4214
(678) 461-4444

KERIN-GOLDBERG ASSOCIATES
155 East 55th Street
New York, NY 10022
(212) 838-7373

KERWIN WILLIAM AGENCY
1605 N. Cahuenga Blvd, Suite #202
Hollywood, CA 90028
(323) 469-5155

KIDS INTERNATIONAL TALENT AGENCY
938 East Swan Creek Rd., Suite 152
Ft. Washington, MD 20744
(301) 292-6094

KING, ARCHER
317 West 46th Street, Suite #3A
New York, NY 10036
(212) 765-3103

KLASS, ERIC AGENCY
139 S Beverly Drive, Suite 331
Beverly Hills, CA 90212
(310) 274-9169

KM AND ASSOCIATES TALENT AGENCY
4051 Radford Ave, Suite A
Studio City, CA 91604
(818) 766-3566

SAG Franchised Talent Agents

KMA ASSOCIATES
11 Broadway Rm #1101
New York, NY 10004-1303
(212) 581-4610

KOHNER, PAUL INC.
9300 Wilshire Blvd., Suite 555
Beverly Hills, CA 90212
(310) 550-1060

KRASNY OFFICE INC., THE
1501 Broadway, Suite 1303
New York, NY 10036
(212) 730-8160

L A TALENT
7700 Sunset Blvd
Los Angeles, CA 90046
(323) 436-7777

L'AGENCE INC.
5901-C Peachtree-Dunwoody Road
Suite 60
Atlanta, GA 30328
(770) 396-9015

LALLY TALENT AGENCY
630 Ninth Avenue, Suite 800
New York, NY 10036
(212) 974-8718

LANGE GREER & ASSOCIATES
40 Lloyd Avenue, Suite 104
Malvern, PA 19355
(610) 647-5515

LANTZ OFFICE
200 West 57th Street, Suite 503
New York, NY 10019
(212) 586-0200

LARNER, LIONEL LTD.
119 West 57th Street, Suite 1412
New York, NY 10019
(212) 246-3105

LEAVITT TALENT GROUP
6404 Wilshire Blvd, Suite 950
Los Angeles, CA 90048
(323) 658-8118

LEE ATTRACTIONS, BUDDY
38 Music Square East, Suite 300
Nashville, TN 37203
(615) 244-4336

LEIGHTON AGENCY INC.
2375 E. Camelback Road, 5th Floor
Phoenix, AZ 85016
(602) 224-9255

LENHOFF & LENHOFF TALENT AGENCY
9200 Sunset Blvd, Suite 830
Los Angeles, CA 90069
(310) 550-3900

LENZ AGENCY
1591 East Desert Inn Road
Las Vegas, NV 89109
(702) 733-6888

LEVIN AGENCY, THE
8484 Wilshire Blvd., Suite 750
Beverly Hills, CA 90211
(323) 653-7073

LEVY, ROBIN & ASSOCIATES
9220 Sunset Blvd, Suite 305
Los Angeles, CA 90069
(310) 278-8748

LICHTMAN/SALNERS CO
12216 Moorpark Street
Studio City, CA 91604
(818) 655-9898

LIGHT AGENCY, ROBERT
6404 Wilshire Blvd, Suite 900
Los Angeles, CA 90048
(323) 651-1777

LILY`S TALENT AGENCY
1301 W. Washington, Suite B
Chicago, IL 60607
(312) 601-2345

LINDNER & ASSOCIATES, KEN
2049 Century Park East, Suite 3050
Los Angeles, CA 90067
(310) 277-9223

LJ AND ASSOCIATES
7949 Woodley Avenue, Suite 102
Van Nuys, CA 91406
(818) 345-9274

LOOK MODEL & TALENT AGENCY
166 Geary Blvd, Suite 1406
San Francisco, CA 94108
(415) 781-2841

LORENCE, EMILIA
325 W. Huron, Suite #404
Chicago, IL 60610
(312) 787-2033

LOUISE'S PEOPLE MODEL & TALENT AGENCY
863 13th Avenue North
St. Petersburg, FL 33701
(727) 823-7828

LOVELL & ASSOCIATES
7095 Hollywood Blvd., Suite 1006
Los Angeles, CA 90028
(323) 876-1560

LUKER, JANA TALENT AGENCY
1923 1/2 Westwood Blvd., Suite #3
Los Angeles, CA 90025
(310) 441-2822

LUND AGENCY/INDUSTRY ARTISTS
3330 Barham Blvd., Suite 103
Los Angeles, CA 90068
(323) 851-6575

LW 1 INC.
8383 Wilshire Blvd, Suite 649
Beverly Hills, CA 90211
(323) 653-5700

LYNNE & REILLY AGENCY
Toluca Plaza Building
10725 Vanowen Street
North Hollywood, CA 91605
(323) 850-1984

MADEMOISELLE TALENT AGENCY
10835 Santa Monica Blvd, Suite 204-A
Los Angeles, CA 90025
(310) 441-9994

MAGGIE INC.
35 Newbury Street
Boston, MA 02116
(617) 536-2639

MALAKY INTERNATIONAL
10642 Santa Monica Blvd., Suite 103
Los Angeles, CA 90025
(310) 234-9114

MANNEQUIN AGENCY, THE
2021 San Mateo Blvd NE
Albuquerque,, NM 87110
(505) 266-6823

MARIANNE'S MODELS INC.
1065 Kane Concourse
Bay Harbor Island, FL 33154
(305) 864-8041

MARIE, IRENE AGENCY
728 Ocean Drive
Miami Beach, FL 33139
(305) 672-2929

MARSHALL MODEL & COMML AGENCY, ALESE
22730 Hawthorne Blvd, Suite 201
Torrance, CA 90505
(310) 378-1223

SAG Franchised Talent Agents

MARTIN & DONALDS TALENT AGENCY INC.
2131 Hollywood Boulevard, #308
Hollywood, FL 33020
(954) 921-2427

MARY ANNE CLARO TALENT AGENCY INC.
1513 West Passyunk Ave
Philadelphia, PA 19145
(215) 465-7788

MASHIA TALENT MANAGEMENT
2808 NE MLK Jr. Blvd, Suite L
Portland, OR 97212
(503) 331-9293

MATTAS TALENT AGENCY
1026 W. Colorado Avenue
Colorado Springs, CO 80904
(719) 577-4704

MAXIMUM TALENT INC.
1660 S. Albion Street, Suite 1004
Denver, CO 80222
(303) 691-2344

MAXINE'S TALENT AGENCY
4830 Encino Avenue
Encino, CA 91316
(818) 986-2946

MCCARTY TALENT INC.
4220 So. Maryland Pkwy
Bldg. B, Ste. 317
Las Vegas, NV 89119
(702) 944-4440

MCCULLOUGH ASSOCIATES
8 South Hanover Avenue
Margate, NJ 08402
(609) 822-2222

MCMILLAN TALENT AGENCY, ROXANNE
12100 NE 16th Avenue, Suite #106
North Miami, FL 33161
(305) 899-9150

MEDIA ARTISTS GROUP
6404 Wilshire Blvd, Suite 950
Los Angeles, CA 90048
(323) 658-5050

MEREDITH MODEL MANAGEMENT
10 Furler Street
Totowa, NJ 07512
(973) 812-0122

MERIDIAN ARTISTS AGENCY
9255 Sunset Blvd, Suite 620
Los Angeles, CA 90069
(310) 246-2600

METROPOLITAN TALENT AGENCY
4526 Wilshire Boulevard
Los Angeles, CA 90010
(323) 857-4500

MGA/MARY GRADY AGENCY
221 E Walnut Street, Suite 130
Pasadena, CA 91101
(818) 567-1400

MICHAEL THOMAS AGENCY INC.
134 East 70th Street
New York, NY 10021

MIRAMAR TALENT AGENCY
7400 Beverly Blvd., Suite 220
Los Angeles, CA 90036
(323) 934-0700

MODEL CLUB INC.
115 Newbury St Ste 203
Boston, MA 02116-2935
(617) 247-9020

MODELS GROUP, THE
374 Congress Street, Suite #305
Boston, MA 02210
(617) 426-4711

MODELS GUILD OF CALIFORNIA, THE
8489 West 3rd. Street,
Suite 1106, 1107 & 1109
Los Angeles, CA 90048
(323) 801-2132

MODELS ON THE MOVE
1200 Route 70
Barclay Towers, #6
Cherry Hill, NJ 08034
(856) 667-1060

MOORE CREATIVE TALENT INC.
1610 West Lake Street
Minneapolis, MN 55408
(612) 827-3823

MORGAN AGENCY
129 West Wilson, Suite 202
Costa Mesa, CA 92627
(949) 574-1100

MORRIS AGENCY INC., WILLIAM
1325 Avenue Of the Americas
New York, NY 10019-6011
(212) 586-5100

MORRIS AGENCY, WILLIAM
151 El Camino Dr
Beverly Hills, CA 90212
(310) 274-7451

MORRIS AGENCY, WILLIAM
2100 W End Avenue, Suite 1000
Nashville, TN 37203
(615) 385-0310

MOSS & ASSOC, H. DAVID
733 North Seward Street, Penthouse
Hollywood, CA 90038
(323) 465-1234

MULLER TALENT AGENCY, KATHY
619 Kapahulu Ave, Penthouse
Honolulu, HI 96815
(808) 737-7917

N T A TALENT AGENCY
8899 Beverly Blvd, Suite 612
Los Angeles, CA 90048
(310) 274-6297

NAKED VOICES INC.
865 North Sangamon Avenue, Suite 415
Chicago, IL 60622
(312) 563-0136

NATHE & ASSOCIATES, SUSAN/C P C
8281 Melrose Avenue, Suite 200
Los Angeles, CA 90046
(323) 653-7573

NOUVEAU MODEL MANAGEMENT TALENT AGENCY
909 Prospect Street, Suite 230
La Jolla, CA 92037
(858) 456-1400

NOUVELLE TALENT MANAGEMENT INC.
20 Bethune Street, Suite 3B
New York, NY 10014
(212) 645-0940

OMNIPOP INC.
10700 Ventura Blvd
Second Floor, Suite 2C
Studio City, CA 91604
(818) 980-9267

OMNIPOP INC.
55 West Old Country Road
Hicksville, NY 11801
(516) 937-6011

OPPENHEIM/CHRISTIE ASSOCIATES, LTD.
13 East 37th Street
New York, NY 10016
(212) 213-4330

ORANGE GROVE GROUP INC.
12178 Ventura Blvd., Suite 205
Studio City, CA 91604
(818) 762-7498

SAG Franchised Talent Agents

ORIGIN TALENT
3393 Barham Blvd
Los Angeles, CA 90068
(323) 845-4141

OSBRINK TALENT AGENCY, CINDY
4343 Lankershim Blvd., Suite 100
North Hollywood, CA 91602
(818) 760-2488

OSCARD AGENCY INC., FIFI
24 West 40th Street, Suite #17
New York, NY 10018
(212) 764-1100

OTIS, DOROTHY DAY PARTNERS
215 S La Cienega Blvd
Penthouse Suite 209
Beverly Hills, CA 90211
(310) 289-8011

PACIFIC WEST ARTISTS TALENT AGENCY
25255 Cabot Road, Suite 103
Laguna Hills, CA 92653
(949) 458-7996

PAGE.713
2727 Kirby, Penthouse
Houston, TX 77098
(713) 622-8282

PAKULA KING & ASSOCIATES
9229 Sunset Blvd., Suite 315
Los Angeles, CA 90069
(310) 281-4868

PALMER TALENT AGENCY, DOROTHY
235 West 56th Street, #24K
New York, NY 10019
(212) 765-4280

PANDA AGENCY
3721 Hoen Avenue
Santa Rosa, CA 95405
(707) 576-0711

PANTERA MEG, THE AGENCY
1501 Broadway, Suite 1508
New York, NY 10036
(212) 278-8366

**PARADIGM, A TALENT &
LITERARY AGENCY**
200 West 57th Street, Suite 900
New York, NY 10019
(212) 246-1030

PARADIGM TALENT AGENCY
10100 Santa Monica Blvd, Suite 2500
Los Angeles, CA 90067
(310) 277-4400

PARKES MODELS, PAGE
763 Collins Avenue, 4th Floor
Miami Beach, FL 33139-6215
(305) 672-4869

PARTOS COMPANY, THE
6363 Wilshire Blvd., Suite 227
Los Angeles, CA 90048
(310) 458-7800

PASTORINI BOSBY TALENT AG
3013 Fountain View Drive, Suite 240
Houston, TX 77057
(713) 266-4488

PAULINE'S TALENT CORPORATION
379 West Broadway, Suite 502
New York, NY 10012
(212) 941-6000

PEAK MODELS & TALENT
27636 Avenue Scott, Suite C
Valencia, CA 91355
(661) 288-1555

PEOPLE NEW YORK, INC.
137 Varick Street, Suite 402
New York, NY 10012
(212) 941-9800

PEOPLE STORE, THE
2004 Rockledge Road NE, Suite 60
Atlanta, GA 30324
(404) 874-6448

PHOENIX AGENCY, THE
4121 Cutler Avenue NE
Albuquerque, NM 87110-3811
(505) 881-1209

PIERCE AGENCY, JOHN
8380 Melrose Ave, Suite 106
Los Angeles, CA 90069
(323) 653-3976

PINNACLE COMMERCIAL TALENT
5757 Wilshire Blvd, Suite 510
Los Angeles, CA 90036
(323) 939-5440

PLAYERS TALENT AGENCY
13033 Ventura Blvd., Suite N
Studio City, CA 91604
(818) 528-7444

PLAZA 7
160 N Gulph Road
King Of Prussia, PA 19406
(610) 337-2693

POLAN TALENT AGENCY, MARION
10 NE 11th Avenue
Ft Lauderdale, FL 33301
(954) 525-8351

PREMIER TALENT ASSOCIATES
1790 Broadway, 10th Floor
New York, NY 10019
(212) 758-4900

PRIVILEGE TALENT AGENCY
14542 Ventura Blvd, Suite 209
Sherman Oaks, CA 91403
(818) 386-2377

PRODUCTIONS PLUS
30600 Telegraph Road, Suite #2156
Birmingham, MI 48025
(248) 644-5566

PROFESSIONAL ARTISTS UNLTD.
321 West 44th Street
New York, NY 10036
(212) 247-8770

PROGRESSIVE ARTISTS
400 S Beverly Drive, Suite #216
Beverly Hills, CA 90212
(310) 553-8561

PTI TALENT AGENCY, LLC
9000 Sunset Blvd., Suite 506
West Hollywood, CA 90069
(310) 205-5290

PYRAMID ENTERTAINMENT GROUP
89 Fifth Avenue
New York, NY 10003
(212) 242-7274

Q MODEL MANAGEMENT
6100 Wilshire Blvd., Suite 710
Los Angeles, CA 90048
(323) 692-1700

QUINN ASSOCIATES, CLAUDIA
533 Airport Boulevard, Suite #400
Burlingame, CA 94010
(650) 615-9950

RADIOACTIVE TALENT INC.
240-03 Linden Blvd.
Elmont, NY 11003
(516) 445-9595

**RBC STUDIOS HOLLYWOOD
TALENT AGENCY**
5723 Melrose Ave.
Los Angeles, CA 90038
(323) 461-0800

SAG FRANCHISED TALENT AGENTS

REICH AGENCY, NORMAN
1650 Broadway, Suite 303
New York, NY 10019
(212) 399-2881

REINHARD AGENCY
2021 Arch Street, Suite 400
Philadelphia, PA 19103
(215) 567-2008

**ROMANO MODELING & TALENT
AGENCY, CINDY**
414 Village Square West
Palm Springs, CA 92262
(760) 323-3333

ROOS, LTD. GILLA
16 West 22nd Street, 7th Floor
New York, NY 10010
(212) 727-7820

RUNWAYS, THE TALENT GROUP INC.
1688 Meridian Avenue, Suite 500
Miami Beach, FL 33139
(305) 538-3529

RYAN ARTISTS INC.
239 NW 13th Avenue, Suite #215
Portland, OR 97209
(503) 274-1005

S D B PARTNERS INC.
1801 Avenue of the Stars, Suite 902
Los Angeles, CA 90067
(310) 785-0060

SALAZAR & NAVAS INC.
760 N. Ogden Ave, Suite 2200
Chicago, IL 60622
(312) 751-3419

SAMANTHA GROUP TALENT AGENCY
300 S. Raymond Avenue, Suite 11
Pasadena, CA 91105
(626) 683-2444

SAMES & ROLLNICK ASSOCIATES
250 West 57th Street, Suite 703
New York, NY 10107
(212) 315-4434

SAN DIEGO MODEL MANAGEMENT
438 Camino Del Rio South, Suite #116
San Diego, CA 92108-3546
(619) 296-1018

**SAN FRANCISCO TOP MODELS
AND TALENT**
870 Market Street, Suite 1076
San Francisco, CA 94102
(415) 391-1800

SARNOFF COMPANY INC.
3500 W. Olive, Suite 300
Burbank, CA 91505
(818) 973-4555

SAVAGE AGENCY, THE
6212 Banner Ave
Los Angeles, CA 90038
(323) 461-8316

SCAGNETTI TALENT AGENCY, JACK
5118 Vineland Avenue, Suite 102
North Hollywood, CA 91601
(818) 762-3871

SCHECHTER COMPANY, THE IRV
9300 Wilshire Blvd, Suite 400
Beverly Hills, CA 90212
(310) 278-8070

**SCHIFFMAN, EKMAN, MORRISON
AND MARX**
22 West 19th Street, 8th Floor
New York, NY 10011
(212) 627-5500

SCHILL AGENCY INC., WILLIAM
250 West 57th Street, Suite 2402
New York, NY 10107
(212) 315-5919

SCHIOWITZ/CLAY/ROSE INC.
165 West 46th Street, Suite 1210
New York, NY 10036
(212) 840-6787

SCHNARR TALENT, SANDIE
8500 Melrose Avenue, Suite 212
West Hollywood, CA 90069
(310) 360-7680

SCHOEN & ASSOCIATES, JUDY
606 N Larchmont Blvd, Suite 309
Los Angeles, CA 90004
(323) 962-1950

SCHUCART, NORMAN ENT
1417 Green Bay Rd
Highland Park, IL 60035-3614
(847) 433-1113

SCHULLER TALENT INC.
AKA NEW YORK KIDS
276 Fifth Avenue, 10th Floor
New York, NY 10001
(212) 532-6005

SCHWARTZ ASSOCIATES, DON
1604 N Cahuenga Blvd, Suite 101
Hollywood, CA 90028
(323) 464-4366

SCREAM MODEL AND TALENT AGENCY
1436 S La Cienega Blvd, Suite 207
Los Angeles, CA 90035
(310) 659-3030

SCREEN ARTISTS AGENCY
12435 Oxnard Street
North Hollywood, CA 91606
(818) 755-0026

SELECT MODEL & TALENT AGENCY
(SMT) LLC
8271 Melrose Ave, Suite 203
Los Angeles, CA 90046
(323) 653-6732

SEM TALENT INC.
282 Pavonia Avenue
Jersey City, NJ 07302
(201) 656-3919

SHAMON FREITAS & COMPANY
9606 Tierra Grande Street, Suite #204
San Diego, CA 92126
(858) 549-3955

SHAPIRA & ASSOC
15821 Ventura Blvd, Suite 235
Encino, CA 91436
(818) 906-0322

SHAPIRO-LICHTMAN TALENT AGENCY
8827 Beverly Blvd
Los Angeles, CA 90048
(310) 859-8877

SHEFFIELD AGENCY INC.
Palm Beach Ocean Studios
2121 Vista Parkway
West Palm Beach, FL 33411
(954) 523-5887

SIEGEL ASSOCIATES, JEROME
1680 North Vine Street, Suite 613
Hollywood, CA 90028
(323) 466-0185

SIERRA TALENT AGENCY
14542 Ventura Blvd., Suite 207
Sherman Oaks, CA 91403
(818) 907-9645

SIGNATURE ARTISTS AGENCY
6700 W 5th Street
Los Angeles, CA 90048
(323) 651-0600

SIGNATURE MODELS & TALENT
2600 N. 44th St., Suite #209
Phoenix, AZ 85008-1521
(480) 966-1102

SAG Franchised Talent Agents

SILVER, MASSETTI & SZATMARY EAST, LTD.
145 West 45th Street, #1204
New York, NY 10036
(212) 391-4545

SILVER, MASSETTI & SZATMARY/ WEST LTD.
8730 Sunset Boulevard, Suite #440
Los Angeles, CA 90069
(310) 289-0909

SLESSINGER ASSOC, MICHAEL
8730 Sunset Boulevard, Suite 220
Los Angeles, CA 90069
(310) 657-7113

SOK TEENS AND SOK TALENT
335 Plaza Central
Los Altos, CA 94022
(650) 947-1210

SORICE TALENT AGENCY, CAMILLE
13412 Moorpark Street, Suite C
Sherman Oaks, CA 91423
(818) 995-1775

SOUTH OF SANTA FE TALENT GUILD INC.
6921-B Montgomery Boulevard NE
Albuquerque, NM 87109
(505) 880-8550

SPECIAL ARTISTS AGENCY
345 North Maple Drive, Suite 302
Beverly Hills, CA 90210
(310) 859-9688

STANDER & ASSOCIATES INC., SCOTT
13701 Riverside Drive, Suite 201
Sherman Oaks, CA 91423
(818) 905-7000

STANLEY KAPLAN TALENT
139 Fulton Street, Suite 503
New York, NY 10038
(212) 385-4400

STARCRAFT TALENT AGENCY
3330 Barham, Suite 105
Los Angeles, CA 90068
(323) 845-4784

STARWILL TALENT AGENCY
433 N. Camden Drive, 4th Floor
Beverly Hills, CA 90210
(323) 874-1239

STEELE AGENCY, ANN
330 W. 42nd Street, 18th Floor
New York, NY 10036
(212) 629-9112

STELLAR TALENT AGENCY
407 Lincoln Road, Suite 2K
Miami Beach, FL 33139
(305) 672-2217

STERN AGENCY, CHARLES H.
11845 W. Olympic Blvd., Suite 1177
Los Angeles, CA 90064
(310) 457-0048

STEVENS GROUP, THE
14011 Ventura Blvd, Suite 201
Sherman Oaks, CA 91423
(818) 528-3674

STEWART TALENT MANAGEMENT
58 West Huron
Chicago, IL 60610
(312) 943-3131

STEWART'S MODELING, EVELYN
911 Samy Drive
Tampa, FL 33613
(813) 968-1441

STONE AGENCY, IVETT
14677 Midway Road, Suite 113
Addison, TX 75001
(972) 392-4951

STONE MANNERS AGENCY
8436 West Third Street, Suite 740
Los Angeles, CA 90048
(323) 655-1313

STRAIN, PETER AND ASSOCIATES
5724 West Third Street, Suite 302
Los Angeles, CA 90036
(323) 525-3391

STRAIN, PETER AND ASSOCIATES
1501 Broadway, Suite 2900
New York, NY 10036
(212) 391-0380

STUBBS, MITCHELL K & ASSOCIATES
1450 S Robertson Blvd
Los Angeles, CA 90035
(310) 838-1200

SUMMERS' TALENT, DONNA
8950 Laurel Way, Suite #200
Alpharetta, GA 30202
(770) 518-9855

SUTTON, BARTH & VENNARI INC.
145 S Fairfax Avenue, Suite 310
Los Angeles, CA 90036
(323) 938-6000

SWB THEATRICAL GROUP TALENT AGENCY
8383 Wilshire Blvd., Suite 850
Beverly Hills, CA 90211
(323) 655-0069

T.G. AGENCY, THE
2820 Smallman Street
Pittsburgh, PA 15222
(412) 471-8011

TALENT GROUP INC.
6300 Wilshire Blvd, Suite 900
Los Angeles, CA 90048
(323) 852-9559

TALENT GROUP THE/HOT SHOT KIDS
3300 Buckeye Road, Suite 405
Buckeye Tower
Atlanta, GA 30341
(770) 986-9600

TALENT & MODEL LAND
4516 Granny White Pike
Nashville, TN 37204
(615) 321-5596

TALENT PLUS AGENCY/LOS LATINOS TALENT
2801 Moorpark Ave #11
Dyer Building
San Jose, CA 95128
(408) 296-2213

TALENT PLUS INC.
1222 Lucas Avenue, Suite 300
Saint Louis, MO 63103
(314) 421-9400

TALENT REPRESENTATIVES INC.
20 East 53rd Street
New York, NY 10022
(212) 752-1835

TALENT SHOP, THE
30100 Telegraph Road, Suite #116
Birmingham, MI 48025
(248) 644-4877

TALENT SYNDICATE, LLC
1680 N. Vine Street, Suite 614
Los Angeles, CA 90028
(323) 463-7300

TALENT TREK AGENCY
406 11th Street
Knoxville, TN 37916
(865) 977-8735

TALENT UNLIMITED, LLC
4049 Pennsylvania, Suite 300
Kansas City, MO 64111
(816) 561-9040

SAG Franchised Talent Agents

TAMAR WOLBROM INC.
130 West 42nd Street, Suite #707
New York, NY 10036
(212) 398-4595

TANNEN & ASSOC
10801 National Blvd, Suite #101
Los Angeles, CA 90064
(310) 446-5802

TAYLOR ROYALL AGENCY
6247 Falls Road
Baltimore, MD 21209
(410) 321-5958

TAYLOR TALENT, PEGGY
437 Southfork, Suite 400
Lewisville, TX 75067
(214) 651-7884

THE KOLSTEIN TALENT AGENCY
85 Lafayette Avenue
Suffern, NY 10977
(845) 357-8301

THE LUEDTKE AGENCY
1674 Broadway, Suite 7A
New York, NY 10019
(212) 765-9564

THE STARS AGENCY
23 Grant Avenue, 4th Floor
San Francisco, CA 94108
(415) 421-6272

THIRD COAST ARTISTS INC.
641 W Lake Street, Suite 402
Chicago, IL 60661
(312) 670-4444

THOMAS TALENT AGENCY
6709 La Tijera Blvd., Suite 915
Los Angeles, CA 90045
(310) 665-0000

THORNTON & ASSOCIATES, ARLENE
12711 Ventura Blvd, Suite 490
Studio City, CA 91604
(818) 760-6688

TILMAR TALENT AGENCY
4929 Wilshire Blvd, Suite 830
Los Angeles, CA 90010
(323) 938-9815

TISHERMAN AGENCY INC.
6767 Forest Lawn Drive, Suite 101
Los Angeles, CA 90068
(323) 850-6767

TOMAS AGENCY
14275 Midway Road, Suite 220
Addison, TX 75001
(972) 687-9181

TONRY TALENT AGENCY
885 Bryant Street, Suite 201
San Francisco, CA 94103
(415) 543-3797

TOPO SWOPE TALENT AGENCY
1932 1st Avenue, Suite 700
Seattle, WA 98101
(206) 443-2021

TOTAL ACTING EXPERIENCE, A
20501 Ventura Blvd., Suite 399
Woodland Hills, CA 91364
(818) 340-9249

ULTRA MODEL MANAGEMENT
1688 Meridian Avenue, Suite 400
Miami Beach, FL 33139
(305) 538-5445

UNITED ARTISTS TALENT AGENCY
14011 Ventura Blvd., Suite 213
Sherman Oaks, CA 91423
(818) 788-7305

UNITED TALENT AGENCY INC.
9560 Wilshire Blvd, 5th Floor
Beverly Hills, CA 90212
(310) 273-6700

US TALENT AGENCY
485 S Robertson Blvd., Suite 7
Beverly Hills, CA 90211
(310) 858-1533

V TALENT & MODEL MANAGEMENT INC.
904 Kohou Street, #303
Honolulu, HI 96817
(808) 842-0881

VE MODEL & TALENT AGENCY
9615 Brighton Way, Suite 302
Beverly Hills, CA 90210
(310) 399-9800

VISION ART MANAGEMENT
9200 Sunset Blvd., Penthouse 1
Los Angeles, CA 90069
(310) 888-3288

VOICE CHOICE
1805 S. Bellaire Street, Suite 510
Denver, CO 80222
(303) 756-9055

VOICES UNLIMITED INC.
541 N. Fairbanks Ct., Suite 2735
Chicago, IL 60611-3319
(312) 832-1113

WALLIS AGENCY
4444 Riverside Dr, Suite 105
Burbank, CA 91505
(818) 953-4848

WARDLOW AND ASSOCIATES
1501 Main Street, Suite 204
Venice, CA 90291
(310) 452-1292

WATERS & NICOLOSI
1501 Broadway, Suite 1305
New York, NY 10036
(212) 302-8787

WATERS & NICOLOSI TALENT AGENCY
9301 Wilshire Blvd., Suite 300
Beverly Hills, CA 90210
(310) 777-8277

WAUGH TALENT AGENCY, ANN
4741 Laurel Canyon Blvd, Suite 200
North Hollywood, CA 91607
(818) 980-0141

WAUHOB, DONNA AGENCY
3135 Industrial Road, Suite #204
Las Vegas, NV 89109-1122
(702) 733-1017

WEHMANN MODELS/TALENT INC.
1128 Harmon Place, Suite 205
Minneapolis, MN 55403
(612) 333-6393

WESTSIDE TALENT AGENCY
17631 S Susana Rd
Rancho Dominguez, CA 90221
(310) 475-5991

WILHELMINA-MIAMI
927 Lincoln Road, Suite 200
Miami Beach, FL 33139
(305) 672-9344

WILSON & ASSOCIATES, SHIRLEY
5410 Wilshire Boulevard, Suite #806
Los Angeles, CA 90036
(323) 857-6977

WILSON TALENT, ARLENE INC.
430 W Erie Street, Suite #210
Chicago, IL 60610
(312) 573-0200

SAG Franchised Talent Agents

WORLD CLASS SPORTS
880 Apollo Street, Suite 337
El Segundo, CA 90245
(310) 535-9120

WORLD OF KIDS INC.
1460 Ocean Drive, Suite 205
Miami Beach, FL 33139
(305) 672-5437

WRITERS AND ARTISTS AGENCY
8383 Wilshire Blvd, Suite 550
Beverly Hills, CA 90211
(323) 866-0900

WRITERS & ARTISTS AGENCY
19 West 44th Street, Suite 1000
New York, NY 10036
(212) 391-1112

YOUNG AGENCY, SHERRY
2620 Fountain View, Suite #212
Houston, TX 77057
(713) 266-5800

ZANUCK, PASSON & PACE
13317 Ventura Blvd., Suite I
Sherman Oaks, CA 91423
(818) 783-4890

WGA Signatory Agents and Agencies

A PICTURE OF YOU
1176 Elizabeth Drive
Hamilton, OH 45013
(513) 863-1108

A TOTAL ACTING EXPERIENCE
5353 Topanga Cyn Rd #220
Woodland Hills, CA 91364
(818) 340-9249

ABOVE THE LINE AGENCY
9200 Sunset Blvd #804
West Hollywood, CA 90069
(310) 859-6115

ABRAMS ARTISTS AGENCY
275 Seventh Ave, 26th Fl
New York, NY 10001
(646) 486-4600

ACME TALENT & LITERARY AGENCY
4727 Wilshire Blvd #333
Los Angeles, CA 90010
(323) 954-2263

ADAMS, BRET LTD.
448 West 44th St
New York, NY 10036
(212) 765-5630

ADLEY, PHILIP AGENCY
157 Tarmarack Dr
May, TX 76857-1649
(915) 784-6849

AGENCY FOR THE PERFORMING ARTS
9200 Sunset Blvd #900
Los Angeles, CA 90069
(310) 888-4200

AGENCY, THE
1800 Avenue of the Stars #400
Los Angeles, CA 90067
(310) 551-3000

AGENCY CHICAGO
601 South La Salle St #600-A
Chicago, IL 60605

AGENCY FOR THE PERFORMING ARTS
888 7th Ave
New York, NY 10106
(212) 582-1500

ALJOUNY, JOSEPH S.
29205 Greening Blvd.
Farmington Hills, MI 48334-2945
(248) 932-0090

ALLAN, LEE AGENCY
7464 North 107th St
Milwaukee, WI 53224-3706
(414) 357-7708

ALLEN TALENT AGENCY
3832 Wilshire Blvd 2nd Floor
Los Angeles, CA 90010-3221
(213) 896-9372

WGA Signatory Agents and Agencies

ALPERN GROUP, THE
15645 Royal Oak Road
Encino, CA 91436
(818) 528-1111

AMATO, MICHAEL AGENCY
1650 Broadway, Suite 307
New York, NY 10019
(212) 247-4456

AMRON DEVELOPMENT, INC.
77 Horton Pl
Syosset, NY 11791
(516) 364-0238

AMSTERDAM, MARCIA AGENCY
41 West 82nd St
New York, NY 10024-5613
(212) 873-4945

ARTISTS AGENCY, INC.
230 West 55th Street #29D
New York, NY 10019
(212) 245-6960

ARTISTS GROUP, LTD., THE
10100 Santa Monica Blvd #2490
Los Angeles, CA 90067
(310) 552-1100

AUTHOR'S AGENCY, THE
3355 North Five Mile Rd #332
Boise, ID 83713-3925
(208) 376-5477

BEACON ARTISTS AGENCY
630 Ninth Ave #215
New York, NY 10036
(212) 765-5533

BERG AGENCY, INC.
15908 Eagle River Way
Tampa, FL 33624
(813) 877-5533

BERMAN, BOALS & FLYNN, INC.
208 West 30th Street, #401
New York, NY 10001
(212) 868-1068

BEVY CREATIVE ENTERPRISES
7139 Azalea
Dallas, TX 75230
(214) 363-5771

BIGGAR, LOIS & ASSOCIATES
8885 Southwest O'Mara St
Portland, OR 97223
(503) 639-3686

BOHRMAN AGENCY, THE
8899 Beverly Blvd. #811
Los Angeles, CA 90048
(310) 550-5444

BORCHARDT, GEORGES INC.
136 East 57th St
New York, NY 10022
(212) 753-5785

BOYLE, THOMAS D.
2001 Ross Ave #3900
Dallas, TX 75201
(214) 661-8913

BROWN, BRUCE AGENCY
1033 Gayley Ave #207
Los Angeles, CA 90024
(310) 208-1835

BROWN, CURTIS, LTD.
10 Astor Pl
New York, NY 10003
(212) 473-5400

BROWN, ELLEN AGENCY
211 Clubhouse Dr
Middletown, NJ 07748
(201) 615-0310

BROWNE, PEMA, LTD.
Pine Rd, HCR Box 104B
Neversink, NY 12765
(914) 985-2936

BRYAN, MARCUS & ASSOCIATES
2970 Maria Avenue #224
Northbrook, IL 60062
(847) 579-0030

BUCHWALD, DON & ASSOCIATES
6500 Wilshire Blvd #2200
Los Angeles, CA 90048
(323) 655-7400

BUCHWALD, DON & ASSOCIATES
10 East 44th St
New York, NY 10017
(212) 867-1070

BULGER, KELVIN C., ATTORNEY AT LAW
11 East Adams #604
Chicago, IL 60603
(312) 692-1002

BURNAM, CAROLYN AGENCY, THE
4207 Valleyfield St
San Antonio, TX 78222-3714
(210) 337-8268

CALIFORNIA ARTISTS AGENCY
3053 Centerville Rosebud Rd
Snellville, GA 30039
(770) 982-1477

CAMERON, MARSHALL AGENCY
19667 NE 20th Lane
Lawtey, FL 32058
(904) 964-7013

CANO AGENCY, THE
8257 Latona Ave, Northeast
Seattle, WA 98115
(206) 522-5974

CAREER ARTISTS INTERNATIONAL
11030 Ventura Blvd #3
Studio City, CA 91604
(818) 980-1315

CARVAINIS, MARIA AGENCY
1350 Ave of the Americas #2950
New York, NY 10019
(212) 245-6365

CATALYST LITERARY & TALENT AGENCY
(818) 597-8335

CAVALERI & ASSOCIATES
178 S. Victory Blvd #205
Burbank, CA 91502
(818) 955-9300

CEO CREATIVE ENTERTAINMENT OFFICE
1801 S. Catalina Ave #103
Redondo Beach, CA 90277
(310) 791-4494

CHASIN AGENCY, INC., THE
8899 Beverly Blvd. #716
Los Angeles, CA 90048
(310) 278-7505

CLIENT FIRST AGENCY
2134 Fairfax Ave #A-3
Nashville, TN 37212
(615) 325-4780

COCONUT GROVE TALENT AGENCY
3525 Vista Ct
Coconut Grove, FL 33133
(305) 858-3002

CONTEMPORARY ARTISTS, LTD.
610 Santa Monica Blvd #202
Santa Monica, CA 90401
(310) 395-1800

COPPAGE COMPANY, THE
5411 Camellia Avenue
North Hollywood, CA 91601
(818) 980-8806

CORALIE JR. THEATRICAL AGENCY
4789 Vineland Ave #100
North Hollywood, CA 91602
(818) 766-9501

CREATIVE AUTHORS AGENCY
12212 Paradise Village Pkwy
South #403-C
Phoenix, AZ 85032
(602) 953-0164

CREATIVE CAREER MANAGEMENT
84 Spruce Run Dr
Brewster, MA 02631
(508) 896-9351

CREATIVE COMMUNICATIONS
6919 SE Holgate Blvd
Portland, OR 97206
(503) 323-4366

DEE MURA ENTERPRISES, INC.
269 West Shore Dr
Massapequa, NY 11758
(516) 795-1616

DEITER LITERARY AGENCY, THE
6207 Fushsimi Court
Burke, VA 22015
(703) 440-8920

DEUCE TALENT & LITERARY AGENCY
197 Lamplighter Dr #6C
Winnsboro, SC 29180
(803) 712-0805

DISCOVERED AGENCY
21 St. James
West Hartford, CT 06107

DIVERSE TALENT GROUP, INC.
1875 Century Park East #2250
Los Angeles, CA 90067
(310) 201-6565

DONADIO & ASHWORTH, INC.
121 West 27th St
New York, NY 10001
(212) 691-8077

DOUROUX & CO.
815 Manhattan Ave. Suite D
Manhattan Beach, CA 90266
(310) 379-3435

DUVA-FLACK ASSOCIATES, INC.
200 West 57th Street #1008
New York, NY 10019
(212) 957-9600

DYTMAN & ASSOCIATES
9200 Sunset Blvd #809
Los Angeles, CA 90069
(310) 274-8844

EARTH TRACKS ARTISTS AGENCY
4809 Ave, North #286
Brooklyn, NY 11234

ELLECHANTE TALENT AGENCY
231 West 75th Street
Los Angeles, CA 90003
(323) 750-9490

ENDEAVOR AGENCY, THE
9701 Wilshire Blvd, 10th Floor
Beverly Hills, CA 90212
(310) 248-2000

EPSTEIN-WYCKOFF-CORSA-ROSS & ASSOCIATES
280 South Beverly Dr #400
Beverly Hills, CA 90212
(310) 278-7222

ES AGENCY, THE
110 East D Street #B
Benicia, CA 94510
(707) 748-7394

FIELD-CECH-MURPHY AGENCY
12725 Ventura Blvd #D
Studio City, CA 91604
(818) 980-2001

FILM ARTISTS ASSOCIATES
13563 1/2 Ventura Blvd, 2nd Floor
Sherman Oaks, CA 91423
(818) 386-9669

FILM-THEATER ACTORS EXCHANGE
390 28th Avenue #3
San Francisco, CA 94121
(415) 379-9308

FILMWRITERS LITERARY AGENCY
4932 Long Shadow Drive
Midlothian, VA 23112
(804) 744-1718

FREED, BARRY COMPANY, INC., THE
2040 Avenue of the Stars #400
Los Angeles, CA 90067
(310) 277-1260

FREEDMAN, ROBERT A.
DRAMATIC AGENCY, INC.
1501 Broadway #2310
New York, NY 10036
(212) 840-5760

FRIES, ALICE AGENCY, LTD.
1927 Vista Del Mar Ave
Los Angeles, CA 90068
(323) 464-1404

GAGE GROUP, INC., THE
14724 Ventura Blvd., Suite 505
Sherman Oaks, CA 91403
(818) 905-3800

GABALDON, THERESA A. LITERARY AGENT
2020 Pennsylvania Ave, NW #222
Washington, DC 20006

GARRICK, DALE INTERNATIONAL
8831 Sunset Blvd
Los Angeles, CA 90069
(310) 657-2661

GARY-PAUL AGENCY, THE
84 Canaan Ct #17
Stratford, CT 06614
(203) 336-0257

GEDDES AGENCY
8430 Santa Monica Blvd #200
West Hollywood, CA 90069
(323) 848-2700

GELFF, LAYA AGENCY
16133 Ventura Blvd #700
Encino, CA 91436
(818) 996-3100

GENESIS
345 N Maple Dr #395
Beverly Hills, CA 90210
(310) 205-5000

GENESIS AGENCY, THE
1465 Northside Dr #120
Atlanta, GA 30318
(404) 350-9212

GERARD, PAUL TALENT AGENCY
11712 Moorpark St #112
Studio City, CA 91604
(818) 769-7015

GERSH AGENCY, INC., THE
130 West 42nd St
New York, NY 10036
(212) 997-1818

GOOD WRITERS AGENCY, THE
113 Henry Hudson Dr
Delmont, PA 15626
(724) 468-0237

GORDON, MICHELLE & ASSOCIATES
260 South Beverly Dr #308
Beverly Hills, CA 90212
(310) 246-9930

GRACE COMPANY, THE
829 Langdon Ct
Rochester Hills, MI 48307
(248) 868-5994

GURMAN, SUSAN AGENCY, THE
865 West End Ave #15A
New York, NY 10025
(212) 749-4618

**GUSAY, CHARLOTTE LITERARY AGENT/
ARTISTS REPRESENTATIVE**
10532 Blythe Ave.
Los Angeles, CA 90064
(310) 559-0831

GROSSMAN, LARRY & ASSOCIATES
211 South Beverly Dr #206
Beverly Hills, CA 90212
(310) 550-8127

HAMILBURG, MITCHELL J. AGENCY
8671 Wilshire Blvd #500
Beverly Hills, CA 90211
(310) 657-1501

HAMILTON, SHIRLEY, INC.
333 East Ontario Ave #302b
Chicago, IL 60611
(312) 787-4700

HANAR COMPANY
34 Fairbanks Ave
Pascoag, RI 02859

HART LITERARY MANAGEMENT
3541 Olive Street
Santa Ynez, CA 93460
(805) 686-7912

HAYES, GIL & ASSOCIATES
5125 Barry Rd
Memphis, TN 38117
(901) 818-0086

HERMAN, RICHARD TALENT AGENCY
124 Lasky Dr, 2nd Floor
Beverly Hills, CA 90212
(310) 550-8913

HODGES, CAROLYN AGENCY
1980 Glenwood Dr
Boulder, CO 80304
(303) 443-4636

HOGENSON, BARBARA AGENCY, INC.
165 West End Ave #19-C
New York, NY 10023
(212) 874-8084

HOHMAN, MAYBANK, LIEB
9229 Sunset Blvd. #700
Los Angeles, CA 90069
(310) 274-4600

HUDSON AGENCY, THE
3 Travis Ln.
Montrose, NY 10548
(914) 737-1475

HURT AGENCY, INC.
400 New York Ave, North #207
Winter Park, FL 32789
(407) 740-5700

HWA TALENT REPRESENTATIVES, INC.
3500 West Olive Ave. #1400
Burbank, CA 91505
(818) 972-4310

INNOVATIVE ARTISTS
1505 Tenth Street
Santa Monica, CA 90401
(310) 656-0400

INTERNATIONAL CREATIVE MGMT
8942 Wilshire Blvd
Beverly Hills, CA 90211
(310) 550-4000

INTERNATIONAL CREATIVE MGMT
40 West 57th St
New York, NY 10019
(212) 556-5600

INTERNATIONAL LEONARDS CORP
3612 North Washington Blvd
Indianapolis, IN 46205

J F GLAVAN AGENCY
10401 E McDowell Mtn Ranch Rd
Suite A2-161
Scottsdale, AZ 85259
(480) 515-5157

JACKSON ARTISTS CORPORATION
7251 Lowell Drive
Overland Park, KS 66204
(913) 384-6688

JEZ ENTERPRISES
227 Village Way
South Bend, IN 46619
(219) 233-3059

JOHNSON, SUSAN AGENCY, THE
13321 Ventura Blvd #C-1
Sherman Oaks, CA 91423
(818) 986-2205

JOHNSON, SUSANNE TALENT AGENCY, LTD.
108 West Oak St
Chicago, IL 60610
(312) 642-8151

JOINT VENTURE AGENCY
2927 Westbrook Dr #110B
Fort Wayne, IN 46805
(219) 484-1832

K.P. AGENCY
300 North State St #4526
Chicago, IL 60610
(312) 832-9777

K.T. ENTERPRISES
2605 Ben Hill Rd
East Point, GA 30344
(404) 346-3191

KALLIOPE ENTERPRISES, INC.
15 Larch Dr
New Hyde, NY 11040
(516) 248-2963

KAPLAN-STAHLER-GUMER AGENCY, THE
8383 Wilshire Blvd #923
Beverly Hills, CA 90211
(323) 653-4483

KERIN-GOLDBERG ASSOCIATES, INC.
155 East 55th St
New York, NY 10022
(212) 838-7373

KETAY, JOYCE AGENCY, INC., THE
1501 Broadway #1908
New York, NY 10036
(212) 354-6825

KICK ENTERTAINMENT
1934 East 123rd St
Cleveland, OH 44106
(216) 791-2515

KING, ARCHER, LTD.
317 West 46 St #3A
New York, NY 10036
(212) 765-3103

KINGDOM INDUSTRIES LTD.
118-11 195th St
P O Box 310
Saint Albans, NY 11412-0310
(718) 949-9804

KLANE, JON AGENCY
120 El Camino Dr #112
Beverly Hills, CA 90212
(310) 278-0178

KMA AGENCY
11 Broadway, Suite 1101
New York, NY 10004
(212) 581-4610

KOHNER, PAUL INC.
9300 Wilshire Blvd #555
Beverly Hills, CA 90212
(310) 550-1060

KOZAK, OTTO LITERARY &
Motion Picture Agency
114 Coronado Street
Atlantic Beach, NY 11509

KOZLOV, CARY LITERARY REPRESENTATION
11911 San Vicente Blvd. #348
Los Angeles, CA 90049
(310) 843-2211

LAKE, CANDACE AGENCY, INC., THE
9200 Sunset Blvd #820
Los Angeles, CA 90069
(310) 247-2115

LARCHMONT LITERARY AGENCY
444 North Larchmont Blvd. #200
Los Angeles, CA 90004
(323) 856-3070

LASERSON CREATIVE
358 13th St
Brooklyn, NY 11215
(718) 832-1785

LAW OFFICES OF JOEL WEISMAN, P.C.
1901 Raymond Drive #6
Northbrook, IL 60062
(847) 400-5900

LE MODELN, INC.
7536 Market St #104
Boardman, OH 44512
(330) 758-4417

LEADING ARTISTS
800 S. Robertson Blvd. #5
Los Angeles, CA 90035
(310) 855-0565

LEGACIES
501 Woodstork Circle, Perico Bay
Bradenton, FL 34209
(941) 792-9159

LENHOFF & LENHOFF
9200 Sunset Blvd #830
Los Angeles, CA 90069
(310) 550-3900

LENNY, JACK ASSOCIATES
9454 Wilshire Blvd #600
Beverly Hills, CA 90212
(310) 271-2174

LICHTMAN/SALNERS CO.
12216 Moorpark Street
Studio City, CA 91604
(818) 655-9898

LIONIZE, INC.
2020 Broadway #2A
New York, NY 10023
(212) 579-5414

LITERARY GROUP INT'L, THE
270 Lafayette St #1505
New York, NY 10012
(212) 274-1616

LORD, STERLING LITERISTIC, INC.
65 Bleecker St.
New York, NY 10012
(212) 780-6050

LUEDTKE AGENCY, THE
1674 Broadway, #7A
New York, NY 10019
(212) 765-9564

LUKER, JANA TALENT AGENCY
1923 1/2 Westwood Blvd #3
Los Angeles, CA 90025
(310) 441-2822

LYNNE & REILLY AGENCY
10725 Vanowen St
North Hollywood, CA 91605-6402
(323) 850-1984

MARIS AGENCY
17620 Sherman Way #213
Van Nuys, CA 91406
(818) 708-2493

MARKSON, ELAINE LITERARY AGENCY
44 Greenwich Ave.
New York, NY 10011
(212) 243-8480

MARKWOOD COMPANY, THE
1813 Victory Blvd
Glendale, CA 91201
(818) 401-3644

MATSON, HAROLD, CO., INC.
276 Fifth Ave.
New York, NY 10001
(212) 679-4490

MC BRAYER LITERARY AGENCY
2483 Wawona Dr
Atlanta, GA 30319
(404) 634-1045

MC INTOSH AND OTIS, INC.
353 Lexington Ave.
New York, NY 10016
(212) 687-7400

MCMAHAN, KELLY AGENCY
5686 S Crocker St #3A
Littleton, CO 80120
(303) 703-3723

MEDIA ARTISTS GROUP/CAPITAL ARTISTS
6404 Wilshire Blvd #950
Los Angeles, CA 90048
(323) 658-7434

METROPOLITAN TALENT AGENCY
4526 Wilshire Blvd
Los Angeles, CA 90010
(323) 857-4500

MEYERS, ALLAN S. AGENCY
105 Court St.
Brooklyn, NY 11201

MILESTONE LITERARY AGENCY
247 West 26th St #3A
New York, NY 10001
(212) 691-0560

MILLER, STUART M. CO., THE
11684 Ventura Blvd #225
Studio City, CA 91604
(818) 506-6067

MIRAGE ENTERPRISES
5100 Stage Road #4
Memphis, TN 38134
(901) 761-9817

MITNIK, ROBERT AGENCY
211 Nw Forest Street, Suite B
Hillsboro, OR 97124
(503) 615-4288

MONROE-PRITCHARD-MONROE
722 Ridgecreek Dr
Clarkston, GA 30021
(404) 296-4000

MORGAN AGENCY, INC.
129 W. Wilson St. #202
Costa Mesa, CA 92627
(949) 574-1100

MORRIS, WILLIAM AGENCY, INC.
1325 Ave of the Americas
New York, NY 10019
(212) 586-5100

MORRISON, HENRY, INC.
105 South Bedford Rd #306-A
Mount Kisco, NY 10549
(914) 666-3500

NIMBUS PRODUCTION GROUP, INC
19999 Ebenezer Church Road
Bluemont, VA 20135
(540) 554-8587

OMNIBUS PRODUCTIONS
184 Thompson St #1-G
New York, NY 10012
(212) 995-2941

OMNIPOP, INC.
10700 Ventura Blvd, 2nd Fl
Studio City, CA 91604
(818) 980-9267

OMNIPOP, INC. TALENT AGENCY
55 West Old Country Rd
Hicksville, NY 11801
(516) 937-6011

OPFAR LITERARY AGENCY
1357 West 800 South
Orem, UT 84058
(801) 224-3836

ORANGE GROVE GROUP, INC., THE
12178 Ventura Blvd #205
Studio City, CA 91604
(818) 762-7498

ORENTAS, DALIA LITERARY AGENT
6128 North Damen Ave
Chicago, IL 60659
(312) 338-6392

ORIGINAL ARTISTS
9465 Wilshire Blvd. #840
Beverly Hills, CA 90212
(310) 277-1251

OSCARD, FIFI AGENCY, INC.
24 West 40th St, 17th Floor
New York, NY 10018
(212) 764-1100

OTITIS MEDIA
1926 Dupont Ave, South
Minneapolis, MN 55403
(612) 377-4918

PALMER, DOROTHY AGENCY
235 West 56th St. #24K
New York, NY 10019
(212) 765-4280

PANDA TALENT AGENCY
3721 Hoen Ave
Santa Rosa, CA 95405
(707) 576-0711

PARAMUSE ARTISTS ASSOCIATION
25 Central Park West, #1B
New York, NY 10023
(212) 758-5055

PEREGRINE WHITTLESEY AGENCY
345 East 80th Street
New York, NY 10021
(212) 737-0153

PLESHETTE, LYNN LITERARY AGENCY
2700 North Beachwood Dr
Hollywood, CA 90068
(323) 465-0428

POWLEY, M.A. LITERARY AGENCY
56 Arrowhead Road
Weston, MA 02193
(781) 899-8386

PREFERRED ARTISTS
16633 Ventura Blvd #1421
Encino, CA 91436
(818) 990-0305

PREMIER ARTISTS AGENCY
400 S. Beverly Dr. #214
Beverly Hills, CA 90212
(310) 284-4064

PRICE, FRED R. LITERARY AGENCY
14044 Ventura Blvd #201
Sherman Oaks, CA 91423
(818) 763-6365

PRIVILEGE TALENT AGENCY
14542 Ventura Blvd. #209
Sherman Oaks, CA 91403
(818) 386-2377

PROFESSIONAL ARTISTS UNLTD.
321 West 44th Street #605
New York, NY 10036
(212) 247-8770

PROMOTE-IT!
501 Hahaione Street #10J
Honolulu, HI 96825
(808) 395-1613

QCORP LITERARY AGENCY
4245 SW 185th Ave
Aloha, OR 97007
(503) 649-6038

QUILLCO AGENCY
3104 West Cumberland Ct
Westlake Village, CA 91362
(805) 495-8436

RAINES AND RAINES
103 Kenyon Road
Medusa, NY 12120
(518) 239-8311

REGENCY LITERARY INT'L AGENCY
285 Verona Ave
Newark, NJ 07104
(201) 485-2692

REVERIE LITERARY AGENCY
6822 22nd Ave, North #121
Saint Petersburg, FL 33710
(727) 864-2106

REYNOLDS, SUZANNE J. AGENCY
167 Church St
Tiverton, RI 02878

ROBBINS OFFICE, THE
405 Park Avenue, 9th Floor
New York, NY 10022
(212) 223-0720

ROBERTS, FLORA, INC.
393 West 49 Street #5G
New York, NY 10019
(212) 355-4165

ROBINS, MICHAEL D & ASSOCIATES
23241 Ventura Blvd. #300
Woodland Hills, CA 91364
(818) 343-1755

ROLLINS AGENCY, THE
2221 NE 164th Street #331
North Miami Beach, FL 33160
(305) 354-7313

**ROMANO, CINDY MODELING &
TALENT AGENCY**
414 Village Square West
Palm Springs, CA 92264
(760) 323-3333

ROSE, BRANT AGENCY
10537 Santa Monica Blvd #305
Los Angeles, CA 90025
(310) 470-4243

SALPETER AGENCY, THE
7461 West Country Club Dr North #406
Sarasota, FL 34243
(941) 359-0568

SANDERS, VICTORIA LITERARY AGENCY
241 Ave of the Americas
New York, NY 10014
(212) 633-8811

SANFORD-GROSS & ASSOCIATES
1015 Gayley Ave #301
Los Angeles, CA 90024
(310)208-2100

SARNOFF COMPANY, INC., THE
3500 West Olive Ave #300
Burbank, CA 91505
(818) 973-4555

SCAGNETTI, JACK
5118 Vineland Ave #102
North Hollywood, CA 91601
(818) 762-3871

SCHECTER, LEONA P. LIT. AGENCY
3748 Huntington St, NW
Washington, DC 20015
(202) 362-9040

SCHULMAN, SUSAN LITERARY AGENCY
454 West 44th St
New York, NY 10036
(212) 713-1633

SCHWARTZ, LAURENS R., ESQ.
5 East 22nd St #15D
New York, NY 10010-5315

SEIGEL, ROBERT L
67-21f 193rd Ln
Fresh Meadows, NY 11365
(718) 454-7044

SELMAN, EDYTHEA GINIS LITERARY AGENT
14 Washington Pl
New York, NY 10003
(212) 473-1874

SHAFER & ASSOCIATES
9000 Sunset Blvd #808
Los Angeles, CA 90069
(310) 888-1240

SHAPIRA, DAVID & ASSOC., INC.
15821 Ventura Blvd #235
Encino, CA 91436
(818) 906-0322

SHAPIRO-LICHTMAN, INC.
8827 Beverly Blvd
Los Angeles, CA 90048
(310) 859-8877

SHERMAN, KEN & ASSOCIATES
9507 Santa Monica Blvd #212
Beverly Hills, CA 90210
(310) 273-8840

SIEGEL, JEROME S. ASSOCIATES
1680 North Vine St. #617
Hollywood, CA 90028
(323) 466-0185

SILVER SCREEN PLACEMENTS INC.
602 65th St
Downers Grove, IL 60516
(630) 963-2124

SINDELL, RICHARD & ASSOCIATES
9301 Wilshire Blvd #300
Beverly Hills, CA 90210
(310) 777-8277

SISTER MANIA PRODUCTIONS, INC.
916 Penn St
Brackenridge, PA 15014
(724) 226-2964

SMITH, GERALD K. & ASSOCIATES
(323) 849-5388

SMITH, SUSAN COMPANY, THE
121 North San Vicente Blvd
Beverly Hills, CA 90211
(323) 852-4777

SORICE, CAMILLE TALENT AGENCY
13412 Moorpark St #C
Sherman Oaks, CA 91423
(818) 995-1775

STAFFORD, GLENDA & ASSOCIATES
14953 Newport Rd #100
Clearwater, FL 33764
(727) 535-1374

STANTON & ASSOCIATES
LITERARY AGENCY
4413 Clemson Dr
Garland TX 75042
(972) 276-5427

STARFLIGHT AGENCY, THE
75 Troy Drive #C
Springfield, NJ 07081
(908) 964-9292

STARS, THE AGENCY
23 Grant Avenue, 4th Floor
San Francisco, CA 94108
(415) 421-6272

STARWILL PRODUCTIONS
433 N. Camden Dr., 4th Floor
Beverly Hills, CA 90210
(323) 874-1239

STEELE, LYLE & COMPANY, LTD.
511 East 73rd #7
New York, NY 10021
(212) 288-2981

STEIN AGENCY, THE
5125 Oakdale Ave.
Woodland Hills, CA 91364
(818) 594-8990

STELLAR MODEL & TALENT AGENCY
407 Lincoln Road #2K
Miami Beach, FL 33139
(305) 672-2217

STERN, MIRIAM, ESQ.
303 East 83rd St
New York, NY 10028
(212) 794-1289

STEWART TALENT MANAGEMENT CORP.
58 West Huron
Chicago, IL 60610
(312) 943-3226

STONE MANNERS AGENCY, THE
8436 W. 3rd Street #740
Los Angeles, CA 90048
(323) 655-1313

STUART, MALCOLM AGENCY
11436 West Burnham Street
Los Angeles, CA 90049
(310) 440-9202

SUMMIT TALENT & LITERARY AGENCY
9454 Wilshire Blvd #203
Beverly Hills, CA 90212
(310) 205-9730

TALENT REPRESENTATIVES, INC.
20 East 53rd St
New York, NY 10022
(212) 752-1835

TALENT SOURCE
107 East Hall St
Savannah, GA 31401
(912) 232-9390

TALESMYTH ENTERTAINMENT, INC.
312 St. John Street #69
Portland, ME 04102
(207) 879-0307

TALL TREES DEVELOPMENT GROUP
301 Old Westport Rd
Wilton, CT 06897
(203) 762-5748

TANNERY HILL LITERARY AGENCY
6447 Hiram Ave
Ashtabula, OH 44004
(216) 997-1440

TARG, ROSLYN LITERARY AGENCY
105 West 13th St
New York, NY 10011
(212) 206-9390

TEL-SCREEN INT'L, INC.
2659 Carambola Circle North
Building A #404
Coconut Creek, FL 33066
(954) 974-2251

TINSLEY, ROBYN L.
2935 Ferndale
Houston, TX 77098

TOAD HALL, INC.
R.R. 2, Box 2090
Laceyville, PA 18623
(570) 869-2942

TRIUMPH LITERARY AGENCY
3000 West Olympic Blvd. #1362
Santa Monica, CA 90404
(310) 264-3959

TURTLE AGENCY, THE
7720 B El Camino Real #125
Carlsbad, CA 92009
(760) 632-5857

TWENTIETH CENTURY ARTISTS
1680 North Vine Street #614
Hollywood, CA 90028
(323) 463-7300

UNITED ARTISTS TALENT AGENCY
14011 Ventura Blvd. #213
Sherman Oaks, CA 91423
(818) 788-7305

UNITED TALENT AGENCY
9560 Wilshire Blvd, 5th Floor
Beverly Hills, CA 90212
(310) 273-6700

VISION ART MANAGEMENT
9200 Sunset Blvd, Penthouse 1
Los Angeles, CA 90069
(310) 888-3288

WALKER TALENT AGENCY, INC.
1080 S. 1500 E #98
Clearfield, UT 84015
(801) 725-2118

WARDLOW & ASSOCIATES
1501 Main Street #204
Venice, CA 90291
(310) 452-1292

WAUHOB, DONNA AGENCY
3135 Industrial Rd. #204
Las Vegas, NV 89109
(702) 733-1017

WENDLAND, JEFFREY T. AGENCY
265 South 38th St
Boulder, CO 80303
(303) 499-2018

WHATEVER... TALENT AGENCY
20917 Gorgonia Street
Woodland Hills, CA 91364
(818) 884-2209

WHISKEY HILL ENTERTAINMENT
1000 South Williams St
P O Box 606
Westmont, IL 60559-0606
(630) 852-5023

WILSON, SHIRLEY & ASSOCIATES
5410 Wilshire Blvd #227
Los Angeles, CA 90036
(323) 857-6977

WINOKUR AGENCY, THE
5575 North Umberland St
Pittsburgh, PA 15217
(412) 421-9248

WORDSWORTH
230 Cherry Lane Rd
East Stroudsburg, PA 18301

WORKING ARTISTS TALENT AGENCY
13525 Ventura Blvd.
Sherman Oaks, CA 91423
(818) 907-1122

WRIGHT, ANN REPRESENTATIVES
165 West 46th St #1105
New York, NY 10036-2501
(212) 764-6770

WRIGHT, MARION A AGENCY
4317 Bluebell Ave
Studio City, CA 91604
(818) 766-7307

WRITERS & ARTISTS AGENCY (LA)
8383 Wilshire Blvd. #550
Beverly Hills, CA 90211
(323) 866-0900

WRITERS & ARTISTS AGENCY (NY)
19 West 44th St #1000
New York, NY 10036
(212) 391-1112

WRITERSTORE
2004 Rockledge Rd, NE
Atlanta, GA 30324
(404) 874-6260

Web Resources for Actors

ACTING A TO Z
Basic advice with lots of links to the *Acting A to Z* book.
http://www.actingatoz.com/

ACTING ADVICE
Information and advice available in article form and recommended books on how to begin your acting career.
http://www.actinggoldmine.com/

ACTING BIZ
Articles on acting, links to resources, and logline reviews of a number of books.
http://www.actingbiz.com/

ACTING DEPOT
Succinct intro to aspects of the acting biz, but after that, $19.95 for three months just gets you lists.
http://www.actingdepot.com/

ACTOR LAUNCH
For $125 an hour, an industry professional will give you advice on how to prepare for your move to NYC or LA, or up a rung in the ladder. (You'd probably be better off with a shrink.)
http://www.actorlaunch.com/

ACTOR FOR YOU
It's free and it's got a pretty comprehensive job board—many don't offer pay, but you've got to hone your craft somewhere, right?
http://www.actor4u.com/

ACTORS CRAFT
"Books, magazine articles, teachers and classes, words of inspiration, interviews, DVD movie reviews, notes from the field, a myriad of resources"...but particularly all about the Sanford Meisner Approach to Acting, and "the world's leading proponent of that approach," Larry Silverberg.
http://www.actorscraft.com/home.html

THE ACTORS SOURCE
Information on how to get started, from step one, all the way to the top. Categories include "auditions, casting calls, talent agent addresses, casting director addresses, adult & kid managers addresses, television network offices & studios addresses, dramatic serial addresses, comedy club & booker addresses, acting colleges & universities, voice over studios & classes, mailing labels & resume service, acting chat rooms, how to get into show business, headshot photographers, headshot reproduction studios, monologues, various acting related links, actors & actresses online, newsgroups, common questions & answers." Good advice and good links too.
http://www.actorsource.com/

THE ACTORS STORE
Just what it says. Shop at home.
http://www.theactorsstore.com/

ANDY'S SHOW BIZ PAGE
Advice about acting. At least it's from a talent agent, and not another actor.
http://www.geocities.com/Broadway/Mezzanine/4089/

DRAMATIST'S PLAY SERVICE
Books and plays for the actor. Find your next audition piece or license an entire play and produce your own debut.
http://www.dramatists.com/

LOS ANGELES ACTORS ONLINE
A monthly fee-based collection of the usual resources.
http://www.laactorsonline.com/

MONOLOGUES
$6.95 per month subscribes you to an ever-growing database of new monologues by would-be writers, as well as some Shakespeare and Moliere.
http://www.themonologueshop.com/frontpage.html

MOVIE EXTRAS
Pay to register as an extra, with no guarantee of jobs. As if the salary wasn't low enough.
http://www.moviex.com/

SAMUEL FRENCH
"Acting editions" of plays (something no serious actor should rehearse with) and lots of theatre books.
http://www.samuelfrench.com/

SHORT TIPS
Some sound and sensible, if simplistic, advice about how to get started as an actor.
http://start.at/theactingpage

STARVING ACTOR
"This Web site has been designed with two purposes in mind. First, I have created an information source to help actors in all stages of their careers, everything from dry information (resources in New York, Chicago, and LA, links to other acting related sites, bimonthly articles) to more entertaining sections (top ten lists, monthly recipes). I've done this so that someone out there can avoid some of the mistakes I made. The second purpose is to shamelessly hype myself and my career." Hey, he's honest, and he's got a good-looking Web site with good links and good advice.
http://www.starvingactor.com/

THEATRE WAREHOUSE
Trying to do everything, this Web site accomplishes little. It's free, which may be the best thing about it.
http://www.theatrewarehouse.com/

YOUR ACTING AGENT
Actor Peter Jazwinski gives you a step-by-step plan for finding an agent, getting auditions, and roles. But then, Jazwinski hasn't yet made himself a household name.
http://www.myactingagent.com/

YOUR TYPE
Cartoony Web site with helpful hints, tips, and lists for the struggling actor.
http://www.yourtype.com/

SCHOOLS & ONLINE LESSONS

ACTING LESSONS

"Do you want to act? Want to take your shot in movies and TV? Want to perform local theatre in your own town and be good at it? Want to improve your communication skills for business? We can teach you how to act right over the Internet. Our working professionals offer lessons and monologues that you can study and perform right now! FREE of charge! Once you're comfortable with your lesson, you can videotape your performance and send it to us for a professional critique." Sounds like a good deal for the actor too shy to leave his room. On the other hand, how much of a career can an artist like that have?
http://www.actingontheweb.com/

ACTING WORKSHOP ONLINE

While sitting in front of your computer is not going to make you much of an actor, this Web site does have some strong essays about the art of acting and the business as well, and is a guide to acting books you can buy on the Web.
http://www.redbirdstudio.com/AWOL/musical.html

AN ACTORS RESOURCE FOR BASIC TECHNIQUE

Outline of a basic acting technique by an actress, and a good reading list for actors as a bonus.
http://free.prohosting.com/~jez/

AMERICAN ACADEMY OF DRAMATIC ARTS

Located in both Hollywood and New York, AADA was founded in 1884, as the first conservatory in the United States dedicated to the training of professional actors. And still going strong.
http://www.aada.org/

BIOMECHANICS OF ACTING

An acting teacher in Fairbanks, Alaska, believes you don't need talent, admits he has none, and has created an acting technique that has something to do with Meyerhold. Overwritten, but amusing.
http://afronord.tripod.com/biomx/title.html

BOSTON CONSERVATORY

"The musical theatre curriculum is designed to provide comprehensive training for the actor-singer-dancer. Acting, voice and speech for the actor, applied voice lessons and dance form the basis of the program and musical theatre performance courses are specifically designed to synthesize these four disciplines. Integral to the course work is a schedule of major productions and workshops which aim at provid-

ing immediate and continuous performance experience to test and stretch the developing performer." And with seventy-five colleges and universities in the immediate area, Boston is a hotbed of students, many interested in media of all sorts.
http://www.bostonconservatory.edu/

CARNEGIE-MELLON SCHOOL OF DRAMA
Their Web site starts with "You've Arrived!"—and you have, if you're a theatre-lover about to enter college, and the college you pick is Carnegie-Mellon.
http://drama1.cfa.cmu.edu/web/front.html

THE JUILLIARD SCHOOL
Located in Manhattan's Lincoln Center for the Performing Arts, Juilliard is America's premiere college for music, but has a fine drama department as well, from which Kevin Kline and Patti Lupone both graduated to stardom.
http://www.juilliard.edu/index-flash.html

LEE STRASBERG THEATRE INSTITUTE
If you're an actor, you've heard of The Method. This is it, as propounded by acting guru and Group Theatre alumni Lee Strasberg (seen in *The Godfather, Part II* as Hyman Roth because Al Pacino was a student). Info here on the studios in both Hollywood and New York, but if the truth be told, it's Hollywood that benefited more than the stage from the worn-T-shirt school of utter realism.
http://www.strasberg.com/

LONDON ACADEMY OF MUSIC AND DRAMATIC ART
LAMDA is possibly the most famous drama school in the English speaking world...and the oldest, dating back to 1861. In London, it accepts American students, who often go there for post-graduate work in the craft of acting, particularly for the stage.
http://www.lamda.org.uk/

MARGIE HABER STUDIOS
Acting coach to the stars Margie Haber has created a revolutionary phrase technique to get actors through readings without stumbling over the script. Her client list has included Heather Locklear, Gabriel Byrne and Kelly Preston, among others.
http://www.margiehaber.com

THE METHOD
Descriptions of the various techniques and procedures of the so called "Method." Definitions, analogies, descriptions and examples from an experienced devotee of the technique. Plus links to books on the subject, with descriptions of their content. Hey, it worked for Brando.
http://www.theatrgroup.com/Method/

NEIGHBORHOOD PLAYHOUSE
"Located in the heart of New York City, The Neighborhood Playhouse School of the Theatre provides a full-time conservatory atmosphere that concentrates on the artistic growth of the actor through a fusion of technical training in acting, movement, speech, voice and singing, combined with a deeper understanding of the cultural values underlying a life of the highest and most demanding artistic principles. The school offers the serious and committed student something few other acting schools can provide: a unique combination of devotion to a rich, specific tradition and a forward-looking concern for innovation, presented in a two year program and in summer workshops." As not every first year student gets invited back the second year, this is notoriously one of the most rigorous conservatories, concentrating on techniques, skills and commitment (to the profession, and the character).
http://www.the-neiplay.org/

NORTH CAROLINA SCHOOL OF THE ARTS
In Winston-Salem, North Carolina, this university is one of the first built for and devoted to performing; a good transition between playing Henry Higgins or Eliza Dolittle in high school, and braving the wild woods of Hollywood or New York.
http://www.ncarts.edu/

ONE TEACHER'S GUIDE TO ACTING
A Web site for the method (and book for sale) of acting/directing teacher Don Richardson (1919-1996), written by one of his followers.
http://www.abwag.com/

PLAYWRIGHTS HORIZONS
"Playwrights Horizons Theater School is a professional training program for theatre artists: actors, directors, designers, playwrights and dramaturgs. During the academic year, the student body consists of Drama Department students from New York University's Tisch School of the Arts. Independent courses are available during the Summer Theater Training Program, and our Playwrighting Workshops are open to the public."
http://www.phtschool.org

SANFORD MEISER CENTER
A two year professional acting program following the precepts of one of America's renown acting teachers. "Training begins with a three month period of intensive improvisational work.... Students then apply this strong beginning in their ability to "live truthfully" to modern scene work. The rest of the year is devoted to a heightening of this sense of truth and the actors' emotional depth through more improvisational work and scenes. There is no character work in the first year. After eight months, the actors emerge more honest human beings with instruments ready to act

truthfully in film, television, and the stage. The second year is by invitation only; students will be asked back, based on the quality of their work in the first year. The work moves into advanced and highly emotional improvisational work, script analysis and interpretation, character work and advanced scene study." If you can make it through nine months of improvisation, you can work with any Hollywood Hack without tearing your hair out.
http://www.themeisnercenter.com/

STELLA ADLER STUDIO OF ACTING
"Located in the heart of Midtown Manhattan's West Side, the Stella Adler Studio of Acting provides the student with an opportunity to experience the diverse cultures of New York while studying the dramatic arts in the center of the world theatre. The Studio offers a full-time, professional, two-year conservatory training program; a part-time evening program; summer programs; programs for young people; and a wide range of individual workshops. In addition, students may study at the Studio through New York University's Tisch School of the Arts bachelor of fine arts program." However you enroll, this school promotes one of the best and most efficient acting methods ever devised.
http://www.stellaadler.com/

UCLA SCHOOL OF THEATRE, FILM AND TELEVISION
There's no better beginning to a career in Hollywood than four years in the neighborhood.
http://www.tft.ucla.edu/tfthome.htm

NEWS FOR ACTORS

BACKSTAGE/BACKSTAGE WEST
Online version of the actors trade paper. Almost all legitimate auditions are listed with *Backstage*, as well as schools, news, and articles.
http://www.backstage.com/backstage/index.jsp

BREAKDOWN SERVICES
Begun as a hard copy service that collected daily information on casting directors needs and forwarded it to agents who would then submit their clients for available roles, Breakdown now has an online component, more Internet savvy. Their "actor access" section has lots of rules in student films, a great way to get started.
http://www.breakdownservices.com/

HOLLYWOOD ACTOR
Box office figures, news and gossip, even a "Babe-of-the-Day" section. But lists agents and—here's something original—lists actors who have their own production companies. Want to know where to submit your "Robin Williams" film? To Blue Wolf Productions, of course. Addresses included.
http://www.hollywoodactor.com/

HOLLYWOOD ACTORS NETWORK
Free to register as an actor, but not so the Inner Circle, which gives you access to their "Log Line & Pitch Rooms, Dealmaking Desks, Box Office & In Production Charts, Script Sales, Pros Profiles, Chat Rooms, Producers Acquisition Boards, and listings of talent agents and casting directors among other inside information." $60 yearly.
http://actors.com/actingindex.html

PERFORMINK
Living in Chicago? Thinking of moving there, because you heard so much about the Goodman? This is the online version of Chicago's trade paper for actors.
http://www.performink.com/

ROSS REPORTS
Here you can subscribe to the major industry listings, updated monthly, for talent agencies, casting directors, TV network studios and offices, primetime network series, talk/variety shows (NY & LA), daytime serials companies, films in preparation, and films in development on both coasts.
http://www.backstage.com/backstage/rossreports/index.jsp

ORGANIZATIONS

ACTORS EQUITY ASSOCIATION
With your first professional job in the theatre, you'll want to join the union that has represented actors for 88 years. Their bulletin boards are a good place for local news, sublets when a member gets a job on the road, and sometimes even free tickets to shows in need of audiences before they open.
http://www.actorsequity.org/home.html

AMERICAN FEDERATION OF RADIO & TELEVISION ARTISTS
You've been cast on a sitcom. Which union do you join? If it's filmed, SAG. If it's taped, AFTRA. News of the TV biz, latest contract negotiations, and schedules of minimum salaries. "They offered you *what*?!"
http://www.aftra.org/

LATIN ACTORS
Can you play Latino? This is the homepage of the Hispanic Organization of Latino Actors. Casting news and other useful tips for the next Ricardo Montalban? Salma Hayek? Antonio Banderas? Penelope Cruz?
http://www.hellohola.org/

SCREEN ACTORS GUILD
The Union's Web site. Lots of news for those in the business of acting.
http://216.10.108.22/index.html

ADVERTISE YOUR ACT!

ACADEMY PLAYERS DIRECTORY
The big book of actors. Once upon a time, everyone who was anyone was in it, and casting directors thumbed through with every project to refresh their memory.
http://www.acadpd.org/

ACTORS AND ACTRESSES
Post your photo and resume. You may get as many perverts as you do casting directors responding, but at least the calls will go to your agent.
http://www.onlinetheater.com/actrs.html

ACTORS DATABANK
Although so far you can count the actors on one hand that have their photo and resume posted here, it's free, and it's surely a good idea. "Cathy" started it, and who knows—one day, instead of photos and resumes, you'll only have to give out your Web address.
http://www.geocities.com/cathy78uk/

ACTORS POST
For $29.95 a year (beginning with a free trial) you get an interactive online portfolio (your pictures and resume online), your demo reel video online (streaming real-video format), your own Web address (www.actorspost.com/yourname) linked to your online portfolio, access to casting notices in your area and beyond, updated daily, weekly email newsletter containing notification of new casting notices. On the other hand, without becoming a member, you can access lists of talent and casting agencies, lists of acting schools, lists of photographers in your area, and answers to questions regarding acting and the biz.
http://www.actorspost.com/

CREATE A RESUME
Online method of putting together a slick looking resume by using their forms (and paying them $19.95). Of course, to be impressive, your resume needs credits, not bold type.
http://www.actingresume.com/index.htm

FILM ACTORS DIRECTORY
The most comprehensive listing of actors, their credits and their agent information, all cross-referenced by film title. Over 6,000 film actors, over 15,000 film listings. Not exactly light reading, but pretty fascinating nonetheless.
http://shop.hcdonline.com/merchant2/merchant.mv

Web Resources for Writers

ABOUT SCREENWRITING
Articles about screenwriting from synopsis to final draft, and lots more, including a great collection of popular film screenplays you can read for free.
http://screenwriting.about.com/

ABSOLUTE WRITE
All the usual links for writers, with a section especially for screenwriters.
http://www.absolutewrite.com

CINEMA
From the non-profit Corporation of Public Broadcasting, a good introduction for young people to the craft of making movies.
http://www.learner.org/exhibits/cinema/screenwriting.html

CRAFTY SCREENWRITING
Good, in-depth discussion of screenwriting with lots of FAQs well answered.
http://www.craftyscreenwriting.com/

CREATIVE SCREENWRITING
The magazine. Lots of online articles on the subject. Interviews with successful writers and directors.
http://www.creativescreenwriting.com/

DONE DEAL
"Your Internet news resource for screenplay, pitch, treatment, and books sales in the film industry, in addition to interviews, software & book reviews, advice, agency & production company listings, contests, news, and more." Just that. And well-organized.
http://www.scriptsales.com/

DRAMATICA
A Theory of Story, linked to its books and software.
http://www.dramatica.com/

ESCRIPT
Online courses in screenwriting.
http://www.singlelane.com/escript/

FADE IN MAGAZINE
Web site for one of the more popular film magazines.
http://www.fadeinmag.com/

FILM SCHOOL ONLINE
Online courses in screenwriting, directing, cinematography, sound, editing and producing using the new digital medium.
http://www.2learnfilm.com/

FINAL DRAFT
Final Draft is pretty much the end-all-be-all of screenwriting software these days. Founded in 1991 by writer Marc Madnick and software engineer Benjamin Cahan, who recognized the need for a screenwriting software package, Final Draft eventually recreated and revolutionized the way an entire industry writes and revises its scripts. It has been used worldwide by professional film and TV writers to create such Oscar®-winning hits as *American Beauty* and *The Usual Suspects* and is endorsed by industry talents such as Oliver Stone, James L. Brooks, Tom Hanks and Michael Bay.
Final Draft is also available in a French language version. Final Draft AV, first released in 2001, is the only word processor specifically designed for dual-column scriptwriting. Final Draft kicks ass over your old Smith-Corona.
http://www.finaldraft.com

GHOSTWRITING
Not happy with your own writing? These people turn your idea into a screenplay, and you get the credit.
http://www.ghostscribes.com/

GOT YA COVERED
Script critique service. $100 gets you "an objective review of screenplays for television or feature productions. Reports contain a coverage of premise, characters, plot development, visual expression, risk and motivation and marketability. The review suggests areas to focus on in rewrites to improve the script's overall marketability. Detailed page notes make comments easy to follow. References by experts in the field of screenwriting are given for specific areas, such as chatty dialogue and direc-

tion balance, character revealed through action, cutting extraneous scenes, etc." Or you could ask your best friend to read it.
http://www.apokolips.com/gotya/gotya.html

HOLLYWOOD LIT SALES
Good site for news of daily spec sales, run by two established production companies that will accept your inquiries via email.
http://www.hollywoodlitsales.com/

HOLLYWOOD SCRIPTWRITER
International trade paper for screenwriters, features in-depth interviews with writers, producers, agents et al. Subscription offer and little else.
http://hollywoodscriptwriter.com/aboutus.html

HOLLYWOOD WRITERS BLOC
"Founded in January 2001, Hollywood Writers Block meets once every two weeks in the KCAL Building on the Paramount Lot. Every meeting, the group critiques a member's feature-length script. During the critique, the group helps the writer mold his vision into a marketable screenplay. Positive and constructive feedback that helps the writer understand what would make the story great. If interested in joining, the group requires a writing sample and a sample critique." In fact, every writer should belong to a club of writers criticizing each other. If you can take it, you'll learn a lot.
http://www.hollywoodwritersblock.com/

INTERNET THEATRE BOOKSHOP
Screenwriters should write, and screenwriters should read, so if you don't want to leave your computer for all that crosstown traffic to the bookstore, browse here.
http://www.stageplays.com/index.htm

JOHN TRUBY'S SCREENWRITING COURSE
One of Hollywood's screenwriting gurus.
http://www.truby.com/

THE MAD SCREENWRITER
Mostly a central hub.
http://www.madscreenwriter.com/

MEGAHIT MOVIES
"This Web site analyzes those films which have generated more than $250 million in North American Box Office receipts. It presents principles of story construction that can be used to develop popular movies by providing an analysis of cinematic techniques. It also offers stimulating ideas that can be helpful in the creative process.

The fundamentals of dramatic structure, the human emotions, and the construction of humorous characters and situations are explained, with examples drawn from some of the most popular motion pictures ever produced." Well, no, it only offers you the opportunity to buy the book. Still, if you're going to steal from the best, this might be the place to start.
http://www.megahitmovies.com/

MOVIE BYTES
Everything, and we do mean everything, about screenplay contests everywhere. The site is a little clunky, but the information is top-notch and there is a ton of it.
http://www.moviebytes.com

ORGANIZATION OF BLACK SCREENWRITERS
"The Organization of Black Screenwriters began in 1988 to address the lack of black writers represented within the entertainment industry. Our primary function is to assist screenwriters in the creation of works for film and television and to help them present their work."
http://www.obswriter.com/

SANFORD MEISNER SCREENWRITING PROGRAM
"The screenwriting program consists of a three-hour workshop each week devoted to the theory and craft of successful screenwriting. During the first eight weeks, students are introduced to the concepts of story, structure, and character development, and will complete an outline of their original screenplay. During the second eight weeks, students will write their actual screenplays. The goal of the program is to have students write and complete a first draft screenplay." (If it takes you sixteen weeks to write a first draft, you're too slow for television.)
http://www.themeisnercenter.com/

SCENARIO
The Magazine of the Screenwriting Art. You can subscribe here, but the site offers little else.
http://www.scenariomag.com/subscribe/info.html

THE SCREENSCRIBE
Home to a variety of fun and useful movie-related links. Focused on "sites that relate to TV Studios and Networks, Movie Fan Links and Resources for aspiring screenwriters (or movie fans who just enjoy knowing more about the craft of screenwriting)." These are well-introduced links by another writer more successful with his Web site than his screenplays.
http://ns2.rt66.com/cedge/index.html

SCREENWRIGHT: THE CRAFT OF SCREENWRITING
An electronic screenwriting course ($240) and hypertext ebook ($40) from Charles Deemer. A self-guided course in writing the Hollywood screenplay. Perhaps you can't learn to act at your monitor, but that's where you're going to write.
http://www.pcez.com/~cdeemer/index.htm

SCREENWRITERS'S RESOURCE CENTER
Links and software.
http://www.screenwriting.com/

THE SCREENWRITERS STORE
Order software, books, magazines and merchandize online.
http://www.screenstyle.com/

ANOTHER SCREENWRITERS' STORE
This one based in England. Check it for English books.
http://www.screenwriterstore.co.uk/index.taf?

SCREENWRITERS'S UTOPIA
News and links.
http://www.screenwritersutopia.com/

THE SCRIPT DUDE
Software for the writer and others.
http://www.scriptdude.com/

SCR(I)PT MAGAZINE
Subscription opportunity, back issues, a few links.
http://www.scriptmag.com/

SCRIPT SERVICES
You've got to wonder how word processing services are still in business, when everyone and his brother owns a computer that prints out great-looking, if ineptly written, screenplays. But if you need one, this one is handily located on the Universal lot.
http://www.universalstudios.com/scriptservices/

SCRIPT SUPPLIES
Brads, card stock, mailers, books & scripts...a regular Office Depot for the screenwriter.
http://www.scriptsupplies.com/

SCRIPT THING
Software for writers called Movie Magic Screenwriter 2000 and Power Structure.
http://www.scriptperfection.com/

SCRIPTSHARK
ScriptShark is comprised of studio and development executives currently searching for new screenwriting talent and material. Submit your script for studio-style coverage.
http://www.scriptshark.com

STUDIO SCRIPT SALES
Fee-based service for getting your work to producers and executives. Services like these are popping up, but bear in mind the old axiom you'll find on many FAQ sights: Stay away from any agent who asks for a fee in advance.
http://www.studioscriptsales.com/

SUNDANCE INSTITUTE
Web site of the countries most renowned "community," includes invitation only seminars for writers, directors.
http://www.sundance.org/jsps/site.jsp?resource=pag_ex_home

UCLA
Features professional programs in screenwriting and producing.
http://www.filmprograms.ucla.edu/

UNIVERSITY OF IOWA
Renowned for its writers workshop, it also boasts strong programs in cinema and theatre. Combine the two, and you're off to a screenwriting career.
http://www.uiowa.edu/homepage/index.html

WORDS FROM HERE
Get your script critiqued by a community of writers.
http://www.wordsfromhere.com/

THE WRITER'S STORE
An excellent resource for writers who can't make it to the Los Angeles location. Their Web page can lead you to hardware, software, books, and much more.
http://www.writersstore.com/

WRITER'S SCRIPT NETWORK
For $30 they'll post your logline, genre, synopsis and full script on the Web. And who knows, maybe an agent or producer will say, "Eureka! I found it!"
http://www.writersscriptnetwork.com/home.html

WRITING CLASSES
Ten week online classes in screenwriting and other forms, from the Gotham Writer's Workshop. If you live in New York, take the class in person and network.
http://www.writingclasses.com/

WRITING SCHOOL
Live in Northern Alaska? Writing classes conducted by email.
http://www.WritingSchool.com/

WRITTEN BY
The magazine of the Writers Guild.
http://www.wga.org/WrittenBy/

WRITERS GUILD OF AMERICA
The union of film and television writers has a script registration service you can access here without getting out of bed, a list of literary agents, research links, news from the scribbler's biz...and a great library, but for the latter, you'll have to visit their headquarters.
http://www.wga.org/

Hollywood Creative Directory
– *The Insider's Guide to the Insiders* –

Hollywood Creative Directory publishes the most complete and up-to-date directories featuring film and television professionals. Our directories are meticulously researched and compiled using strict listing qualifications. Each company listing contains staff names, titles, addresses, phone and fax numbers, email addresses, and Web sites. All books feature comprehensive indices for easy reference.

PRODUCERS

Over 9,900 Film and TV Producers, and Studio and Network Executives. Includes Development Deals, Projects, and Credits. Also features TV Show section. Published every March, July, and November. Spring/Summer 2002. **ISBN 1-92893-661-9**

PDBK0 Single Issue	$59.95 (+$6.00 shipping)
PDBK1 1-Year Subscription	$149.95 (+$18.00 shipping)
PDBK2 2-Year Subscription	$249.95 (+$36.00 shipping)

AGENTS & MANAGERS

Over 5,500 Agents, Managers, and Casting Directors nationwide. Also includes Publicity Companies. Published every February and August. Spring/Summer 2002. **ISBN 1-92893-618-0**

ADBK0 Single Issue	$59.95 (+$6.00 shipping)
ADBK1 1-Year Subscription	$94.95 (+$12.00 shipping)
ADBK2 2-year Subscription	$169.95 (+$24.00 shipping)

DISTRIBUTORS

Over 4,500 US Film and TV Distribution Executives, Sales Agents, Marketing and Merchandising Executives, Producer and Distributor Reps, and Financing Company Executives. Also includes Publicity Companies, and over 500 International Film and TV Buyers and Distributors worldwide. Published every January. 2002 Edition. **ISBN 1-92893-617-2**

DDBK0 Single Issue	$59.95 (+$6.00 shipping)

To order, call 323.308.3490 or
visit www.hcdonline.com

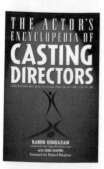
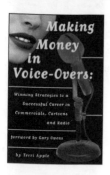

Filmmaking Books from IFILMPublishing

DIGITAL BABYLON

Hollywood, Indiewood and Dogme 95

by Shari Roman

In an exploration of the influence of Dogme 95 style filmmaking and the new technologies that have brought film and video making within reach of the layman, Shari Roman has created an entertaining and clear-sighted account with *Digital Babylon: Hollywood, Indiewood and Dogme 95*. Exclusive, in-depth discussions with maverick filmmakers Lars von Trier, Mike Figgis, Wim Wenders, Harmony Korine, Rick Linklater, and Gus Van Sant. **ISBN 1-58065-036-8**
$19.95 (+$4.50 shipping)

THE INDIE PRODUCER'S HANDBOOK

Creative Producing from A to Z

by Myrl A. Schreibman

Myrl Schreibman has written a straightforward, insightful, and articulate account of what it takes to make a successful feature film. Filled with engaging and useful anecdotes, Schreibman provides a superlative introduction and overview to all of the key elements in producing feature films. Useful to film students and filmmakers as a theoretical and practical guide to understanding the filmmaking process. **ISBN 1-58065-037-6**
$21.95 (+$4.50 shipping)

THE IFILM DIGITAL VIDEO FILMMAKER'S HANDBOOK

by Maxie D. Collier

Maxie D. Collier's book covers the creative and technical aspects of digital shooting and is designed to provide detailed, practical information on DV filmmaking. Collier delves into the mechanics and craft of creating personal films and introduces the reader to the essential terminology, concepts, equipment, and services required to produce a quality DV feature film. Includes DVD. **ISBN 1-58065-031-7**
$24.95 (+$4.50 shipping)

THE ULTIMATE FILM FESTIVAL SURVIVAL GUIDE, 2ND EDITION

by Chris Gore

Learn the secrets of successfully marketing and selling your film at over 600 film festivals worldwide. Author Chris Gore reveals how to get a film accepted and what to do after acceptance, from putting together a press kit to putting on a great party to actually closing a deal. Gore includes an expanded directory section, new interviews as well as a new chapter that details a case study of the most successful independent film to date, *The Blair Witch Project*. **ISBN 1-58065-032-5**
$19.95 (+$4.50 shipping)

To order, call 323.308.3490 or visit www.hcdonline.com